GREATEST GAMES
CARDIFF CITY

GREATEST GAMES
CARDIFF CITY

SEAN WOZENCROFT

First published by Pitch Publishing, 2013
Reprinted 2017

Pitch Publishing
A2 Yeoman Gate
Yeoman Way
Durrington
BN13 3QZ
www.pitchpublishing.co.uk

A CIP catalogue record is available for this book from the British Library

ISBN 978-1-90917-868-7

Typesetting and origination by Pitch Publishing

Printed in India by Replika Press Pvt. Ltd.

Contents

Acknowledgements 6

Introduction 7

1. v Wolverhampton Wanderers 1921 9
2. v Sheffield United 1925 12
3. v Arsenal 1927 16
4. v Dynamo Moscow 1945 21
5. v Leeds United 1952 25
6. v Liverpool 1957 29
7. v Liverpool 1959 32
8. v Aston Villa 1960 36
9. v Knighton Town 1961 40
10. v Arsenal 1961 43
11. v Tottenham Hotspur 1961 47
12. v Newcastle United 1962 51
13. v Sporting Lisbon 1964 55
14. v Real Zaragoza 1965 59
15. v Middlesbrough 1966 63
16. v Moscow Torpedo 1968 66
17. v Hamburg SV 1968 70
18. v Pezoporikos Larnaca 1970 74
19. v Real Madrid 1971 77
20. v Crystal Palace 1974 81
21. v Hereford United 1976 85
22. v Tottenham Hotspur 1977 89
23. v Wrexham 1977 92
24. v Swansea City 1980 96
25. v Leyton Orient 1983 99
26. v Chelsea 1984 103
27. v Scunthorpe United 1993 107
28. v Middlesbrough 1994 111
29. v Manchester City 1994 115
30. v Fulham 1997 119
31. v Chester City 1998 123
32. v Scunthorpe United 1999 127
33. v Cambridge United 1999 131
34. v York City 2001 135
35. v Leeds United 2002 139
36. v Oldham Athletic 2002 144
37. v Stoke City 2002 148
38. v Bristol City 2003 152
39. v Queens Park Rangers 2003 156
40. v Middlesbrough 2008 161
41. v Barnsley 2008 165
42. v Portsmouth 2008 169
43. v Bristol City 2010 174
44. v Swansea City 2010 178
45. v Leicester City 2010 182
46. v Blackpool 2010 186
47. v Leeds United 2010 190
48. v Liverpool 2012 194
49. v Charlton Athletic 2013 199
50. v Burnley 2013 204

Bibliography 207

Acknowledgements

THIS WONDERFUL football club has played a major role in my family for more than 100 years. Indeed, our support for the club can be traced back to its very formation in 1899.

For my own obsession I have my late grandfather John Wozencroft and my father Paul Wozencroft to thank. John was born in 1916 and started supporting Cardiff City as a young boy after being encouraged by his uncle. In 1927 he was among the thousands to line the streets of Cardiff to welcome home the FA Cup heroes. His passion for the club was unfailing throughout his life and we would spend hours talking about the most minuscule piece of news. John stopped attending matches shortly before City moved to the new stadium as his eyesight deteriorated, but his support continued from his armchair. He died in 2011 aged 95.

My dad started going to City games in the late 1950s. He caught the bug and has been a regular ever since and a long-standing season ticket holder. He started taking me to Ninian Park in the 1992/93 season when City won the Third Division championship. What a way to start, but it could never last and the years that followed turned out to be some of the worst in the club's history. With City languishing towards the bottom of the fourth tier of English football by 1995/96 and playing in front of crowds of less than 3,000, I'm sure there were times when my dad wondered whether his Saturday afternoons could be better spent elsewhere. But he persevered and in the last decade the rewards have been plentiful with cup finals and thrilling football. I will always be grateful that he chose to share his passion with me.

A word of thanks, too, for my wonderful wife, Dani. She is a staunch Crystal Palace supporter but humours me and my childlike love for Cardiff City. She has also been very supportive of this book, even though its production has left me with little time to help her around the house. I'll get the washing up gloves back on soon, I promise!

Tribute must also be paid to staff at libraries across the country who have helped me dig out the information required, particularly the helpful folk at Cardiff Central Library.

A big thank you, too, to Ann Lumley, who ploughed through the draft version of this book with her red pen to eliminate mistakes and typos.

But above all the praise must go to the Cardiff City heroes of the last 114 years who have produced such a large amount of incredible games and unforgettable moments. I salute you all.

Sean Wozencroft

Introduction

CARDIFF CITY are the ultimate rollercoaster club. Supporters old enough will have witnessed victories over Real Madrid, Sporting Lisbon and Arsenal as well as defeats against Maidstone United, Weymouth and Scarborough. In the last 25 years the Bluebirds have been amongst the dead men in the bottom division and have also played in two major cup finals. And now they are ready to soar on the biggest stage of them all – the Premier League.

This book aims to be a celebration of the best moments since the club's formation in 1899. "Have there been 50 great Cardiff games?" was a joke I heard regularly as I began to tell my friends and family that I was going to be writing this book. There have, of course, been many more. When I started looking through results of seasons gone by it became abundantly clear that 100 games would have been possible. Some great victories – even a League Cup semi-final win over Crystal Palace in 2012 – have been left out as I struggled to pick the games to be featured.

Some matches, of course, were obvious choices for inclusion. The 1927 FA Cup Final against Arsenal remains the most famous day in the club's history while the European Cup Winners' Cup successes over Real Madrid, Sporting Lisbon and Moscow Torpedo in the 1960s and 1970s were very special.

But I have deliberately strayed away from the obvious where possible to include some fixtures which might not have been great games in their own right but have gone down in folklore because of what they meant to the supporters. A 0-0 draw at Cambridge United in 1999 might not sound like a candidate for this book, but any City fan worth their salt will know that this was the day when Frank Burrows's team held out for a point with just eight men. Likewise, the 3-0 win over Scunthorpe United in 1993 might not have won any awards for football brilliance from pundits, but City fans remember it as the day more than 4,500 Bluebirds supporters invaded North Lincolnshire for a promotion party of epic proportions.

I have tried to select games from as many different decades as possible but it is inevitably the case that many are from the 1960s and 1970s when City plied their trade almost exclusively in the top two divisions. There were big wins against Liverpool, Chelsea, Arsenal and Spurs during those years of relative success. But despite lurking in the bottom two divisions for much of the 1980s and 1990s, there were still some memorable games, including a 3-3 draw against Chelsea on a feisty afternoon and 2-0 win against Leyton Orient which secured promotion.

But there is no escaping the fact that the last ten years have seen unprecedented success for the club, including a play-off promotion against QPR and a play-off final defeat against Blackpool as well as an FA Cup Final and a League Cup Final, and promotion to the top tier.

Nothing excites supporters more than a cup shock, and there have been one or two for City fans to savour over the years. The 2-1 win at Middlesbrough in 1994 was excellent while Nathan Blake's winner against Manchester City just weeks later will never be forgotten. And of course, that win against top-of-the-Premier-League Leeds in 2002 was out of this world.

Some games have been featured simply because they showed City at their best. They include a 6-0 trouncing of Chester City, a win by the same scoreline at rivals Bristol City and a 7-1 win at Oldham Athletic. The 16-0 Welsh Cup win over Knighton Town earns a chapter simply as it is the club's record scoreline. A 10-1 loss against Moscow Dynamo is one of only a handful of defeats featured but is there because of the political importance of the match and the excitement it created around the country at the time.

It is my hope that this book will in a small way help to revive memories among supporters of a certain vintage while helping to reinforce the history and traditions of the club to younger folk. The greats like Brian Clark, Derek Tapscott, Ivor Allchurch and Willie Anderson – not to mention Phil Dwyer, John Toshack and John Charles – should never be forgotten. And then there are the modern-day heroes like Graham Kavanagh, Phil Stant, Carl Dale, Peter Whittingham and Robert Earnshaw. So much of this great club has changed over the years, including the move of stadium and the recent alteration of home colour from blue to red. I hope that this simple book will go some way to keeping yesteryear alive for us all.

It is also worth remembering that the story of Cardiff City Football Club will run and run. As long as there is football being played in this country there will be a 'Cardiff' in one form or another. In 200 years the supporters of today will be considered the early trailblazers.

It is inevitable that some readers will not agree with some of the games I have decided to include and will question why others have been omitted. Whether or not that is the case, I sincerely hope you enjoy reading about what were undoubtedly 50 great days in the club's history.

1 v Wolves 2-0

2 May 1921. Attendance: 40,000
Ninian Park. Second Division

CARDIFF CITY:	WOLVERHAMPTON WANDERERS:
Ben Davies	Teddy Peers
Jack Page	Maurice Woodward
Jimmy Blair	George Marshall
Fred Keenor	Val Gregory
Bert Smith	Joe Hodnett
Billy Hardy	Alf Riley
Billy Grimshaw	Tansey Lea
Jimmy Gill	Frank Burrill
Fred Pagnam	George Edmonds
Harry Nash	Richard Richards
Joe Clark	Sammy Brooks

Referee: Mr Scholey (Sheffield)

IT WAS May Day 1921. Britain was getting back on its feet two and a half years on from the end of the First World War, George V was King, car tax discs had just been introduced – and fledgling Cardiff City Football Club was taking flight.

City's directors had worked wonders in re-establishing the club after the war years and in 1919/20 the Bluebirds had finished a very respectable fourth in the Southern League Division One, with crowds topping 20,000 at times. The following season, after persistent lobbying by secretary-manager Fred Stewart, City were accepted into the Football League. They would play in a reconstructed Second Division just a decade on from turning professional.

And what a first season in the Football League City had enjoyed. A clutch of players had been signed, including inside-forward Jimmy Gill for the princely sum of £750 from The Wednesday, as the Sheffield club was known until 1929. Ninian Park, too, saw major changes with the erection of the Canton Stand, complete with enough wooden benches for several thousand spectators.

Stewart's men had kicked off the season with an encouraging 5-2 win at Stockport County, new boy Gill with the honour of scoring the club's first Football League goal. And the Cardiff juggernaut had powered on from there. By Christmas Day 1920, City sat proudly at the top of the table with 12 wins and six draws from their opening 20 games. There followed a stutter with City winning just four of their next 11, but the Bluebirds regained their poise to march back into the top two.

In fact, a 2-2 draw between The Wednesday and third-placed Bristol City in the Steel City meant that Cardiff had the luxury of knowing they were guaranteed promotion to the First Division regardless of their result in this evening kick-off against Wolves. It was a feat matched only by Tottenham, who had also won promotion to the top flight in their first season in the League in 1908/09.

Cardiff City's Greatest Games

Even without iPhones and talkSPORT, the news had filtered through the huge 40,000 crowd in Ninian. Hundreds had walked to the ground from The Valleys and, with unemployment rife, many were let in for free. It seems impossible that today's football money men would ever show such generosity.

With promotion in the bag, there was still the small matter of the championship to be decided. With two games to play, City and Birmingham were tied on 54 points, though the Midlanders held the advantage on goal average. And City were out for revenge, too, as it was Wolves who knocked them out of the FA Cup in the semi-finals 40 days earlier, Jack Addenbrooke's side benefiting from two refereeing howlers to win 3-1 in the replay at Old Trafford. Tottenham Hotspur went on to beat Wolves 1-0 in the final on 23 April.

The game got off to a lively start on the hard turf with both teams keen to finish the season with a flurry. City went close first when inside-forward Harry Nash, a February signing from struggling Coventry City, sent a header wide from a Billy Grimshaw cross after good work by Fred Keenor.

Minutes later Nash sent in another powerful shot after the ball had been sprayed from wing to wing in the build-up. It had goalkeeper Teddy Peers beaten all ends up but the FA Cup finalists were fortunate to have George Marshall in the right place to clear.

Left-back Jimmy Blair, whose son Douglas went on to play for City in the 1940s and 1950s, brought an end to a promising Wolves attack after neat link-up play between Richard Richards and Joe Hodnett, but it was City on the front foot. Northerner Joe Clark stung the bare palms of Peers, while at the other end Jack Page read the game well to snuff out a long ball.

Soon afterwards, centre-forward Fred Pagnam, who had bagged six crucial goals since his £1,500 March move from Arsenal, headed goalwards from a Nash cross but Peers pushed it out for a corner.

Wolves were getting themselves into good positions but were wasteful with their final ball. Lanky goalkeeper Ben Davies easily dealt with the danger of a Tansey Lea cross before in a City counter-attack a quick throw-in by Grimshaw nearly sent Pagnam away but Hodnett rescued the situation for the visitors.

The crowd, keen to see attractive football on the floor, roared with excitement as the game switched from end to end at a lightning pace. Richards fired a shot over the bar for Wolves, though Davies would probably have saved it had it been on target, while Peers saved well from Pagnam and Gill.

Just before half-time the City faithful were left bemoaning poor refereeing again as Maurice Woodward prevented a Gill goal by handling, but no penalty was given.

At the end of a long season, a slower pace in the second half could have been excused, but both teams continued to show impressive stamina to carry on where they left off. City began to click with Bert Smith, one of City's greatest ever defenders, instrumental. It was the Irish international who nearly created the opening goal, but Gill could not provide the finish.

Minutes later Pagnam flicked on a Clark cross which Nash was nearly on the end of but Val Gregory cleared before Peers had to get down to save a strong shot from Gill. A City goal was coming – and it was no surprise that it was Gill who got it with a low drive from a left side cross.

South Wales Echo reporter Arthurian wrote, "Huge shouts went up all over the ground and as the players swarmed around Gill to congratulate him an excited spectator – an *Echo* seller – dashed on to the field of play and shook the scorer by the hand."

That goal allowed City to open up and play some of the best football of the season. And within five minutes it was 2-0 through a little piece of Pagnam magic. The good-looking 29-year-old evaded a Hodnett tackle by hooking the ball over the defender's head, dodged past Marshall and then smacked the ball into the corner of the net. City's £2,250 investment in Pagnam and Gill had paid dividends.

Wolves continued to fight until the end – Grimshaw's shot was saved for a corner and Hodnett tried to catch Davies out with a long distance lob – but they never really looked like troubling City's lead.

So City's first season as one of 66 Football League members had finished in resounding success. Birmingham City's 4-0 win at home to Port Vale meant the title race went right to the wire. The following weekend saw a reverse of the Bank Holiday fixtures with City travelling to Wolves and Birmingham making the short trip to Port Vale. City needed to better Birmingham's result to get their hands on the trophy – and they did their bit with a 3-1 win at Molineux with goals from Pagnam, Nash and Gill, but Birmingham won 2-0 and City had to settle for second.

A Wolves director sidled up to the *Echo* reporter at the end of the game and told him that he believed City would hold their own in the First Division. And he was proved to be right as City, despite a woeful start, went on to finish fourth the following season, earning the respect of football bosses across the land.

2 v Sheffield United 0-1

25 April 1925. Attendance: 91,763
FA Cup Final. Wembley Stadium

CARDIFF CITY:	SHEFFIELD UNITED:
Tom Farquharson	Charles Sutcliffe
Jimmy Nelson	Bill Cook
Jimmy Blair	Ernest Milton
Harry Wake	Harry Pantling
Fred Keenor	Seth King
Billy Hardy	George Green
Billy Davies	Dave Mercer
Jimmy Gill	Tommy Boyle
Joe Nicholson	Harry Johnson
Harry Beadles	Billy Gillespie
Jack Evans	Fred Tunstall

Referee: G.N. Watson

WITH ALL the fame of 1927, the historic Cup run of 1925 is largely overlooked. Fred Stewart's Bluebirds had enjoyed a meteoric rise since joining the Football League in 1920 and were now rubbing shoulders with the powerhouses of English football. They had missed out on being crowned First Division champions by the most slender of margins the season before. Now they had a chance to make history by becoming the first team outside of England to win the FA Cup – and in the competition's 50th 'Jubilee' year.

City had put together some impressive performances to reach the final, the highlight of the football calendar. It took City three attempts to get past Third Division Darlington and they were less than convincing against Fulham in the second round, winning by a single goal in monsoon conditions. City then beat Notts County 2-0 and then Leicester City 2-0 in front of more than 50,000 at Ninian Park. The Bluebirds saved the best for the semi-final, smashing Blackburn Rovers 3-1 with three goals inside the opening 20 minutes.

Sheffield United had already won the Cup on three occasions, in 1899, 1902 and 1915, and had also been beaten finalists in 1901 – but this was their first appearance at Wembley, which had only been opened two years earlier. They had enjoyed some good fortune on their way to the 1925 Cup Final having not had to play a single game away from Bramall Lane until the semi-final on neutral ground. The superstitious among the United support were encouraged that all of their previous Cup opponents – Corinthian FC, Sheffield Wednesday, West Bromwich Albion and Southampton – had been disposed of while wearing blue and white. Cardiff, of course, would run out wearing those traditional colours.

City went into the game as slight favourites in most people's eyes – but really it was too close to call. City were 13th in the First Division, just two points above the Blades. In the league the pair had drawn 1-1 at Ninian and United had won 1-0 at their home just seven days later.

The Daily Express and The Times both agreed that man-for-man City had the better side. "Sheffield are good Cup fighters with a workmanlike rather than polished team, and from that point of view Cardiff can point to superiority," the Express said. But while City held the edge in defence, United had the upper hand in attack. Cardiff captain Jimmy Blair said beforehand: "Whether the Cup will be dashed from our lips on our first appearance at Wembley, I cannot say. What I do say most definitely, however, is that we have a chance, a great chance, of winning."

Almost 92,000 packed into Wembley, including tens of thousands from Wales. What an atmosphere there must have been as 22,000 journeyed from Cardiff on 54 special trains. The first train left at 9.30pm the day before and the last at 1.30am. Of that army, 10,000 came from the mining valleys. Many more hired cars to make the journey to be part of the momentous occasion.

And London was ready for the invasion. According to the Express, restaurants opened at 5am. Lyons' Corner House, a huge eatery on four floors, was well prepared with 13,000 eggs, 6,000 rashers of bacon, 50,000 slices of bread and butter, 700 gallons of coffee, 1,000lbs of marmalade and a quarter of an acre of watercress.

The Times appeared surprised that these "doughty Welsh citizens" made no attempt to conceal their origin. Many wore huge home-made hats covered in the blue and white – while others arrived in England's capital clutching the biggest leeks they could find. The paper remarked that City fans "never relaxed their grip of their leeks", giving Londoners a chance to study the apparently exotic vegetable which they had only seen before in Shakespeare plays. London road sweepers must have had a shock to find thousands of these strange green vegetables strewn across their streets the following morning.

The Sheffield fans, meanwhile, demonstrated their support with hand bells and rattles. The noise was not as great as it had been at previous finals, newspaper reports state. But despite the strong displays of national pride, there was never any danger of crowd trouble. These were, after all, men who had fought side by side in the First World War less than ten years earlier.

Stewart stuck with the same side that impressed in the semi-final meaning there was no place for ace marksman Len Davies, who had scored 22 goals that season but had lost his place to converted wing-half Joe Nicholson after an injury.

With referee Watson suitably attired in shirt and bow tie, Sheffield United won the toss to get the game under way. It was an exciting match by Cup Final standards with plenty to keep the crowd interested, even if the football was not always of the highest quality. There had been little rain in the days leading up the game, making the surface hard and causing the heavy leather ball to bounce irregularly.

Sheffield United were far and away the better side in the first half. They were on the front foot from the off with a couple of smart attacks but Scotland's international backs Blair and Jimmy Nelson offered good protection for keeper Tom Farquharson. United wasted a handful of opportunities with Billy Gillespie and Harry Johnson off target.

Johnson ought to have done better when he found himself unmarked from a Dave Mercer cross but he couldn't get it under control and Blair stormed in to prevent him getting his shot away. At the other end Jimmy Gill was not too far over with a piledriver and Nicholson, who scored in the semi-final success, tried his luck from a tight angle.

It was shaping up to be a good, clean contest between two sides desperate to not let their opponents get into the ascendancy. The Daily Express described the play as "not colourless by any means but it was not picturesque".

The Blades had the breakthrough they deserved after 31 minutes. City were looking to make some ground down the left but Harry Pantling intercepted and tried to feed the ball out to the right. Right half-back Harry Wake was there ahead of Fred Tunstall but he badly misjudged the speed of his opponent. He dallied on the ball and instead of just thumping it to safety allowed Tunstall to nip in. Blair and Nelson, convinced Wake had it under control, had switched off and the flying outside-left had a clear run on goal. With impressive coolness Tunstall placed the ball into the net despite Farquharson's best efforts.

Despite later being absolved of blame by captain Fred Keenor, it was a moment Wake would never forget. *The Daily Mail* said: "'What was Wake thinking about?' was the mildest remark applied to the poor half-back."

City were playing against the wind but responded to the setback well. Minutes later leek-waving Cardiffians were ready to tip their caps when a fine Gill shot grazed the crossbar.

City were not without their chances, many coming from Sheffield United mistakes, but momentary hesitations cost them dear.

United legend Tunstall went close to putting his side two goals up shortly before half-time in a similar move to the opener. This time, though, Wake, Nelson and Blair all went charging desperately towards the ball and managed to clear.

The second half was dull in comparison to the first. City had come out the blocks like Usain Bolt but faded in the spring sun after just a few minutes. *The Sunday Pictorial*, later renamed *The Sunday Mirror*, said both sides were "working hard without having, apparently, any definite aim in view". And the same reporter added: "One might have taken it to be a league match in which Cardiff were content to be narrowly beaten; they did not seem to bestir themselves at all until the closing quarter of an hour was entered on."

The Blades goal had come from a horrible blunder – and the team in red and white stripes almost returned the favour. A string of mistakes gave City a glorious chance but three forwards were unable to force the ball the final few yards over the line. Each in turn flung a boot towards the ball but failed to make the necessary connection and it was eventually scrambled clear.

United came close with a decent header from a corner and both sides tried reasonable efforts from distance, but both Charles Sutcliffe and Farquharson in between the sticks were largely untested.

The United half-backs were dominating the game and keeping Cardiff away effectively. Outside-left Jack Evans, nicknamed 'Bala Bang' for his legendary powerful shot, was isolated and visibly frustrated with a host of poor passes by Harry Beadles.

But no matter how bad teams are in Cup Finals, there is always one big chance. City's opportunity to take the tie to extra time came when Gill picked up the ball after good work by Beadles and Nicholson. United keeper Sutcliffe was unsighted but with Seth King and Ernest Milton closing in, Gill – the scorer of City's first ever Football League goal in 1920 – rushed his shot and it flew wide.

City's play was lacking composure. Perhaps they had been affected by the occasion just a little bit more than Cup Final veterans United. *The Daily Express* described City's movements as "jerk-like", though there were some good dashes down the wing. United's play was more purposeful and confident. The Blades always looked like they could step up a gear if necessary but were more than happy with their single goal.

But City were always in the match right up to the closing minutes. For two exciting minutes the United defence was put under a barrage of pressure. Had sharp-shooter Len Davies been on the pitch, the record books might have looked very different. The Bluebirds picked up the pace and got into some good positions but the final shots were poor. Three times efforts cannoned off brave Blades defenders.

United had a chance to make it 2-0 in the final minute when Tommy Boyle was clattered to the ground when he looked to be surging through on goal. A free kick was awarded on the edge of the area but nothing came of it and the final whistle was immediately blown.

City's dreams of taking the Cup out of England for the first time were over. The Bluebirds had failed to reach the heights that they achieved in the magnificent semi-final win while Sheffield United had played beyond themselves.

The stand-out player and ultimately the difference between the sides was Blades skipper Gillespie. The Irish international, who signed for United in 1912 for the maximum wage of £4 a week, was 33 years old but looked like he was in his mid-50s. *The Times* said of Gillespie's performance, "He used his brains and his feet to such good purpose that he was continually building up positions like a clever billiard player."

There was criticism from many of the national newspapers for City-legend-in-the-making Keenor. The Welsh international centre-half was a man mountain in the opening minutes as City were put under the cosh. But Keenor faded as the game drew on and allowed his defensive duties to stifle his usual attacking attributes.

G.P. Smith in *The Sunday Pictorial* reported, "Keenor, Cardiff's match-winning asset, was too much concerned in looking after Johnson and Gillespie to be able to nurse his own forwards." *The Daily Express* said Keenor failed to deal with the "wiles and stratagems" of Gillespie.

Blades fans invaded the pitch as Sheffield United collected the Cup from the Duke and Duchess of York in front of a sea of bowler hats and cigarette smoke. The City players looked on, wondering what might have been. There was praise for City from the press – but the nationals made little attempt to hide their glee that the Cup had remained in England.

The Times said: "Whenever scoffers point to our loss of athletic prestige, we can still proudly declare that England has once again won the England FA Cup." *The Times* made no reference to the fact that all but two of the 64 teams in the first round proper were from England, weighting the odds somewhat. The *Express*, which described the Welsh as "clannish folk", said, "St George succeeded in slaying the Red Dragon at Wembley."

City travelled back to Cardiff as beaten heroes but confident that their time would come. And just two years later it did with Keenor making up for his abject performance by leading the Bluebirds to a famous success.

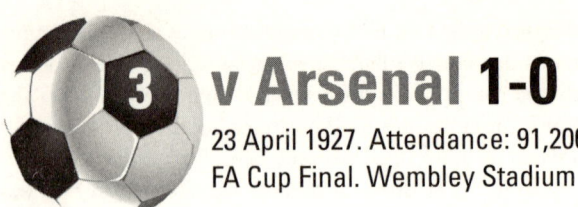

3 v Arsenal 1-0

23 April 1927. Attendance: 91,206
FA Cup Final. Wembley Stadium

CARDIFF CITY:	ARSENAL:
Tom Farquharson	Dan Lewis
Jimmy Nelson	Tom Parker
Tom Watson	Andy Kennedy
Fred Keenor	Alf Baker
Tom Sloan	Jack Butler
Billy Hardy	Bob John
Ernie Curtis	Joe Hulme
Sam Irving	Charles Buchan
Hughie Ferguson	Jimmy Brain
Len Davies	Billy Blyth
George McLachlan	Sid Hoar

Referee: W.F. Bunnell (Lancashire)

T HE DATE 23 April 1927 is etched on the heart of any Bluebirds supporter worth their salt. Despite modern-day success, it's still the greatest day in the club's history: the day the FA Cup was snatched from English soil.
It was a day of many firsts.

There was a spine-tingling atmosphere at Wembley before the game as 91,206 fans – including tens of thousands from Wales – indulged in a new craze sweeping the country: community singing. Football supporters had long sung songs during matches, but now it was pre-planned, structured and controlled by the organising bodies. A black painted platform had been erected on the side of the pitch for conductor Thomas Ratcliff, who stood on top leading the masses in song with vigorous arm waving. *The Times* likened the structure to a "scaffold and an execution". The crowds belted out renditions of the Froth Blowers' anthem, 'Land of my Fathers', and, for the first time, 'Abide with Me'. Community singing died out in the early 1970s but 'Abide with Me' is still sung with gusto at FA Cup finals.

The 1927 showpiece was also the first Cup Final to be broadcast live on BBC radio. Thousands of people gathered to listen to the match outside City Hall in Cardiff on mounted speakers. Some newspapers printed a grid with squares numbered one to eight so that listeners would have a clearer idea of where the play was taking place. There is a regularly repeated myth that this was the origin of the phrase "back to square one", but it's more likely to be from hopscotch or snakes and ladders.

Most importantly, it was the first time (and possibly the last time) that a team not from England won the famous knock-out competition. It is a fact which has earned City fans many quiz points over the years. Fred Stewart's Cardiff had invaded the English capital and come back with the trophy – and on St George's Day to boot.

Arsenal were slight favourites to win their first major trophy. The Gunners were taken over by legendary manager Herbert Chapman in 1925 after he was tempted away from

Huddersfield Town. They had spent two seasons struggling against relegation from the top flight before Chapman's arrival but he immediately signed 34-year-old marksman Charles Buchan from Sunderland and reacted to changes in the offside laws by bringing in a 3-4-3 formation.

Arsenal went on to finish the 1925/26 season in second position and Chapman moved to sign Joe Hulme, Jack Lambert and Tom Parker. Their league form in 1926/27 was indifferent, going into the Cup Final in 14th position, level on points with City in 12th – but the revolution had begun.

Cardiff, meanwhile, were beaten Cup finalists in 1925 and desperate to go one better this time after another momentous run all the way to Wembley. City had retained the backbone of the team with Tom Farquharson, Jimmy Nelson, Fred Keenor and Billy Hardy the survivors from 1925. And there were some useful new additions including local amateur Ernie Curtis, well-travelled Sam Irving and speedy outside-left George McLachlan. Len Davies, still the club's all-time top scorer today, had a point to prove after being left out of the 1925 Cup Final 11.

City had a tough run to the final with wins against Aston Villa, Darlington, Bolton, Chelsea and Reading. City had tonked Second Division Reading 3-0 in the semi-final with Hughie Ferguson scoring two goals either side of a Harry Wake header. Wake was desperate to play to make up his costly mistake in the final two years earlier but picked up an injury and, with Billy Thirlaway cup-tied, manager Stewart named Curtis at outside-right, making the 19-year-old the youngest player to appear in an FA Cup Final at the time.

The backbone of the side, of course, was iconic captain Keenor. The Roath-born half-back signed for his home-town club before it turned professional in 1912 and is considered to be Cardiff's most inspirational leader of all time. He suffered shoulder and knee injuries in the First World War but returned to the club afterwards and scored in the club's first league game in 1920. After bitter disappointment in the 1925 final, Keenor vowed to return to Wembley to win – and he was good to his word.

But the uncompromising tackler almost missed out on City's finest hour after requesting a transfer in January having been left out of the side for a few games, partly through injury. The City history books might have looked very different if Keenor hadn't settled his differences with the club before this April showdown.

There was another key member of this historic City squad – a lucky black cat called Trixie. According to the BBC, Ferguson found the stray wandering around on the Royal Birkdale golf course as City prepared for their fifth round tie at Bolton, when they were clear underdogs. Ferguson believed she was a lucky omen and is said to have tracked down the cat's owner, who agreed to lend the animal as a mascot in exchange for two Cup Final tickets. A deal was struck and a couple of months later Trixie found herself parading with the Cup in front of huge crowds.

The City team bus was pelted with leeks as it arrived at Wembley, which only served to motivate the players. Led by Keenor, the Bluebirds came bounding out of the tunnel while Arsenal marched robotically.

With King George V and Britain's two 20th century war-time prime ministers, David Lloyd George and Winston Churchill, watching from the stands, it was a nervy opening to the ticket-only match. Balls were being ballooned into the air by anxious legs, or over-hit, or mis-controlled. Frequent free kicks for offsides or mistimed tackles broke up the play and made life easy for two notoriously good defensive units.

But Arsenal soon started to exert some pressure and for a time it looked like they might be just too powerful for City. The first shot came from Arsenal captain Parker, a £3,250 signing from Southampton in 1926. His 30-yard free kick did not lack venom but was straight at Farquharson. Soon after Parker tried an audacious dipping shot from long range that Farquharson, widely considered the club's best ever goalkeeper, had to punch away with Jimmy Brain lurking ominously.

Arsenal were enjoying the majority of possession but City's defensive masters Nelson, Tom Watson, Keenor, Hardy and Tom Sloan looked almost impenetrable.

The Times mused, "Hardy, with his bald head and sturdy figure, looked more of a veteran even than the long-legged, keen-faced Buchan, but he is still a player of the international class – none the less so because he has never been capped."

Buchan and Hulme put together a number of tidy Arsenal moves down the right but it was more often than not Hardy who stuck his foot in and relieved the danger.

Meanwhile, Irish international Sloan was too strong for Brain. In its match report *The Sunday Pictorial* said, "Sloan, the Cardiff centre-half, was easily master of Brain, the Arsenal centre-forward. The Londoner is frail of build and had not the physique to force his way past this resolute defender." And on the odd occasion that Brain did get the better of Sloan, there was Nelson or Watson ready to mop up.

Arsenal star forward Buchan was 35 years old and had lost some of his devastating pace, but he still had bags of skill. City knew all about his ability to control games and marked him closely – putting in a couple of crunching tackles along the way. He was kept largely quiet but a wonderful first-time pass to Hulme did force the first corner of the game. Three more quick-fire corners followed but not one of them was good enough to endanger the City goal.

Farquharson was largely untroubled. When it did look like he would be forced into a save, Sid Hoar lost his nerve and his effort landed on top of the net.

City did have the occasional counter-attack that went close to breaking the deadlock. Ferguson, who had led the line well in the first half, broke through with a fine solo run but just as he looked likely to get his shot away Arsenal defenders raced back to shepherd him out of play.

With half-time approaching, neat link-up play between Hulme and Buchan left the City midfield chasing shadows. The ball was then swung out to Hoar but his attempted pass went astray.

It had not been the flowing football match that the capacity crowd had been hoping for. "A rather bored crowd settled down in silence to hope for better things to come during the second 45 minutes," said *The Times*.

The Arsenal started the second half like a team given a changing-room ear-bashing. Brain sent a header just a yard wide with Farquharson badly positioned. Buchan, who eventually retired having scored 257 goals in the Football League, started to pull the strings and on one occasion sold a City player a wonderful dummy.

Hulme got away from his man shortly after and sent a cross over from Hoar. Hard man Nelson, one of the best full-backs of his era, charged him down just in time.

But City slowly forced their way back into the game. Half-backs Keenor, Sloan and Hardy were beginning to find a little space and McLachlan and Curtis were able to use their pace down the wings. McLachlan, a £2,000 signing from Clyde in 1925, looked to have finally found a way through to goal after a clever Ferguson dribble but the final pass was lacking.

A report in *The Daily Express* read, "When the game did begin to look like a football match after the interval, I thought Cardiff were going to win. They seemed suddenly to feel full of hope. Despite the distance, I could almost detect the sparkle in their eyes. Fifteen minutes after the interval, I made a note: 'Cardiff look like scoring.'"

After about 70 minutes, good work by Hardy gave Ferguson his first real opportunity. The Scot had scored 28 goals that season, including one in City's 2-0 win against Liverpool five days earlier – but he missed the target this time.

That woke the huge Wembley crowd from its slumber – but nobody could have foreseen the drama that was to come. The decisive goal, undoubtedly the most famous in City's colourful history, came on 74 minutes with extra time looming.

It started with a throw-in to McLachlan. He switched it inside to Davies, who quickly touched it to Ferguson. The forward got it under control and with little room to move tried a speculative low shot from a tight angle. Flickering Pathe newsreel footage shows Rhondda-born Dan Lewis go to ground and appear to have it under control.

But somehow, with Davies and 'pretty boy' Irving charging towards him, the ball squirmed under his body like a bar of soap. He desperately tried to turn and grab it but only succeeded in elbowing it into his own net. The Welshman would famously blame the blunder on his new jersey, claiming the wool was too greasy. According to legend, since that day Arsenal goalkeeper jerseys have always been washed before use. Despite the blunder, the goal was credited to Ferguson.

Conspiracy theorists claimed that Lewis had let the goal in to support his fellow countrymen – or perhaps even for a bribe. That was denied by Lewis's son Dave. Speaking in an interview with *The Telegraph* in 2008, he said, "That mistake preyed on my dad's mind for years. He never spoke about it much but the memory of what happened was always there. The idea my dad let the ball in deliberately is ludicrous – he desperately wanted to win."

Arsenal attempted to stage a fightback in the last quarter of an hour and the game saw its best spell of attractive football but the City defence stood firm. Brain did have the ball in the net once but it was correctly ruled out for offside.

Keenor admitted afterwards that City had been fortunate. "I think we were very lucky to win, because, to be candid, I think the Arsenal deserved to," he said honestly. "I hope, though, that although we are taking the Cup out of this country, we shall return to Wales with the good wishes of all English sportsmen. Arsenal played a clean, hard, sporting game."

Elated Welshmen poured on to the pitch to celebrate what remains today one of the nation's proudest sporting achievements. Chain-smoker Keenor grinned from ear to ear as he collected the Cup from the Royal Box. There had been a fair portion of luck to City's success, but that took nothing away from a marvellous achievement just seven years after entering the Football League. The dynamic trio of manager Stewart, highly-praised coach George Latham and founder Batley Wilson, who held the purse strings, had delivered something very special indeed.

A crowd of about 150,000 thronged the streets as the City heroes returned to Cardiff to parade the trophy. Dozens of police officers kept the ecstatic fans at bay as the ridiculously overcrowded open-top car crawled its way through the city centre. There were wild cheers and hankies and hats were waved in the air as the legends passed.

In an interview with *Sports Budget* shortly after the success, Keenor said, "As a Cardiff boy I was overwhelmed with our home-coming, and Len Davies, Ernie Curtis and myself felt ever so proud to be natives of this great city. The scenes outside City Hall will remain with us long after our playing days are over."

It took the club 81 long years to return to Wembley. City might have changed almost inconceivably in that time – but the heroes of 1927 must never be forgotten, even as those old enough to recall that great day dwindle.

4 v Moscow Dynamo 1-10

17 November 1945. Attendance: 31,000
Friendly. Ninian Park

CARDIFF CITY:	MOSCOW DYNAMO:
Kevin McLoughlin	Alexei Khomich
Arthur Lever	Vsevolod Radikorsky
Marsh Raybould	Ivan Stankevich
Ken Hollyman	Sergei Blinkov
Fred Stansfield	Mikhail Semichastny
Danny Lester	Leonid Soloviev
Beriah Moore	Evgeny Archangelski
Ernie Carless	Vassili Kartsev
Colin Gibson	Konstantin Beskov
Terry Wood	Vsevolod Bobrov
Roy Clarke	Sergei Soloviev
Sub not used: Billy Foulkes	

Referee: A.E. Davies (Pontyclun)

BY THE end of 1945, the country was taking the first tentative steps towards normality following the long-awaited conclusion of the Second World War. Football had been on the back-burner during the six-year conflict – now the Football League and the FA wanted a glittering event to relaunch the national game.

An England XI international against Russia was considered but officials thought it would be a mismatch. At the end of October it was announced that crack Russian team Dynamo FC of Moscow would play a series of games against Britain's leading teams – and Division Three South part-timers Cardiff City, of course!

There was immediate excitement about the visit of the Russians. There was an air of curiosity and mystery about Britain's communist allies, as well as some suspicion about their peculiar leader, Joseph Stalin.

Dynamo, Russian suits decided, were the best team to demonstrate the country's credentials. That season they had run away with the Russian championship, winning 19 of their 23 games – including 17 on the bounce – and smashing 73 goals.

Dynamo agreed to play Cardiff, Arsenal, Chelsea and Rangers but they came with an exhaustive list of demands. They highlighted concerns over differing perceptions of the laws of the game. Body charging, for example, was legal in the British game but not in Russia, while they also stressed the need for substitutes, allowed in Russia but not yet in this country. They also demanded to eat all meals in the Soviet Embassy. The FA agreed to all of their demands, except games would not necessarily be played on Saturdays and neither would they be limited to one a week.

The visitors had been written off by the British press. *The Sunday Express* told its readers "not to expect much from this bunch of factory workers". But people were soon taking them seriously after they began their tour with an entertaining 3-3 draw against a strong Chelsea side. Then it was the turn of the Welsh capital to welcome this classy bunch of footballers – and the red carpet was rolled out.

Cardiff City's Greatest Games

The 40-strong Russian party arrived in Cardiff by train on Thursday ahead of the Saturday kick-off and were greeted on the platform by chairman Herbert Merrett. "May I extend to you a hearty welcome to the city of Cardiff," the businessman told them. The directors of the club were at Dynamo's disposal and nothing would be too much trouble, he assured.

Cardiff was still dressed with thousands of flags following the visit of King George VI and Queen Elizabeth just days earlier – but red flags with the iconic hammer and sickle and a huge portrait of Stalin had also gone up.

Club officials were keen to give their guests a taste of South Wales. On the eve of the match 12 of the party visited a coal mine at Abercynon while other groups went to the City Hall, museum and Cardiff Docks. The previous evening, according to the *South Wales Echo*, some of the Russian officials enjoyed a dance with some Cardiff lasses but the players had to settle for dominoes and magazines.

Such was the hysteria around the city that rugby had been pushed out of the newspapers – and *The Western Mail* felt the need to remind readers that the Dynamo players were only human. The reporter wrote, "They are strong, silent men of fiction, but actually underneath the surface they are just like you and I. Most of them are artisans and engineers who live in Moscow. So let us preserve a proper sense of proportion. Anyway, football and hysteria will never mix."

The crowd was expected to break the Ninian Park record at the time of 55,000 for an international fixture between Wales and England in 1938. Almost 75,000 had been at Chelsea's Stamford Bridge four days earlier, including some sat on the roof. But in the end, somewhat disappointingly, just 31,000 turned out. *The Western Mail* blamed morning rain, pre-match predictions of huge queues to get into the ground and increased ticket prices of 2s 6d for the terraces.

Nevertheless, the match brought in about £4,500 in gate receipts at a time when the average price of a UK house was £500. Half of that amount after tax went to the Russians to help rebuild bombed Stalingrad. And there was some extra pocket money for a group of enterprising youths, too, who, according to an article in *FourFourTwo* in 2004, sold pirate programmes on Sloper Road at twice the official price (threepence).

There was a shock in store for supporters as with half an hour until kick-off the visitors came on to the pitch for an organised warm-up, something unheard of in British football. "They used not one, but about half a dozen balls, passing and kicking to one another," said the gobsmacked *South Wales Echo* reporter.

The excitable crowd responded with a rendition of 'Hen Wlad Fy Nhadau' and the Russians immediately halted their exotic routine to listen. The match was broadcast from Ninian Park to Russia on radio and producers had made a special request to hear some Welsh singing before kick-off and during the interval. They had their wish.

The teams exchanged gifts before kick-off. City skipper Fred Stansfield received a bunch of flowers from his Dynamo counterpart while the visitors each went home with a miniature silver plated miners' lamp. Just what they always longed for, I'm sure. The original idea of a bunch of leeks as a gift had been rejected.

Dynamo wore blue with a white trim, meaning City were forced to play in red. Maybe Vincent Tan knew more about the club's heritage than he was given credit for.

There was a last-minute change to the City line-up with experienced Beriah Moore preferred to 18-year-old Billy Foulkes at outside-right. Cardiff-born Moore had been a prolific goalscorer during the war-time competitions. Regulars Alf Sherwood and Billy

Rees were missing for City while reserve keeper Kevin McLoughlin started between the sticks.

As with all clubs across the country, the war had a big impact on Cardiff. Goalkeeper Jackie Pritchard lost his life at sea while Billy Baker, Bobby Tobin and Billy James were taken prisoners by the Japanese. The captured trio did later return to action for the Bluebirds with varied success. But City had been able to keep Cyril Spiers on their books as secretary-manager and he had been busy in setting up feeder teams such as Cardiff Nomads as well as encouraging local talent into the club.

Spiers, 43 and a brave goalkeeper in his day, had watched Dynamo against Chelsea and was convinced that his City team could put up a decent fight. He had said that Chelsea had approached the game with too slow a tempo and was banking on the energy of his youngsters to cause Dynamo problems, despite some of his players putting in a shift down the pits before the match. And for the first five minutes it looked like being a close game with City passing the ball around well, even if the final killer ball was lacking.

But the Moscovites soon found their stride and were ahead after seven minutes following a foul by centre-half Stansfield. The free kick was taken quickly, catching the City defence on the hop and blond forward Vsevolod Bobrov headed home. Bobrov, who also excelled in bandy and ice hockey, had earned rave reviews after capping an impressive performance with a goal against Chelsea.

Things began to look ominous for the Bluebirds just two minutes later when Vassili Kartsev carried the ball forward and pushed a pass through for Konstantin Beskov to fire into the bottom corner from 12 yards.

But despite the scoreline, City continued to look dangerous on the attack. City might have found a breakthrough had it not been for the sharpness of Soviet goalkeeper Alexei Khomich, nicknamed 'Tiger' because of his excellent reflexes. On one occasion the theatrical 25-year-old pounced off his line to take the ball away from Colin Gibson.

City then appealed for a penalty after a goalmouth scramble but the Pontyclun referee waved play on and Khomich eventually made a good save from close range.

A third goal for the lightning fast Russians soon followed after 25 minutes, though, when Evgeny Archangelski added to his strike against Chelsea by latching on to a pass from the right and finishing with aplomb past McLoughlin.

Roy Clarke, a future Wales international, thundered a shot goalbound but Khomich was able to clear for a corner and the first half finished 3-0. City may have had nine shots to Dynamo's ten – but the visitors were running them ragged.

Spiers's men gave the mammoth crowd plenty to cheer with a spirited start to the second half – a Gibson shot even brushed the outside of the post – but they lacked the poise to make their possession count. And Dynamo were further ahead with their first meaningful attack on 55 minutes when a quick one-two bamboozled the City back-line and Beskov was able to finish the move with a simple back-heel.

Minutes later there was rapturous applause for show-off Khomich when he leapt to save a fierce shot by tough-tackling wing-half Ken Hollyman. Despite the chasm in the score, City were holding their own, but maybe the Russians were just toying with the home side as in the next ten minutes they doubled their lead.

When they put their foot down, they played football like never before seen in the UK. Their movement was fast and intelligent and the ball was always under control. *The Western Mail* reporter said, "To my way of thinking the most devastating feature of their football is the uncanny way they have of suddenly developing an attacking movement with each man thinking about three or four moves ahead." This, the reporter suggested, could be partly attributed to foreign players being encouraged to play chess to develop their minds and strict diets to improve fitness.

The Queen's English commentator on British Pathé footage said, "They're a machine and not an ordinary football team. They shoot before they see the whites of their opponent's eyes."

Quick-fire goals from Bobrov and then Archangelski made it 6-0 before Beskov bagged his third of the game and Dynamo's seventh after sharp passing which left the City defence rooted to the spot. Archangelski's goal to make it half a dozen was described by Peter Wilson in the *Sunday Pictorial* as "the greatest piece of football wizardry" he had seen in six years.

There was, though, some light relief for the now flailing Bluebirds when Glamorgan wicketkeeper-turned-footballer Ernie Carless won a penalty. Inside-left Terry Wood stepped up full of confidence and fired low and hard – but Tiger Khomich lived up to his nickname, pouncing to his left to palm the ball on to the post.

Bobrov completed his hat-trick after McLoughlin had fumbled a corner but then came City's consolation, and a moment to savour for Moore. The 25-year-old finally caught Khomich out of position as he hooked in a shot from a tight angle to give the huge crowd something to cheer at last.

Dynamo's ninth goal came with four minutes to go as the visitors started to take the mickey. Sharp passing saw three Russian forwards get in behind the City defence. Any one of them could have shot but instead they toyed with keeper McLoughlin. "They played with it like two kittens would play with a ball of wool so completely was City's defence beaten," said *The Western Mail*. Eventually Beskov smashed it in – and Archangelski finished the rout with a tenth goal in the closing minutes.

It had been a humbling experience for City and it was seen as a sign that the British game was falling behind other European countries previously thought of as footballing minnows. Spiers said afterwards, "Dynamo are the finest team I've ever seen. They are a match for any side in Britain."

Dynamo went on to beat Arsenal 4-3 in thick fog at White Hart Lane. The clash descended into a farce, though, with Dynamo apparently playing with 12 men for 20 minutes due to the terrible visibility. Dynamo then drew 2-2 in a thunderous encounter at Rangers before returning to Russia as national heroes. A 90-page booklet was produced to commemorate the tour.

The UK was talking about Moscow's super athletes – but it hadn't been the diplomatic success that bosses had hoped. Writing in socialist magazine *Tribune*, George Orwell suggested that if anything Anglo-Soviet relations had been made slightly worse. But Dynamo had proved themselves to be equal to their western European counterparts – and a year later the USSR joined FIFA, signalling a new chapter in Soviet football.

It was a new chapter for City too, who were crowned champions of the Third Division in 1946/47 with their new-look team.

5 v Leeds United 3-1

3 May 1952. Attendance: 45,925
Second Division. Ninian Park

CARDIFF CITY:	LEEDS UNITED:
Ron Howells	Jack Scott
Glyn Williams	Jim Milburn
Alf Sherwood	Grenville Hair
Bobby McLaughlin	Eric Kerfoot
Stan Montgomery	Jim McCabe
Billy Baker	Tom Burden
Roley Williams	Peter Harrison
Doug Blair	Don Mills
Wilf Grant	Frank Fidler
Ken Chisholm	Ray Iggleden
George Edwards	Harold Williams

Referee: Mr G. Pankhurst (Warwick)

NINIAN PARK became a fortress for City in the 1951/52 season. The Bluebirds were in imperious form on their own turf and went into the final game of the season boasting a record of 17 wins, two draws and one defeat, the best in the top two divisions. Only Rotherham United had managed to take maximum points from the Welsh capital – and that was way back on 20 August. Away from South Wales it was a completely different story, though, with just two wins and ten defeats, the second worst record in the Second Division.

With the majority of games already played in the league, City went into their last fixture at home to Leeds United knowing that one more triumph in front of their own fans would see them pip Birmingham City to second place on goal average – and seal a place in the top division after a 23-year absence.

The pressure was immense on Cyril Spiers's men. A cracking run of four wins and a draw – including a vital 3-1 home win against Birmingham – had put the Bluebirds in the ascendancy. But now, 25 years after the club was catapulted into the national spotlight by winning the FA Cup, the job needed to be finished.

And that's exactly what this fine City team did, crossing the line in style like a great marathon runner as he approaches the final 100 metres. Two goals from red-hot forward Wilf Grant and another from Ken Chisholm against his former club gave City an unassailable 3-0 lead. A late Leeds consolation did not stop thousands pouring on to the pitch in celebration. The Bluebirds were back among the elite.

It was a magnificent achievement for the club – and a result of years of intelligent, structured progress by Spiers and the club's bosses.

When City earned promotion to the Second Division in 1947 as football began to return to normal following the Second World War, chairman Herbert Merrett had bravely announced that the club's ambition was to be in the top flight within five years. Spiers had been poached from Norwich City three months into the 1947/48 season following the departure of Billy McCandless. It was the second spell at Ninian Park for the former Villa and Spurs keeper, who had served in a secretary-manager role from 1939 to 1946 before a contractual disagreement saw him leave for Carrow Road.

Spiers was renowned for nurturing home-grown talent and he had been steadily building a squad capable of realising Merrett's dreams. He had achieved four consecutive top-ten finishes, and had missed out on promotion in 1950/51 by just two points.

Local lads in this great team included skipper Alf Sherwood, Glyn Williams, Billy Baker, Roley Williams, George Edwards, Ron Howells, Ken Hollyman, Ron Stitfall and Derrick Sullivan. City used 21 players throughout the season and only three – Hollyman, Stitfall and Griff Norman – were actually born in Cardiff, but the surrounding towns and villages were well represented with players from Aberaman to Swansea, Penrhiwceiber to Newport.

And the South Walians were complemented by some shrewd cross-border transfers since Spiers's second coming. Londoner Stan Montgomery arrived from Southend United in 1948 and the giant centre-half had become one of the first names on the team-sheet, while inside-forward Doug Blair, from Sheffield, was shining in his fifth season with the Bluebirds.

But the star of the team was Grant. The former Manchester City man had switched from winger to centre-forward the previous season and in 1951/52 was City's only ever-present player, hitting 26 goals in the league and another in the FA Cup.

Leeds, managed at the time by the legendary Major Frank Buckley, would pose a test for City. United, whose home colours were blue and yellow, had enjoyed a respectable season. Going into this game they were just two points behind City but would have needed to win 10-0 to leapfrog the Bluebirds on goal average.

Twenty-year-old legend-in-the-making John Charles had been in and out of the side due to National Service and cartilage problems. He proved to be virtually irreplaceable, but Leeds did have some decent players, not least skilful inside-forward Don Mills, who moved to Elland Road from City in September 1951 for £12,000. Ray Iggleden had also enjoyed a good season with 18 goals.

The game was dubbed "the most important to be played at Ninian Park" by *The Western Mail* and was expected to attract a crowd of 60,000. The whole of South Wales was abuzz with excited chatter. Edwards, one of the outstanding wingers of his era, interviewed for *The Official History of Cardiff City Football Club* video in 1993, said, "That week in Cardiff you couldn't go out without someone talking to you about the game. The tension built throughout the week. There was tremendous excitement."

City had to share the limelight with the FA Cup Final between Newcastle and Arsenal, which was taking place on the same day. There were also two First Division games being played – and without the uproar that has been seen in recent years when Premier League games have been scheduled for Cup Final day.

Despite competition from the Wembley showpiece, supporters started queuing outside Ninian Park four hours before the 3.15pm kick-off. According to the *South Wales Echo*, some had travelled from Liverpool, Plymouth and London to be part of an historic occasion. About 7,000 fans came from The Valleys on 19 special trains and there were also three specials from Newport. Secretary Trevor Morris, who would later go on to manage the Bluebirds, told the *Echo* he had been inundated with requests for tickets, including from Birmingham supporters, who would be celebrating promotion if City slipped up. Telegrams of support "poured in from all parts of the British Isles", according to the *Echo*.

Spiers stuck with the same team that showed nerves of steel to beat Bury 3-0 in a do-or-die game a week earlier. That meant hard man Glyn Williams was preferred ahead of Stitfall and came up against fellow Welsh international Harold Williams in the opposite position.

As the rain poured at Ninian Park and made for a heavy surface, there were signs of the inevitable early jitters from City. The home side went close with long-range shots from Glyn Williams and Grant. Blair then looked to have beaten Jack Scott but the ball swerved wide at the last moment before there was a real heart-stopping moment for the huge crowd when former Wrexham man Frank Fidler clipped the top of the crossbar with a header for Leeds.

That served as a wake-up call for City, who began to pile on the pressure. Jim Milburn and Jim McCabe produced a series of last-ditch tackles for United while Scott made a string of good saves as the Bluebirds peppered their goal. Blair thundered another shot towards goal which was pushed wide at the expense of a corner.

City were spraying the play from one wing to another at every opportunity to try and pull their opponents out of position, but Leeds were playing with the coolness of a team with nothing to win nor lose on the final day. It took the individual brilliance of Grant to break the deadlock after 28 minutes. The 31-year-old forward jinked past McCabe and Grenville Hair before sliding a left-footed shot into the bottom corner with ease.

United looked to reply immediately and nearly did when Peter Harrison centred for Fidler, but he didn't get enough on his shot and Howells saved on the line. Moments later Fidler was involved in a race for possession with Howells after a ball through the middle, but the City keeper won by inches.

And then two minutes before half-time, Grant was at it again. This time the well-spoken goal machine, who was brought to the club in a swap deal with Southampton involving Ernie Stevenson, drew three defenders with his magnetic control. Everyone in the ground – including the Leeds defence – expected him to roll the ball to Chisholm or Blair in space, but instead he cracked the ball into the net via hapless defender Tom Burden and a post.

There was now little doubt that City were heading for the First Division. Away from home Spiers's team were not averse to conceding goals – they had even shipped half a dozen in an embarrassing 6-1 defeat at Sheffield United in March. But at Fortress Ninian they had conceded more than one goal on just one occasion and had only let in 14 in the league all season up to this point.

There was nothing wrong with Leeds' midfield play. They knocked it around with some guile at times, but they lacked the killer instinct in front of goal. The City back-line never looked in any serious trouble.

City's attractive play continued into the second half, and the bumper crowd had to wait only ten minutes before it was 3-0. Roley Williams, having one of his best games since signing from Welsh League minnows Milford United three years earlier, won a strong challenge with Hair and played over a trademark accurate cross. Chisholm was caught off balance but managed to arch backwards to produce a clever header which beat the advancing Scott and trickled over the line into the Grange End net. Chisholm, a fighter pilot during the Second World War, was a £12,000 signing from struggling Second Division rivals Coventry in March 1952 and scored eight crucial goals in just 11 appearances. It turned out to be another Spiers master-stroke.

Spiers, who had been number two to Leeds counterpart Buckley at Wolves, had been visibly stressed before kick-off but could now breathe easy.

The Leeds players had started dreaming of summer holidays in Minehead and City turned on the style. *The Western Mail* said, "The Welsh side settled down to play a brand of football which stamped them as obvious winners," and, "they delighted with fine go-ahead play."

City nearly had a fourth goal on 65 minutes when Chisholm crashed a header against the crossbar from an Edwards cross before Blair tried a cheeky lob which Scott just managed to push over.

City's defence had held the upper hand throughout the game with Leeds rarely threatening, but there was to be a consolation for the visitors through Iggleden with three minutes remaining. The Yorkshireman shot in via a post after Fidler had broken down the right.

It wasn't nearly enough to produce any fears among the supporters though, who had witnessed an incredible season of home dominance. City had sealed promotion by 0.13 of a goal on goal average to finish second behind champions Sheffield Wednesday. This had been a team effort from one to 11, but *Echo* reporter Kelper hailed, "McLaughlin, the magnificent; Glyn Williams, the unconquerable; Wilf Grant, the untameable; and Alf Sherwood, the unshakeable."

Fans leapt on to the pitch for an orgy of backslapping and congratulations. City were back where their directors and supporters believed they ought to be. Indeed, the *Echo* thought it would be the start of City "rivalling those famous clubs in efforts for greater honours".

Supporters congregated in front of the Grandstand and demanded to see their heroes. First up was Sherwood, who would later be described in the same breath as Stanley Matthews by team-mate Montgomery. "I can hardly find words to express my delight," he told the throng in front of him.

Sir Herbert then took the microphone and pledged that City were in the First Division to stay. But the crowd wanted more. "We want Grant, we want Grant," they chanted, hoping for one more glimpse of their two-goal hero. Some of the players had already stripped for their communal bath but got re-dressed to appease the fans from the directors' box.

Sir Herbert called for three cheers and then the players were finally able to return to their champagne in the dressing room, which was shared with the Leeds players. Speaking about the adulation from fans, Grant said, "I don't think I'll ever forget that, ever."

The only shame was that club founder Bart Wilson had missed the game through illness.

Spiers immediately promised the City faithful that his team would survive at the higher level, even suggesting that the slower tempo would suit the Bluebirds. And he was right. City finished 12th the following season, followed by a tenth-place finish in 1953/54 before Spiers moved on to Crystal Palace. City's time in the top division eventually came to an end in 1957.

6 v Liverpool 6-1

28 December 1957. Attendance: 30,622
Second Division. Ninian Park

CARDIFF CITY:	LIVERPOOL:
Ken Jones	Tommy Younger
Ron Stitfall	John Molyneux
Alec Milne	Don Campbell
Alan Harrington	Ronnie Moran
Danny Malloy	Dick White
Colin Baker	Alan A'Court
Brian Walsh	John Wheeler
Brayley Reynolds	Tony McNamara
Joe Bonson	Billy Liddell
Ron Hewitt	Tony Rowley
Colin Hudson	Bobby Murdoch

Referee: D.G. Brandwood (Kidderminster)

T COULD have finished 9-1 – that was the damning verdict of the Merseyside press after City tore league leaders Liverpool apart in this incredible Christmas 1957 goal-fest.

American singer Harry Belafonte was number one in the charts with 'Mary's Boy Child' when Colin Hudson, Brayley Reynolds (two), Ron Hewitt and Joe Bonson (two) fired the Bluebirds to a 6-1 triumph over the mighty Reds. City's hungry forward line had run the five-times First Division champions ragged from the first whistle and had stormed into a 5-0 lead by half-time. Had they not eased off after the break, it might even have been more embarrassing for the visitors.

While Phil Taylor's Liverpool were top of the Second Division – and had been for five weeks – the result was not altogether a surprise. That was because the Bluebirds, who had started the season poorly, had hit a rich vein of form. They had beaten Barnsley 7-0 at Ninian – the club's biggest post-war league victory – but then followed that up with a 2-0 defeat at Fulham.

On 21 December City enjoyed their first ever league win at Swansea, and then Trevor Morris's team beat high-flying Stoke City 5-2 at home on Boxing Day. This demolition job on Liverpool made it 18 goals in three successive home league games, a record which still stands and is unlikely to ever be beaten. Newspaper talk of City challenging for an immediate return to the First Division was premature, but the Blues had certainly turned a corner and looked a different prospect from the team which was bottom of the pile just 14 weeks earlier.

This pre-Shankly Liverpool team was certainly not a classic by the standards of the famous Anfielders but it did include some more than useful players at Second Division level. Legendary striker Billy Liddell, the club's all-time fourth highest goalscorer, was in the 20th of 23 years with Liverpool and had already scored 11 league goals that season. He had netted in Liverpool's 3-0 win over City at Anfield in August, a game which is remembered for a Cardiff fan running on to the pitch to plant leeks before kick-off.

Another popular figure was defender Ronnie Moran. The consistent performer, 23 at the time, played a total of 379 times for Liverpool and even had two stints as caretaker manager in 1991 and 1992. For the trip to South Wales, Taylor stuck with the same team which beat Grimsby Town 3-2 on Boxing Day, local lad Bobby Murdoch keeping his place at inside-left and former Everton star Tony McNamara at outside-right.

For City, five-goal Hewitt passed a fitness test having recovered from the knee problem which saw him miss the Stoke victory. The £7,000 summer signing from Wrexham took the number ten jersey from Cliff Nugent.

Colin 'The Rock' Hudson was married in the morning but raced back for the game. And it was the newly-wed who put the home side ahead after just five minutes. City progressed up the pitch with some intelligent football and Reynolds and Hewitt combined to create the opening for Hudson. He cut in from the left wing and unleashed a thunderous shot which flew past the Liverpool keeper, his third goal in as many games.

Hudson, 22, might have been forgiven for having his mind fixed on post-match activities yet *Western Mail* reporter Dewi Lewis rated his performance the best yet for the club since signing from Newport County months earlier.

The crowds were flocking back to Ninian Park to see what this City transformation was all about. More than 30,000 packed in – and the *South Wales Echo* said they "gasped with amazement" as the rampant Bluebirds put the visitors under intense pressure from the off. Both teams continued to play fast, attractive football with Liverpool a couple of times at full stretch to deal with through balls. Not that it was all one-way traffic. McNamara raced clear down the Liverpool right and an equaliser looked on the cards but the City defence managed to scramble clear.

But it was 2-0 after just 17 minutes when the exceptional Hewitt hit a speculative shot. It seemed to lack any real power but Scottish goalkeeper Tommy Younger went down too late and to the surprise of everyone in the ground, not least Hewitt, the net rippled. To give Younger the benefit of the doubt, he might have been unsighted.

City were now in complete control and playing like the side top of the table rather than the one in 15th. Younger redeemed himself to an extent with a fine save with his foot from Reynolds and John Molyneux twice hacked off the line.

Liddell headed over the bar for the Reds while at the other end Dick White stepped in to stop a Brian Walsh ball going to Benson.

Liverpool were rattled and it was another Younger howler which gifted City their third goal on 31 minutes. Blackwood lad Reynolds hit a hopeful back-heeled lob towards goal but Younger fumbled and the ball embarrassingly spun over his shoulder and trickled over the line.

That goal knocked the stuffing out of Liverpool and two more defensive calamities saw City go five clear. First, just two minutes after City's third, a bad White back-pass was out of Younger's reach and Bonson came charging in to force it home.

City keeper Ken Jones, from Aberdare, made a couple of tidy saves while Bonson cracked the Liverpool post.

Then a minute before half-time White again played a shoddy ball back to his keeper and Reynolds nipped in for one of the easiest goals of his career.

It was completely uncharacteristic of Liverpool, who up until this shambles of an afternoon boasted the meanest defence in the league. Stork wrote in the *Liverpool Echo*,

"Never in my long history of following football have I seen so many defensive errors." But Liverpool's inadequacies should not detract from City's brilliance.

And it wasn't just the Bluebirds' slick passing in attack which impressed. Half-backs Alan Harrington, Danny Malloy and Colin Baker shone and Ron Stitfall put in a captain's display. The *Liverpool Daily Post* reporter said he could see "no earthly chance" of his team recovering, which won't go down in journalism folklore as the bravest of predictions.

City did not go into half-time with a 5-0 lead again until 45 years later when the feat was repeated at Oldham Athletic's Boundary Park.

McNamara had taken a knock to his knee during the first half and came out heavily bandaged.

Unsurprisingly, the second half was not as packed with thrills as the first as City eased off. John Wheeler fired a decent shot goalwards but a deflection took it out for a corner. Meanwhile, Walsh attacked down the right but was successfully stopped by Moran.

A Liddell piledriver then rocked the crossbar and Murdoch spurned the rebound. At last Liverpool were showing glimpses of quality and Jones had to produce impressive acrobatics to tip another Liddell effort over the bar.

Baker was unlucky to see his shot cleared off the line by Moran as City began to re-find their feet. The sixth goal came with 13 minutes remaining – and it was a Bonson special. Burly Bonson had been signed for £7,000 from Wolves just a month earlier to replace flop Johnny Nicholls. The centre-forward thundered a shot with his right foot which Younger blocked but Bonson was there to smash the rebound even harder with his left, almost breaking the net. It was Bonson's sixth goal in as many games and his fourth in three days.

Welshman Tony Rowley had a poor game in general but came close with a header over the City bar. But there was some consolation for the small band of Liverpool fans with two minutes to go when Jones failed to get to a soft long-range Wheeler shot.

The second half might not have produced the excitement of the first, but the City fans went home more than happy with what they had seen. Sure, Liverpool's peculiar defensive frailties led to most of City's goals, but it was the speed of Cardiff's play which unsettled the visitors' defence.

Man of the match was Hewitt – and in front of Welsh selectors, too. His form was rewarded with his first of five caps against Israel in January. He finished the season as City's top scorer with 14 league goals, two more than Bonson.

The win took City up just two places, but now just seven points off new leaders Fulham. But thin hopes of a promotion push in the second half of the season soon disappeared as City went on to win just five of their remaining 17, finishing 15th.

Manager Morris remained at the club just seven more months before accepting a job at Swansea Town.

Liverpool, meanwhile, finished the season in fourth, two points shy of the promotion places. Bill Shankly arrived two years later, took them up in 1961/62 – and Liverpool have been in the top division ever since.

Their supporters don't like being reminded of this gobsmacking afternoon, though.

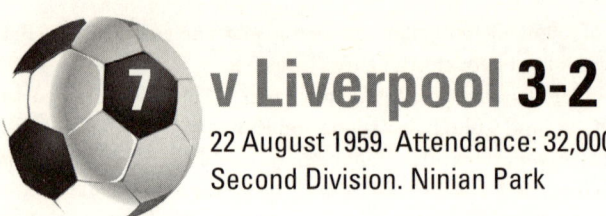

7 v Liverpool 3-2

22 August 1959. Attendance: 32,000
Second Division. Ninian Park

CARDIFF CITY:	LIVERPOOL:
Graham Vearncombe	Bert Slater
Alan Harrington	John Molyneux
Alec Milne	Ronnie Moran
Derrick Sullivan	Johnny Wheeler
Danny Malloy	Dick White
Colin Baker	Geoff Twentyman
Brian Walsh	Fred Morris
Derek Tapscott	Jimmy Melia
Graham Moore	Louis Bimpson
Steve Mokone	James Harrower
Johnny Watkins	Alan A'Court

Referee: Mr J.W. Hunt (Portsmouth)

THERE WAS a time when Liverpool quaked in their boots at the mere thought of a game at Cardiff. And with good reason. Ninian Park had become a major bogey ground for the Scousers. Before this one they had lost all of their last four games in the Welsh capital – and with an aggregate score of 16-2. A 6-1 battering in 1957/58 was still fresh in the memory, and the previous season they had gone down 3-0. They had last won in Cardiff in 1929.

Liverpool boss Phil Taylor was desperate for his team to quash the 30-year hoodoo on the first day of the 1959/60 season. But even though City skipper Danny Malloy put through his own net twice, the Reds faltered again against the Bluebirds.

It was a scintillating start to a wonderful season which ended in City earning promotion to the First Division after a three season absence. But before the big kick-off it was Liverpool rather than City who were being tipped for success. The Anfielders had finished third twice and fourth twice in their last four seasons and had the likes of goal-getter Billy Liddell and winger Alan A'Court in their number.

Bill Jones had been made City manager at the start of the previous season and had guided the club to a good enough ninth-place finish. There hadn't been massive activity during the close-season. Brayley Reynolds left for Swansea Town and, a little surprisingly, Ron Hewitt, the club's top goalscorer for the last two years, was flogged to Wrexham for £5,000. Two players came in; inside-forward Steve Mokone from Dutch club Heracles, and Bristol City outside-left Johnny Watkins, signed for just £2,500.

But City had a youngster coming through their ranks who this season would prove more important than any signing could ever have been. That man was 18-year-old Graham Moore, who despite only having five first team appearances under his belt was already attracting interest from Arsenal. He had delighted Jones by cracking four goals in the public trial the previous week. Two months after impressing in this game he earned the first of 21 Wales caps against England.

Mokone, Watkins and Moore all started for the Bluebirds on a typically sweltering opening day of the season. Jones had been searching for a ball player to bring the best out of Derek Tapscott and Moore but had so far drawn a blank, deciding to instead go with what he had.

But City had to do without goalkeeper Ron Nicholls, who missed just three games the previous season, as he was required by his other employer, Gloucestershire Cricket Club, where he was a highly-regarded batsman. The overlap in the seasons of the two sports caused friction for Nicholls throughout his career, but he remained determined to play both.

Cardiff-born Graham Vearncombe, who had been in and out of the side since breaking into the first team in 1953, was handed the number one shirt – and kept hold of it for most of the campaign.

There was, though, a clever positional change implemented by Jones, Alec Milne switching with Alan Harrington on the right to try to keep A'Court quiet. Milne had got the better of A'Court on previous meetings and Jones was banking on the 22-year-old doing the same again.

There was just one change for Liverpool to the team which finished the previous season, and that was also between the sticks. Scotland Under-23 cap Bert Slater replaced Tommy Younger, who had taken on the manager's job at Falkirk. Younger would have been glad to have escaped another trip to Ninian Park, a ground where he had conceded nine in the last two seasons and had looked decidedly shaky.

And 23-year-old Slater was immediately in action as City started the season with a flurry. Less than a minute was on referee Hunt's wristwatch when Moore slipped a ball to Watkins who, with his very first touch as a Cardiff player, instinctively fired towards the corner. Slater was alive to the danger and pushed it clear.

James Harrower sliced a shot over the bar at the other end before Slater was called upon again, this time to save from Colin Baker. Brian Walsh's corner had beaten Harrower and had fallen to the Welsh international. Baker drilled a shot towards the post but Slater somehow managed to scramble across his goal-line to make a wonderful stop.

It was an electric opening which had the large crowd buzzing with excitement. Vearncombe made a stunning point-blank save from an A'Court thunder-blast before City had a crucial lead through unknown quantity Mokone.

The slight forward became the first black South African footballer to play in Europe when he turned out for Coventry City in the Third Division South two seasons earlier, but he became frustrated and lonely in England and departed. Mokone, nicknamed 'Kalamazoo', had a trial at Real Madrid before joining Heracles and later Cardiff City. There was a sense of the exotic about the 26-year-old, but it remained to be seen whether he could cut it in the Second Division. Mokone appeared to provide an answer after just six minutes when he thumped City in front after Slater had pushed a Tapscott shot square into his path.

The City fans desperately wanted Mokone to be a success but his season was blighted by ankle injuries and he was offloaded at the end of the campaign having played just five games for the Bluebirds. Mokone later signed for Barcelona and went on loan to Marseilles – but didn't play a game for either – before finishing his career in Australia and Canada. Mokone, now in his 80s, spent 12 years in a New York jail for assaults against two women which he insists he did not commit. In 2000 a film was released based on Mokone's topsy-turvy life called *The Black Meteor*.

Despite the early lead, Liverpool continued to look dangerous. Louis Bimpson was sent through on goal by Ronnie Moran and managed to get a good shot away but Vearncombe produced a diving save.

The frantic tempo did eventually calm but chances continued to come. For City, Moore saw a shot on the turn charged down, Dick White almost caught Slater unaware and Walsh's long-range pot shot was punched clear.

Liverpool's Jimmy Melia was a player capable of opening games up with his exceptional footwork and soon after he almost created a chance for Bimpson after ghosting past three blue shirts, but Malloy read the play well to intercept.

Some Mokone magic brought much excitement from the crowd before almost out of nothing Liverpool had an equaliser on 38 minutes. Melia came forward with the ball and with no one with him in support tried a hopeful shot. Vearncombe had it covered – until it struck Malloy's chest and flew past him.

Malloy was a brave, tough-tackling Scot who made himself popular with supporters by launching his body in front of shots, but he was famed for scoring own goals. In 262 appearances for City (including the Welsh Cup) he put through his own net an incredible 14 times – once every 19 games on average – including once in Liverpool's 3-0 home win against City in 1957. Unbelievably, his finishing at the right end was not so sharp, netting just twice in his six seasons at the club.

And Malloy put himself in pole position for the Liverpool golden boot award when he put the visitors 2-1 ahead on 42 minutes. If his first own goal was unfortunate, the second was inexplicable. When A'Court dashed down the wing and crossed, there were four City players near the ball and not a red shirt in sight. Had Malloy done nothing it would have rolled harmlessly out of play, but instead he tried to bring the ball under control while running backwards and put it past Vearncombe. The generous *Western Mail* reporter commented that he had not heard any of the other City players telling Malloy that he didn't need to intervene.

Tapscott tried to pull City level again but Slater was equal to his powerful shot and Liverpool went into half-time with a fortuitous lead.

But City did not waste any time feeling sorry for themselves and drew level within three minutes. Walsh and Mokone combined to give Moore ample space, and he cracked in a beauty from eight yards. Liverpool's defenders cast a hopeful glance to the linesman, but the flag remained locked to his side. It was the youngster's first of 16 goals in all competitions in a season in which he missed just two games and was scouted by the best clubs in the country.

The adventure of both teams made for an exciting second half, and the City faithful roared their approval. They thought City's third was imminent when versatile player Derrick Sullivan swung a cross in and Tapscott came tearing in, but Slater blocked the shot with his body.

City were piling pressure on Liverpool with deadly balls into the area and the winner came on the hour. Walsh beat the visiting defence and picked out Watkins on the corner of the penalty area. With no defenders near, he had all the time he needed to pick his spot, sending a low left-footed drive into the bottom corner. It was an equal measure of good attacking and poor defending.

Like Younger before him, Slater had had a torrid afternoon at Ninian Park, picking the ball out his net on three occasions, but the *Liverpool Echo* exonerated him of any blame. "A less capable player would have been beaten more frequently," the paper said.

Liverpool tried to turn the screw in the last half hour. Fred Morris and A'Court both missed the target before Melia raced on to a Harrower through pass, only to have the ball nicked off his toes by an alert Vearncombe charging off his line.

Vearncombe then saved well from a left foot Harrower drive, while at the other end Walsh almost capitalised from more lax Liverpool defending.

There were one or two hairy moments late on, but City held out for a thoroughly deserved victory to kick-start one of the club's greatest seasons. Malloy, to his enormous credit, delivered a sterling second half display, muting the threat of Bimpson expertly. It was the first time the Bluebirds had won – or even managed a goal – on the opening day of the season in four attempts.

The Western Mail praised City's fighting spirit, but Liverpool came in for a hard time from their local paper. Horace Yates in the *Daily Post* wrote, "Liverpool took these points and in a distressing sort of little ceremony handed them over in the most benevolent fashion to their Welsh foes."

That was followed by an almost desperate call for the club to make a move for Middlesbrough goalscorer Brian Clough. Whatever became of him?

City went on to notch up six wins from their first eight league games, a record good enough to take the Bluebirds up to second. Jones's team remained fairly consistent throughout the season and were eventually promoted with three games to spare.

Liverpool, meanwhile, suffered a poor start to the season and were in 11th position when an emotional Taylor tendered his resignation in November. A month later Huddersfield Town boss Bill Shankly accepted an offer to take over at Anfield. It was an appointment which would change the course of the club – but his reign didn't get off to the best of starts. The usually outspoken coach was subdued after watching his side get tonked 4-0 by Cardiff at Anfield.

8 v Aston Villa 1-0

16 April 1960. Attendance: 54,769
Second Division. Ninian Park

CARDIFF CITY:	ASTON VILLA:
Ron Nicholls	Nigel Sims
Alec Milne	John Neal
Ron Stitfall	Stan Lynn
Steve Gammon	Jimmy Dugdale
Danny Malloy	Vic Crowe
Colin Baker	Pat Saward
Brian Walsh	Jimmy Adam
Derek Tapscott	Peter McParland
Graham Moore	Bobby Thomson
Colin Hudson	Johnny Dixon
Johnny Watkins	Ron Wylie

Referee: Rogers

SOMETIMES IN football, it's just meant to be – and this game could hardly have been better set up. Bill Jones's brilliant Bluebirds knew that a single point against Aston Villa in front of a hysterical Ninian Park crowd would clinch promotion to the First Division with three games to spare.

But better than that, the maximum two points would see the Bluebirds leapfrog leaders Villa to the top of the table and immediately become huge favourites to win the second tier title for the first time.

And as fate would have it, the huge fixture landed on the date selected to celebrate 50 years of Ninian Park. By coincidence and in a neat piece of symmetry, the visitors for the stadium-opening friendly in September 1910 were also Villa.

It all pointed to a magnificent afternoon of sporting theatre. City fans have become all-too-familiar with being let down on big occasions but this was one day when the final whistle brought delirium rather than disappointment.

The atmosphere in Cardiff on the day of the game was incredible as thousands descended on the capital. The official crowd was announced as close to 55,000, but another 5,000 can probably be added to that number. Either way, it was well above the season average of 25,000.

Thousands had travelled down from The Valleys – some on foot due to a 24-hour strike by Rhondda Valley busmen – and hordes of away fans had come from Birmingham on two special trains. And to add to the chaos Cardiff were playing the Barbarians in their annual rugby fixture. More than 100,000 sports fans thronged the streets of Cardiff, the biggest Bank Holiday crowd the city had seen for many years.

City and Villa had tussled for top spot throughout the whole season. Joe Mercer's Villans led the way from the seventh game of the season through to the 31st when City briefly took the baton. There was an intense scrap for the honours for the final 11 games and going into this match just one point separated the clubs. Villa had already guaranteed their immediate return to the First Division after relegation in 1958/59. This clash looked like being the one which either guaranteed the Midlanders the championship or which put City firmly in the driving seat.

Modest City boss Jones had built what is still considered to be one of the most exciting City teams in history. Before this match the Bluebirds had lost just six games and had scored goals in abundance. They had found the net 86 times – more than anyone else in the division – including 20 goals from Derek Tapscott, 14 from winger Johnny Watkins and 18 by strong centre-forward Joseph Bonson.

But the golden boy was undoubtedly Graham Moore, who had just turned 19. The centre-forward, already a full Wales international, had set the division alight with his sparkling natural ability. He had already started working at the Penallta pit coal face when he was offered a route into professional football aged 16. Now three years on Jones was tipping blonde-haired Moore to be better than John Charles.

Jones would often surprise supporters with his team selections – and he had a shock move up his sleeve this day as well by recalling Colin Hudson at inside-left. The man nicknamed 'The Rock' was preferred over utility man Derrick Sullivan, who had filled in for the injured Bonson in the 1-0 win at Stoke City the previous weekend. The *Western Mail* said there were "gasps of amazement" from the City fans.

Skipper Danny Malloy sat out the Stoke match with a knee problem – the only league game he missed in three consecutive seasons from 1958 to 1961 – but was back in at centre-half.

Villa, going into this game on the back of a 2-1 home win over Bristol City, had to do without centre-forward Gerry Hitchens. The England international scored 41 goals in 99 league and cup games for City before being transferred to Villa Park for £22,500 in 1957. To the disappointment of the City crowd, Hitchens missed this match with a shoulder injury.

Even without Hitchens, who scored in Villa's 2-0 win against City in December, there was plenty of talent in the Villa ranks. Probably the most dangerous was Irish winger Peter McParland, who was a goal threat with his head as well as his boot. Also in the visitors' starting line-up was speedy outside-left Jimmy Adam and strong forward Bobby Thomson.

The Ninian Park gates opened at midday and half an hour before the 3.15pm kick-off the gates to both enclosures were locked. The hum of excitement mixed with the stench of Woodbines as supporters anticipated a return to the First Division after a three-year break. There was one more surprise for the masses as City ran out in their second-choice strip of white shirts and shorts with blue piping. The only explanation for this bizarre decision came from Mervyn Thomas at the *South Wales Echo*, who suggested that the players were hoping to somehow "draw greater inspiration from this new outfit than from their traditional gear".

Ninian was absolutely jumping as the match got underway. It was a thrilling start with the ball quickly moving from end to end as both teams tried to find their rhythm. Hudson, who had not played since the beginning of October, was a livewire from the off and produced some decent early touches.

McParland and Ron Wylie were looking threatening at the other end but Steve Gammon and Alec Milne combined to snuff out one move. Shortly after Brian Walsh and Tapscott linked up and Hudson looked set to be in for the opening goal but fast and agile goalkeeper Nigel Sims stole it from his feet.

But the excitable home fans did not have to wait long for the historic goal on 12 minutes – and right on script it was wonderkid Moore. Walsh won the battle with John Neal on halfway and pushed the ball down the right flank for Hudson, who had made an opportunistic run. Hudson was under pressure from Jimmy Dugdale who came charging across but the former Newport County man managed to squeeze the ball across, slicing the Villa defence in two. Moore had looked slightly nervy in the opening minutes but showed no hesitation in cracking his left foot shot in from 12 yards.

The volume cranked up a notch as City took control. The Bluebirds came close on 20 minutes when Tapscott caught the Villa defence out with a clever little chip over the top. Hudson almost burst a blood vessel to get on the end of it but could only volley over the bar from close range.

Villa showed signs of getting back into the game with Pat Saward and Welsh international Vic Crowe looking lively, but City were superbly marshalled by man of the match Malloy. Tackles were robust but fair.

Tapscott and Watkins showed glimpses of their ability at times and on one occasion they combined to set up Hudson, who could only smash over once again. For the visitors McParland had a decent opening but he too ballooned over.

City had a lucky escape seven minutes before half-time when the ball struck Milne on the hand. It looked like referee Rogers would point to the spot but instead the man in black awarded a free kick on the edge of the area. McParland hit the free kick to the side of the wall but Ron Stitfall anticipated it and cleared the danger.

City might have gone into the break two goals up after Moore played a wonderful low pass through the middle, but Hudson was slow to react and Villa recovered.

The Bluebirds were more defensive in the second half with Adam posing a worrying threat for Villa. The home fans held their breath during a melee inside the area during which McParland, Wylie and Thomson all had shots blocked but eventually 34-year-old Stitfall coolly cleared the danger.

There was more drama when Adams slipped the ball through to Wylie but Ron Nicholls managed to grasp the ball.

Tempers flared between Watkins and Crowe in the 50th minute before Walsh thought he should have had a penalty for City when he was sent to ground by Neal but the referee gave a goal kick. And there was another loud appeal from the stands soon after when Tapscott was clattered in the box by Saward after being put through by Gammon but again the referee saw nothing in it. Both would have been penalties – and probably red cards – in today's game.

There was a tense atmosphere around Ninian as the crunching tackles continued. Villa tested Nicholls but the City stopper, starting only his third league game of the season having played second fiddle to Graham Vearncombe for the majority of the campaign, was up to the task.

City's defence remained rock solid as Villa continued to threaten with the long ball. Yet Jones's men still had the bravery to attack and Neal had to head away under pressure after a fierce cross from Walsh.

Colin Baker was then cynically fouled and was left writhing in pain on the floor. Fortunately the wing-half from Cardiff did return to his feet and was able to continue.

There were moments of relief for City as they managed to get the ball in the Villa box. Tapscott's header was well saved by Sims and then Gammon tried a spectacular first time shot after a Watkins free kick and was just inches off target.

The last few minutes were as tense as any witnessed at Ninian during her 99 years. Fans chanted and stamped their feet to encourage the men in white. McParland, who was given licence to roam from wing to wing, was brought down a fraction outside the area. And then in the very last minute Stitfall handled again just inches outside the area. Neither free kick amounted to anything.

The referee added 90 seconds of stoppage time because of the earlier injuries – but eventually the whistle sounded to signal City's return to the elite league of British football. "Pandemonium reigned," said the *Western Mail* as the supporters poured on to the pitch. The report added, "The vast throng on the popular bank surged over the boundary wall and a human wave enveloped the players, who were trying desperately to reach the comparative calm of the dressing room." The last time Ninian had seen such mayhem was on promotion day against Leeds in 1952.

Jubilant fans stayed on the pitch and chanted for their heroes to return. Eventually they did emerge from the changing rooms and chairman Ron Beecher, manager Jones, trainer Wilf Grant and skipper Malloy spoke to the crowds from the directors' box through microphones.

Beecher paid tribute to Jones, the man who in just his second season in charge had instilled a wonderful team spirit right throughout the club. Then it was Jones's turn to take the mic. Jones, who lived in Barry, made no promises. According to the *Western Mail*, he said, "We have a great struggle ahead and we want your support. We are back in the First Division and must stay there. I have had a grand lot of lads under me and I know they will face the task ahead confidently and, we all hope, successfully."

Then Grant, who scored 67 goals in four seasons for City as centre-forward between 1949 and 1954, including 27 in the 1952 promotion campaign, said, "How the lads deserved it! They have worked really hard all season, and no one realised it more than me when they struck a bad patch."

Champagne was presented to both teams, who had proved themselves to be, by some distance, the two best in the division. Former Everton and Arsenal left-half Mercer, who would later go on to manage England briefly, promised that the title race was not over. He told the crowd, "We at Villa Park have had Cardiff much in mind all season – small wonder because you have played some great football. The championship issue is not settled yet and we'll fight to the bitter end. But how grand is it that the Villa and Cardiff City, both steeped in tradition, go hand in hand together to the First Division."

As the congratulatory telegraphs poured in over the next couple of days – one even from Swansea Town – preparations were in full swing for a season against the likes of Wolves, Tottenham and Manchester United. Requests for season tickets started to drop through the Ninian letterbox just hours after promotion was assured even though they could not be allocated until after the Football League's annual meeting.

A poor end to the season in which City lost against Plymouth and drew against Sunderland and Bristol Rovers meant that Villa won the title by a point.

The following season, 1960/61, was as hard as Jones had predicted but some stunning results, including a 3-0 win over Manchester United and a 3-2 success over double-chasing Tottenham, saw the Bluebirds finish five points above the drop zone.

But 1961/62 ended in relegation and after a poor start to 1962/63, Jones was dismissed. But the shy family man will never be forgotten by Cardiff City as the man who delivered top flight football to the capital of Wales – the last to do so until Malky Mackay finally repeated the feat in 2013.

9 v Knighton Town 16-0

28 January 1961. Attendance: 3,800
Welsh Cup Round Five. Ninian Park

CARDIFF CITY:	KNIGHTON TOWN:
Maurice Swan	David Cunnington
Alan Harrington	Ivor Price
Ron Stitfall	Ken Price
Steve Gammon	Johnny Crump
Danny Malloy	Johnny Draycott
Colin Baker	Francis
Brian Walsh	G Price
Derek Tapscott	Bobby Mayle
Graham Moore	Reece
Peter Donnelly	Bodenham
Derek Hogg	Ted Jones

Referee: Mr J. Meredith (Shrewsbury)

CITY COULD have scored 30 – and that is no exaggeration. In the end the Bluebirds settled for a mere 16 goals without reply, their biggest ever win in a recognised first team fixture. The scoreline made an absolute mockery of the Welsh FA's insistence on clubs fielding their strongest team in the Welsh Cup. It had all started the previous season when City, pushing for promotion to the First Division, courted controversy by naming a reserve team to face Swansea in the sixth round of the competition. The decision angered the governing body – and the ill feeling spilled on to the pitch.

Swansea fielded their Second Division team yet the second string Bluebirds outfit took the lead when a Steve Mokone shot was deflected into the net by Alan Woods. Harry Knowles doubled City's lead with 15 minutes to go as tackles became more and more rash. Brayley Reynolds pulled a goal back for the home side before Colin Hudson was sent off for Cardiff. Soon after Mokone and Swansea's Harry Griffiths were both red-carded after wrestling and slinging mud at each other.

The FA of Wales held an inquiry into Cardiff's selection policy and duly fined the club £350 and ordered them to name their strongest 11 in future Welsh Cup matches.

The Knighton tie was a complete mismatch. Bill Jones's City were 12th in the First Division and just two weeks earlier had beaten fourth-placed Burnley 2-1 at Ninian Park. A couple of months before that they had won 3-0 against a Manchester United team which included the likes of Bobby Charlton, Bill Foulkes and Harry Gregg. Now they were coming up against Mid-Wales minnows Knighton, a team of mechanics, salesmen and bank clerks.

Just two of the Radnor Robins' team had any league experience – captain Bobby Mayle and Johnny Draycott, who made just a handful of appearances for Shrewsbury Town between them. Centre-half Draycott had been tipped for a successful career in the game but suffered tuberculosis and lost a lung while young. It is quite remarkable that he continued to play in the Welsh League until he was 42.

Knighton were top of the Mid-Wales League at the time and scoring goals for fun. By the end of their 24-game campaign they had notched a mind-boggling 112 goals, an average of 4.6 goals per game, though they did end up finishing third. In reaching the fifth round of the cup, the twice semi-finalists had already beaten Llandrindod Wells, Welshpool, Macynlleth and Towyn. City, meanwhile, waltzed into the competition at the fifth round stage.

Jones had applied to the Welsh FA for permission to field a weakened team, which was duly rejected. That left the City chief with little room to manoeuvre when it came to picking his team, though there was one change from the side which lost 2-1 at Nottingham Forest a week earlier, Brian Walsh coming in for Johnny Watkins. Watkins paid the price for missing gilt-edged chances against Forest and Manchester City. Former Arsenal man Walsh started on the right flank with Derek Hogg switching to the left wing.

With no European football on offer to the Welsh Cup winners until the following season, the competition was not a priority for City, but this game was seen as a chance to get the misfiring forwards back on the goal trail. There was nothing wrong with City's defence – with just 46 conceded in the league it was the best outside the top three. But at the other end, City had managed just 37 goals in their 27 games. Only bottom of the pile Preston North End had scored less.

Derek Tapscott had netted 16 times, but aside from that there was little to get excited about. Jones had been trailing Bristol Rovers' want-away forward Dai Ward in a bid to add some pace to his attack, a move which eventually materialised in February.

The tie was officially Knighton's home match but both teams agreed to play at Ninian Park. The match programme was printed by City and featured the familiar design but in Knighton's home colour of red. And despite the venue, the match had the feel of an away game for City, too, with more fans from the small Powys village than from the capital. City had pulled in more than 25,000 fans for the home game against Burnley, yet not many more than 1,000 were interested in the early rounds of the Welsh Cup.

The 2,000-or-so Town fans who had made the trip down the A470 were in good spirits with red rosettes, bells and rattles. And their chances looked reasonable when straight from the kick-off they managed a dangerous looking cross into the City box. Unfortunately for Town, that was as good as their afternoon got.

Mechanic David Cunnington's goal was bombarded from all angles in the opening ten minutes. And City had a penalty early on when right-half Johnny Crump showed great goalkeeping skills to leap and palm out a shot from Peter Donnelly. He was mercifully spared a red card. Walsh stepped up and blasted the kick well wide of the post.

Despite almost absolute dominance, it took City 15 minutes to break the deadlock when Graham Moore directed his header home from a Walsh cross for his second goal of the season, and his first since missing three months with a broken leg.

That goal opened the floodgates. On 21 minutes Walsh tore through three Town defenders before setting up Tapscott for his first of the afternoon – and after 36 minutes Moore banged in City's third.

Knighton's young team, average age of just 22, were being ripped to shreds. Only some first-class goalkeeping by Cunnington kept the scoreline sensible. With eight minutes to go before half-time supporters of both sides rose to their feet to applaud a fantastic one-handed save from a Donnelly shot.

Remembering the match, Cunnington said years later, "The pressure was constant. It was good practice I suppose." And Knighton committee member David Isherwood said, "David had a screamer – it could have been 30 if it hadn't been for him."

But Cunnington was helpless to prevent City smashing four goals in four crazy minutes to take a 7-0 lead into half-time. First bustling forward Donnelly made it 4-0 before Moore forced his way through the flimsy Knighton back-line to score from all of two yards. Tapscott then tapped home a cross by Walsh, who was terrorising 19-year-old left-back Ken Price – and ruthless Tappy completed his hat-trick on 44 minutes.

The second half saw City continue to run riot under the new floodlights, which were installed during the summer. It took Moore just four minutes to notch his fourth of the 'contest', making it 8-0.

But the victory came at a price as minutes later stalwart Alan Harrington was clattered to the ground by a Knighton forward and suffered two broken ribs. The full-back was forced off for the remainder of the game, leaving City with ten men, and he missed the next three games. It did nothing to improve the City boss's attitude towards the Welsh Cup.

But even a man light, City continued to pile forward at will and scored another five goals in the next seven minutes. Tapscott pounced twice on 55 and 57 minutes to take his own tally to five before Donnelly headed in another tempting Walsh cross. Tapscott then became the only City player in history to score a 'double hat-trick' just past the hour when he drilled in from 20 yards. And Walsh finally got in on the act a minute later after running straight down the middle for 13-0.

With 28 minutes to play, City had made their point to the FAW bigwigs. Such annihilations did the competition no good at all. As an act of mercy, City switched their defence and attackers around, with Danny Malloy now leading the line.

There were comedy moments aplenty as the new-look attack spurned a string of golden chances, often by falling over the ball or even their own feet. But it was centre-half Malloy, more used to scoring own goals than he was netting at the right end, who registered next with a tidy finish from a tight angle.

Malloy managed just two goals in 262 appearances in all competitions for City, his only other coming from the penalty spot against Manchester United four seasons earlier. No wonder, then, that the goal received the loudest cheer of the day from the City fans. It turned out to be Malloy's last goal in blue and white before his shock summer move to Doncaster Rovers.

Outside-left Hogg bagged another with eight minutes remaining, his fourth of the campaign, before Walsh wrapped up the scoring two minutes later.

The press demanded a change of policy from the FAW to prevent similar massacres in the future. "Such a game as this does no credit for football and it would have been better if Cardiff had been allowed to select a team more in keeping with the strength of their visitors," said Dewi Lewis in the *Western Mail*.

City went on to get knocked out of the cup in a semi-final replay against Swansea Town in Llanelli. Meanwhile Knighton, quite unbelievably, followed up their 16-0 hammering with a 16-1 win against Bala Town. Has a team ever recorded two such contrasting results in succession?

The lure of European football meant that playing strong teams in the Welsh Cup became the norm in the years that followed. City won the competition five times in the 1960s – but they never had it as easy as they did against poor old Knighton.

v Arsenal 3-2

11 February 1961. Attendance: 33,534
First Division. Highbury

CARDIFF CITY:	ARSENAL:
Maurice Swan	Jack McClelland
Trevor Edwards	Len Wills
Ron Stitfall	Billy McCullough
Barrie Hole	Mel Charles
Danny Malloy	Allan Young
Colin Baker	Vic Groves
Brian Walsh	Alan Skirton
Graham Moore	Geoff Strong
Derek Tapscott	David Herd
Peter Donnelly	George Eastham
Derek Hogg	Joe Haverty

Referee: H.G. New (Hampshire)

MANY CONSIDER the 1960s to be football's golden years. There were great players which dazzled British supporters like Bobby Moore, Bobby Charlton and George Best, while overseas some chap called Pele was making a name for himself.

Attendances were good, too, with over a million people across the UK attending games every Saturday afternoon. Men and children, the rich and the poor, donned suits and piled through turnstiles to see their idols in action.

And best of all, Cardiff City were back in the First Division after a three-season absence. City's return had got off to a barely mediocre start with Bill Jones's side lingering in 19th position on Bonfire Night before out of nowhere a run of two defeats in 12 – including a 3-0 win over Manchester United – saw City surge up the table into 12th place. Now City's upturn was about to be put to the test with a trip to face seven times league champions Arsenal. What an afternoon it turned out to be for the 1,000 fans who journeyed from South Wales.

The Gunners were big favourites against the division's newbies, particularly as the Bluebirds' defence had been ravaged by injuries. There seemed no way that a City back-line missing the experience of Alan Harrington and Steve Gammon could cope with a strike-force boasting David Herd and George Eastham, but in the end there was little doubt that City were good value for their two points.

The famous Highbury clock showed six minutes past three when Graham Moore fired City ahead. The home side equalised in the 27th minute but City regained their composure and were in front once again through Derek Tapscott. Peter Donnelly gave City the two-goal cushion their dominance deserved early in the second half. Herd pulled one back for George Swindin's comparatively expensive team, but City held out comfortably for one of their greatest top flight away days. Admittedly, there were only 29 to choose from between the end of the Second World War and the start of the 2013/14 season.

Cardiff City's Greatest Games

Jones had tweaked his team after earning promotion, bringing in busy forward Donnelly from Scunthorpe United, Trevor Edwards from Charlton Athletic, Maurice Swan from Irish club Drumcondra and Brian Edgley from Shrewsbury Town. Derek Hogg was signed from West Bromwich Albion for £12,000 in October as Jones looked to add some experience.

But getting a result at Highbury, where Arsenal had won 21 points from a possible 28, looked unlikely. Dependable right-back Harrington was out with broken ribs and Gammon, considered one of the best defensive wing-halves in the country, had suffered a fractured leg after clashing with Denis Law in a 3-3 draw with Manchester City the previous Saturday. It was the end of Gammon's season and ruined his career. The Welshman who had shown so much promise broke the leg twice more in the next three seasons and managed just a handful of league appearances before admitting defeat.

Welsh international Edwards continued to fill in for Harrington while 18-year-old starlet Barrie Hole came in for Gammon at right-half. Tall and slim, Swansea-born Hole had made just 17 first team appearances and was now facing his toughest task yet – marking Gunners danger man Eastham.

Hole had caught the eye with a mature display for Wales Under-23s against England at Goodison Park three days earlier and he was outstanding again at Highbury. An exceptional talent with the ball at his feet, Hole would go on to reach his potential, later shining for Blackburn Rovers, Aston Villa and Swansea City after making more than 200 appearances for the Bluebirds.

Swan, meanwhile, started in goal in place of injured Graham Vearncombe and Derek Tapscott led the City attack against his former club. Tapscott spent five seasons at Arsenal, scoring 68 goals, before moving to Ninian Park in 1958. This season he had already hit 17 league goals. Also coming up against his former club was speedy right-winger Brian Walsh, who left Arsenal for Cardiff in 1955. He was given the captain's armband for the day.

It would be folly to suggest that this was a vintage Arsenal side. The famous north Londoners had not won the championship since 1953 and in 1959/60 finished a distinctively average 13th.

And they were not without their own injury worries. Most notably Jackie Henderson had picked up an ankle injury after scoring twice in their 3-3 draw at Newcastle United last time out. Centre-forward Herd, though, the third top scorer in the First Division with 23 strikes, had recovered from a bout of flu to start. Nineteen-year-old Arfon Griffiths, who would go on to earn the accolade of Wales legend, signed for Arsenal days before this match but did not feature.

There was one Welshman in the Arsenal line-up in Mel Charles, who returned to right-half after recovering from tonsillitis. The younger of the famous Charles brothers had been in and out of the side throughout the season with injury and illness.

There might have only been four positions and three points between the teams before kick-off but few pundits expected City to pick up their second win on the road. That was despite City beating Arsenal 1-0 at home in September thanks to a controversial Tapscott goal which appeared to come off his hand.

Going against the grain was *South Wales Echo* hack Peter Corrigan, who wrote, "Can City pinch anything from the home stronghold of Arsenal? The tipsters don't seem to think so and I'm yet to discover anyone who even gives City the chance of a draw. But with my usual brash optimism, I say that Cardiff could well provide a coupon shock."

It was City's second visit to Highbury that season as the second FA Cup replay against Manchester City had been played in north London a month earlier. That game finished 2-0 to their opponents – but this was a far more enjoyable trip to the Big Smoke for City's travelling fans.

Arsenal started brightly with Charles leading a couple of early charges, but once City had settled they started to play some neat football. And it took just six minutes for Jones's boys to take the lead. Donnelly picked up Moore's through ball, evaded the challenge of Charles and curled in a cross for Tapscott. The ex-Gunner played in Moore, who belied his recent poor form by slamming a first time shot into the far corner. It was the third league goal of the season for 19-year-old Moore, a former pit worker who would go on to score 32 in 101 first team outings for City.

City continued to pile on the pressure. Moore saw a header pushed over the bar by the Arsenal keeper and then the same player was not too far over with a 30-yard smash.

It came as something of a surprise when Arsenal drew level. Charles made a typical burst upfield and was harshly adjudged to have been fouled by Moore ten yards outside the area. Charles pushed the ball to Eastham, who knocked it on to Herd to fire a low and hard shot just inside the post from 25 yards or so. Players told the *Western Mail*'s Dewi Lewis afterwards that Swan had it covered until the ball swerved at the last moment.

That was harsh on City who had been the better team. Any worries of defensive frailties due to absentees were unfounded with Hole oozing class. The *Western Mail* said, "He had the famous George Eastham in his pocket and was going to keep him there."

The Bluebirds kept battling and had their reward just nine minutes later. The excellent Moore sent Tapscott away and he tried his luck with a shot towards the back post. Jack McClelland managed to get a hand to it, but there was Walsh charging in from the right to tap it home and make it 2-1. It was the third goal of the season for the fans' favourite.

The *Echo* said, "Arsenal were being clearly worried by this City side. They had not expected such class in the Cardiff attack." The *Western Mail* added, "An interval lead of 2-1 did not do Cardiff City justice."

One would imagine there was a contrast of emotions in the opposite dressing rooms at half-time – but just two minutes into the second half, things got worse for Swindin and his team. Tapscott won a corner, which was hit high into the air by Walsh and caught in the wind. McClelland was bamboozled by the ball's movement. He jumped for it but Donnelly got there first to force home his fifth goal of the campaign. The inside-left injured his wrist in the process and but managed to re-emerge a few minutes later complete with bandage.

Arsenal stepped up the pace and started to bombard City as they searched for a way back into the game, but time after time they were thwarted by a City defence which looked like it had been playing together for years. Regular captain Danny Malloy was demonstrating his usual consistency and Colin Baker, too, gave a strong performance.

And the progressively euphoric City fans almost had a fourth goal to celebrate when Donnelly's low volley from Hogg's pass was excellently saved by McClelland. Instead it was Arsenal who bagged the fifth goal of an exciting game on 71 minutes when Scotland cap Herd drilled in from ten yards after Haverty had finally split open the City defence with a killer pass.

Both teams went hammer and tongs for the decisive next goal in the final 19 minutes, but despite Arsenal's desperation and Charles's surging runs from the back, City never looked in any real danger of surrendering the lead they so richly deserved. "Anything

Arsenal did Cardiff did better," wrote Lewis, adding later in his prose, "At times they made Arsenal look like a very poor side indeed."

The Gunners forced two late corners but they came to nothing and the final whistle confirmed City's first league double over Arsenal since the 1923/24 season. It was only Cardiff's second double of the campaign, the other home and away success coming against reigning league champions Burnley.

And this, despite half a dozen attempts in the league and cup since, remains the last time that City won on Arsenal's home turf. Something to put right in the coming years, then.

11 v Tottenham Hotspur 3-2

11 March 1961. Attendance: 45,463
First Division. Ninian Park

CARDIFF CITY:
Ron Nicholls
Alan Harrington
Ron Stitfall
Barrie Hole
Danny Malloy
Colin Baker
Brian Walsh
Graham Moore
Derek Tapscott
Peter Donnelly
Derek Hogg

TOTTENHAM HOTSPUR:
Bill Brown
Peter Baker
Ron Henry
Maurice Norman
Danny Blanchflower
Dave Mackay
Terry Dyson
Leslie Allen
Bobby Smith
Cliff Jones
John White

Referee: E.T. Jennings (Stourbridge)

THIS OUTSTANDING victory over one of the greatest ever British teams cemented City's reputation as First Division giant-killers. Runaway league leaders Tottenham Hotspur were twice ahead but Bill Jones's brilliant Cardiff bounced back and edged a helter-skelter match with goals from Derek Hogg, Brian Walsh and Derek Tapscott. The mighty Spurs had become the latest team to leave Fortress Ninian empty handed, following Arsenal, Burnley, Wolves and Manchester United before them.

Ask any football fan over 60 and they will tell you that this Tottenham side was something special. They had genuine stars running right through the team, from brilliant Irish wing-half Danny Blanchflower to formidable middleman Dave Mackay. By the time they came to Cardiff in March 1961 Bill Nicholson's team were well on the way to becoming the first team to complete the First Division and FA Cup double. The so-called 'Tottenham Terrors' had brought a new style to football, spreading the gospel of soccer wherever they went, said the *South Wales Echo*.

Before this game Spurs were eight points clear of second-placed Wolverhampton Wanderers and had just days earlier booked their place in the semi-final of the FA Cup with a 5-0 replay win over Sunderland. They had led the way in the league since the very first day after kicking off with a sensational 11-game winning spree. It wasn't until mid-November that this £250,000 Spurs side tasted defeat.

They didn't just beat teams, they blew them away. They had already banged in 91 goals in the league – the total would be 115 by the end of the season – scoring three times or more in 19 of their 31 games to date. A key to their success was the way they stamped their authority on games at the start and finish. A graph published by the *Sunday Times* in the build-up to this game showed that in the first 25 minutes and last ten minutes of a match Spurs' superiority in terms of goals was five to one. In the 55 minutes in between that stat dipped to two to one. Spurs could control the speed of play "like a housewife regulates her cooker", as the *Echo* put it.

Sparkling ball players were at the heart of Nicholson's wonders. Inside-right John White was nicknamed 'The Ghost' for his ability to appear suddenly in the opposition's penalty area, while Welsh wizard Cliff Jones was a world-class winger as capable of scoring goals as he was at creating them. Blanchflower and Mackay were the dynamos which powered the Spurs motor while Bobby Smith was the goalscoring battering ram.

But after such a devastating first half to the season, were there now signs of a chink in Tottenham's armour? In their first half-dozen games of 1961 before travelling to South Wales they had lost twice against Manchester United and Leicester City, only their second and third defeats of the campaign. They had also drawn at home to Wolves. But Nicholson, who made over 300 appearances for Spurs as a player, scoffed at suggestions that they were choking under the pressure. "A lot of people seem to think so but it's all nonsense," he told the *Western Mail*. "It is the other teams who are feeling the pressure when they come up against us."

But there were plenty of reasons for optimism for City supporters. The Bluebirds' first season back in the First Division had started a little shakily but Jones's boys soon found their feet and three consecutive 3-2 wins – against Arsenal, Newcastle United and Wolves – had given them breathing space over the relegation zone.

City had been uncharacteristically poor in a 3-0 defeat at Bolton a week earlier but Jones backed his team by naming an unchanged 11. Ron Nicholls remained in goal due to injuries to both Maurice Swan and Graham Vearncombe. Nicholls had conceded five goals in two games since being handed the number one jersey and never exuded confidence.

City, who had not been beaten at home since mid-October, were generally better against teams which came to play football. They played with a confident swagger and had already defeated last year's champions Burnley on home soil as well as Manchester United and high-flying West Bromwich Albion. And Cardiff were unlucky not to take anything from the away game at White Hart Lane in November when a controversial penalty with half an hour to go gifted Spurs a 3-2 win. Blanchflower, a popular figure in British football, had admitted that the Bluebirds had deserved a point.

Attendances at Ninian had varied greatly from close to 35,000 against Aston Villa to little more than 15,000 against Manchester City. The biggest crowd of the season was a certainty, and the gate was boosted by kick-off being put back to 7pm because of the Wales v Ireland rugby international at Cardiff Arms Park. Thousands of supporters of the oval ball – many of whom hadn't been to a 'soccer' game before – made the mile-and-a-half walk from the city centre to see City's most-hyped game of the season. Floodlights had been installed at Ninian Park during the close-season – this was the night that illuminated football in Cardiff really came into its own.

There was an excited buzz as more than 45,000 fans packed into the ground. And centre-forward Peter Donnelly, who had famously scored the winner against Leicester earlier in the season by charging Gordon Banks into his own net, could have put the home side ahead after just two minutes but shot wide.

In a frantic opening Tapscott also slashed wide, but it was Spurs who went ahead just a minute later when Blanchflower knocked a free kick to White, who in turn whipped in a killer cross for Terry Dyson on the left side of the penalty area. The pocket rocket winger, who had risen from obscurity after signing from non-league Scarborough, volleyed low just inside the post.

The *Echo* said City had "trained like beavers" to be ready for Tottenham's lightning fast start to the game – but it had been in vain.

Lesser teams had waved the white flag after falling behind against Spurs, but not City, who were immediately on the offensive in search of an equaliser. Tapscott had already scored 18 league goals but wasted a golden opportunity this time before Hogg showed brilliant individual skill to make it 1-1 after ten minutes. The Stockton-born outside-left ran half the length of the field, jinking and stumbling past three Tottenham players before firing an outstanding shot into the roof of the net.

Late City historian John Crooks rated it as one of the finest goals ever scored at Ninian in his book, *Cardiff City Chronology*.

It had been the blistering start that the press had predicted – and there was more to come on 17 minutes when Spurs went ahead once again. The visitors had been pushing forward in numbers so it came as no real shock when Smith sent in a wicked cross which Nicholls could only palm into the path of Leslie Allen, who stabbed the ball through a crowd of players and into the net.

White had the ball in the net for City soon after but was offside and then Donnelly ballooned over the bar after being played in by Tapscott. Half-time came with Spurs deservedly 2-1 in front – but nobody could have predicted the sensational fightback by the Bluebirds, who scored twice in 67 seconds shortly after the interval.

First after 49 minutes Donnelly did well down the left and hit a low pass to Walsh on the other side of the pitch. The winger turned inside and raised the roof with a precise shot from close range. The Ninian Park roar was still ringing around the ground when, incredibly, Tapscott fired the Bluebirds ahead for the first time. Buoyant Barrie Hole nicked the ball off Smith and came forward at pace. The Welshman found Tappy, who fired low into the far corner through a packed penalty box.

Bill Jones later revealed that he had told his team to target the middle section of the match. Spurs were so strong at the beginning and end of matches that it was inevitable that there would be periods of 'coasting'. Jones told the *Daily Express*, "We expected a tough start and a blistering finish. So we planned our own surprises for the mid-match period when Spurs like to ease off and dictate a slower pace." His plan had worked to perfection. Suddenly Tottenham looked mortal – but there were still 40 minutes for the Bluebirds to see off.

The tension was incredible among the home fans as Spurs launched wave after wave of attacks. *Echo* reporter Peter Corrigan wrote, "I've never known such excitement, such nerve-racking moments, such voluble elation at what was only, after all, a league game." Nicholls, who only played two further games for City, looked edgy and dropped a couple of catches under pressure, but the City defence was always on hand to clear.

More often than not it was super skipper Danny Malloy who was there to complete the escape, though Ron Stitfall and Alan Harrington both played their part, furiously hassling and hurrying their opponents.

The Spurs pressure was relentless in the final 20 minutes. Jones, in his post-match musings, said City could have won by more than a one-goal margin – but *Daily Mirror* reporter Tom Lyons saw things slightly differently: "How Cardiff survived Spurs' non-stop onslaught in the last 20 minutes I don't know. Not for years have I seen such relentless and persistent pressure."

But survive they did and hundreds of thrilled youngsters mobbed the City heroes at the final whistle. "Cardiff City could not have been happier had they just won the FA

Cup," wrote *Daily Express* Welsh correspondent Jim Hill. "Even manager Bill Jones, soccer's soul of discretion, melted in the moonshine of Saturday night's spectacular win over super Spurs."

Today supporters take to Twitter to congratulate or, more often, abuse footballers after games, but in 1961 the humble postcard ruled. Hundreds poured through the Ninian Park letterbox in the days after the match, many heaping praise on the conquerors of Spurs.

The triumph lifted City into sixth position, a height the club has failed to match since. But City's season collapsed after this glorious night with six defeats and three draws from the final nine fixtures, including a 6-1 hammering at Chelsea and a 5-1 loss at Everton. Jones' team finished a season of extreme highs and lows in 15th position, but the following season ended in relegation.

v Newcastle United 4-4

18 August 1962. Attendance: 27,569
Second Division. Ninian Park

CARDIFF CITY:	NEWCASTLE UNITED:
Dilwyn John	Dave Hollins
Alan Harrington	Dick Keith
Alec Milne	Alf McMichael
Barrie Hole	George Dalton
Frank Rankmore	Bill Thompson
Colin Baker	Brian Wright
Alan McIntosh	Alan Suddick
Alan Durban	Jimmy Fell
Mel Charles	Barrie Thomas
Ivor Allchurch	Dave Hilley
Peter Hooper	Jimmy Kerray

Referee: Mr Pickles

THE OPENING day of the 1962/63 season felt vitally important for City. The Bluebirds had yo-yoed between the First Division and Second Division for the past decade, being promoted twice and relegated twice. There was still a sense – probably misguided – that the top flight was City's natural resting place. The dreaded drop at the end of the previous season had been met by dismay by supporters and attendances had dipped below the 20,000 mark. Towards the end of the campaign one home gate plummeted to just 8,608, down more than 16,000 from the first Ninian game of the season. Relegation had been, the *Western Mail* submitted, a "tragedy" for Welsh soccer.

There had been little in the 1961/62 season to encourage South Wales's notoriously fickle football fans to part with their hard-earned cash. City managed just six home league wins all season – the fewest in the First Division – and a paltry 30 goals in front of their own supporters. The club needed to get the fans back on side and promised a new, positive approach.

"I can promise you that City will play attacking football," said City chief Bill Jones. "I would rather win 5-4 than 1-0. If the crowd want goals, we will try and give it to them." This eight-goal cracker against Newcastle United, with City fighting back from 3-1 and 4-3 down, was just the start.

Jones made two important signings during the close-season which suggested that he was serious about improving his team's success in front of goal. Winger Peter Hooper, who at the time boasted one of the hardest shots in football, arrived from Bristol Rovers for £7,000 and Welsh inside-forward Ivor Allchurch signed for £18,000 from Newcastle and took the captain's armband.

Thirty-two when the Swansea City legend returned to South Wales, this time in a blue shirt, some questioned whether Allchurch would still have enough in the tank to terrorise Second Division defences, but he retained a great hunger for the game and kept playing until he was over 50.

Cardiff City's Greatest Games

Hooper and Allchurch both started for City in two of four changes from the team which drew the final game of the last season at Aston Villa. The other two alterations saw 18-year-old goalkeeper Dilwyn John and Alan McIntosh, who had shown encouraging form in the pre-season friendlies, in the starting line-up. There was no place for old favourites Ron Stitfall or Derek Tapscott, who had scored nine the previous season.

Newcastle United, managed by former player Joe Harvey, were also hoping for a big season. The Magpies had been relegated to the Second Division in 1961 after 13 seasons in the top tier and had finished a mediocre 11th in their first campaign. This time more was expected of them, some pundits even predicting a championship trophy come May. They had signed inside-right Dave Hilley for £35,000 from Glasgow outfit Third Lanark to replace Allchurch, who they had been loath to lose. Also in attack was instinctive goal-getter Barrie Thomas, who was signed from Scunthorpe for around £40,000 at the start of the calendar year and was widely tipped to be a future England international, a feat he would never quite achieve. The 25-year-old had smashed 41 goals in his previous season. Scottish ace Jimmy Kerray completed the three-pronged United attack.

If some City fans were still feeling the effects of relegation blues, that did not reflect in the attendance which, at over 27,000, was bigger than all but two home gates the previous season. And basked in glorious sunshine, they were in for an Allchurch-inspired treat. The debutant tormented Newcastle all afternoon, twisting and turning with faultless ball control.

It was the visitors who had the first chance of a ding-dong encounter on a pristine pitch when a Bill Thompson free kick on the halfway line caught City napping and Thomas nipped through on goal, but John was out like a flash and gathered the ball at the forward's feet.

Hooper then sliced a shot badly from inside the area after good work by Mel Charles and McIntosh – and soon after the busy front man pulled another shot wide after cutting in. The best early chance fell to the Magpies, though, on 12 minutes when Kerray brought a wonderful finger tip save from John after storming from halfway.

Rhondda lad John, who in his 40s would become the Welsh amateur snooker champion, was called upon twice more, first tipping a volley over the bar and then gathering a header.

The pressure was mounting and it was no surprise when Newcastle, backed by a reasonable number of travelling Geordies, finally broke the deadlock on the half-hour. Hilley was on his way through on goal when he was upended by a combination of Alec Milne and Frank Rankmore inside the box. John was just inches away from stopping Jimmy Fell's low penalty, but United were 1-0 to the good.

Just five minutes later some of the gloom of the previous season descended on Ninian Park as United made it 2-0. Alan Harrington, usually so reliable, had a torrid afternoon up against the tricky Fell, and it was the full-back's blunder which led to the goal. Harrington, last season's skipper, misjudged the bounce of a high ball down the line and Fell pounced, racing to the byline. He pulled back for Kerray to fire home from 15 yards.

United were living up to their billing of title contenders and City fans feared the worst. Last season just a one-goal deficit was enough to dampen City's fire, the *Echo*'s Peter Corrigan said.

But City showed great defiance and got a goal back three minutes before half-time when Hooper thundered a low shot which deflected off Dick Keith and curled in at the near post. It was Hooper's first of 22 league goals in a season in which he would ask to leave on three occasions before eventually departing at the end of the campaign.

Jones probably would have accepted a one-goal deficit at half-time given the way that the game had gone, but the Magpies restored their two-goal advantage just a minute later – and in embarrassing fashion for one Bluebird. Rankmore, signed from Cardiff Corinthians, was a powerful centre-half who always gave 100 per cent, but this was one of his worst displays for the club. Under no real pressure, the 23-year-old lashed wildly at Fell's low cross and succeeded only in slicing the ball with the outside of his right boot over John's head and into the net.

Whatever Jones said at half-time worked as City came out of the dressing room with a new desire. It was 3-2 and very much game on four minutes in when, eager to impress, Hooper burst down the left and put in an accurate cross for Charles. The Welshman, who just like his brother John was as adept at centre-half as centre-forward, lost his marker Thompson for the first time and at full stretch found the back of the net via a post.

That was just the lift City needed – and after 54 minutes it was 3-3 as the game's blistering pace continued. Referee Pickles awarded City an indirect free kick in the area for obstruction on Alan Durban rather than a penalty. Hooper hit the dead ball hard past the wall and Barrie Hole, playing with a new found aggression, was there to turn in only his second goal as a professional.

John produced a point-blank save from Fell's half volley which earned the applause of his opponent but there was nothing he could do after 71 minutes after another Rankmore blunder. This time Rankmore mis-kicked to set Thompson away down the right and his quick cross was smartly dispatched by Hilley, his first of 33 goals in the famous black and white stripes.

It looked as if City's return to the second tier might end in disappointment, but Jones's boys managed to rescue a point with 11 minutes to go and it was that man Hole again who popped up in the right place. This time Hooper's deep cross was headed back across goal by Charles and Hole had all the time in the world to prod home.

It might not have been the victory that City fans had hoped for, but the opening day thriller – the best curtain raiser in many years in the eyes of the *Western Mail* – had sent them down Sloper Road smiling. The Bluebirds had scored four or more just once the previous season – maybe being in the Second Division wasn't so bad after all.

Jones seemed content. "There were weaknesses in the side but every man gave 100 per cent endeavour," he told the *South Wales Echo*. "That's all a manager can demand and I am satisfied." And Newcastle were pleased, too, Harvey telling the *Sunday Sun*, "It was a great game and we'll not have many matches as hard as that. Both teams look set for a successful season." The *Sun* reporter was just pleased that United wouldn't have to come up against Allchurch every week.

The result set the tone for a season of goals galore. A poor start, which saw City slump to 17th position after four consecutive defeats, cost Jones and coach Wilf Gant their jobs. Coach Ernie Curtis and veteran Ron Stitfall took charge of the first team – and the Bluebirds embarked on an incredible run, winning seven from nine and scoring 29 goals. There were some enthralling games along the way, including 5-3, 5-2 and 6-2 wins over Grimsby, Swansea and Preston, and a 6-0 defeat at Chelsea.

Former Arsenal goalkeeper George Swindin quit his job at Norwich to take over as City manager at the beginning of November, and he guided the club to a solid, if unspectacular, tenth-place finish, three places behind Newcastle. Despite the so-so league standing, City managed 83 goals, ten more than champions Stoke City, and conceded 73, just 11 fewer than bottom club Luton Town. Problems in attack had been fixed – Hooper bagged 22 league goals and Allchurch managed a dozen – but serious defensive frailties remained.

Despite frequent talk of challenging for promotion, it would prove to be the first of 13 consecutive seasons in the Second Division for Cardiff City.

v Sporting Clube De Portugal 2-1

16 December 1964. Attendance: 15,311
European Cup Winners' Cup. Estádio José Alvalade

SPORTING CLUBE De Portugal were one of the most famous names in world football and the current holders of the European Cup Winners' Cup. Cardiff City, meanwhile, were 17th in the old Second Division and in danger of dropping down into the third tier of English football for the first time since 1947. What happened on 16 December 1964 had football fans across the continent shaking their heads in wonderment.

It was City's first foray into European football having qualified by winning the Welsh Cup the previous season, beating Bangor City in the final. The campaign had started in tepid fashion with City scraping past Danish side Esbjerg fB 1-0 over two legs. But now they had the plum draw they craved against the 11-times champions of Portugal.

Sporting had caught the eye by winning the competition last year. They had shown no mercy in beating Cypriot side Apoel FC 18-1 on aggregate before turning a 4-1 first leg deficit on its head against Manchester United to win 5-0 in Lisbon and 6-4 overall.

This was a Lions team with plenty of talent. Goalkeeper Joaquim Carvalho had earned a reputation for his quick reactions while Fernando Mendes, regarded as one of the best half-backs of his time, was captain of both his club and country. Star of the attack was Brazilian Osvaldo Da Silva, but it was Ernesto Figueiredo, the league's top scorer the previous season, who posed the greatest goal threat.

But it is true that Sporting were a club in crisis going into this game. Just two days before kick-off coach Jean Luciano had been suspended after a special meeting of the board of directors to scrutinise the club's diabolical start to the season. The Lions were fourth from bottom in the Portuguese league and were beaten 3-0 by basement boys Torrense the previous week. They had taken just seven points from nine league games and Lisbon reporters were predicting another torrid evening against the Bluebirds, some foreseeing a 3-1 defeat for their team.

Yet despite their recent misery and the frustration of the Sporting fans, there still ought to have been a gulf in class. Eight of their starters – Carvalho, Pedro Gomes, Hilario

Cardiff City's Greatest Games

Rosario da Conceição, Mendes, Jose Carlos, Silva, Figueiredo and João Pedro Morais – played in that drubbing of Manchester United. Jimmy Scoular's City, meanwhile, were a struggling outfit. They had battled to a decent 1-1 draw at Ipswich Town four days earlier but had won just five of their 21 Second Division games. Indeed, the *South Wales Echo* concluded, "Scoular knows that if his team can get away with a narrow defeat they will be lucky." And the *Western Mail* added, "Obviously City's tactics will have to concentrate rather more on preventing goals than scoring them."

Former Portsmouth and Newcastle boss Scoular took over from George Swindin before the start of the season but his reign could hardly have started worse with the Bluebirds taking 12 games before recording their first league win. But things had picked up in November with three wins and a draw before defeat against Norwich and that draw at Ipswich. The Cardiff team arrived in Portugal the day before the match – and were on the training pitch within an hour. The squad were put through their paces the following morning, too, with kick-off not until 9.15pm. Scoular refused to reveal his team until the last possible moment but, with one exception, it picked itself. With first-choice keeper Bob Wilson unavailable, Dilwyn John started in goal. The acrobatic 20-year-old had only played the two European legs against Esbjerg but was well regarded at the club.

The only headache was in the forward line. The *Western Mail* called for the inclusion of six-goal Allchurch, the ageing golden boy of Welsh football. Instead Greg Farrell passed a late fitness test and was given the nod. Ellis, who had scored at Ipswich, was ineligible so Derek Tapscott switched to centre-forward.

Burly John Charles, the only City player known to Sporting after his time with Juventus and AS Roma, was given the role of sweeper. The Welsh legend played with a strip of plaster covering five stitches on his forehead, battle wounds from an earlier clash.

Scoular's tactics were clear – stifle the Sporting attack and hit on the break. And the plan worked to perfection. The Lions were never given enough time on the ball to carry out their intricate passing moves.

City, backed by about 30 hardy Welshmen in the huge Estádio José Alvalade, were on the attack inside the first minute when Bernie Lewis crossed but Carvalho was quickly off his line to grasp the ball.

But seconds later Sporting came close with their first attack on the City goal when Morais headed firmly into the ground and over John's slight frame. The net looked set to bulge until Charles appeared from nowhere to head away from underneath the crossbar. It was the first in a host of heroic interventions on a fantastic night for the colossal defender.

At this stage the game was going to script with the home side having the better of the possession – but there were signs that City's counter-attacking game plan could reap rewards. Barrie Hole sent Gareth Williams through with a good pass but the inside-forward could not quite get on the end of it. Silva flashed a low drive just past the post before at the other end Farrell latched on to a pinpoint Lewis pass but missed the target.

There was a tense atmosphere around the ground as the locals began whistling, but Charles showed nerves of steel to head back to John under pressure.

City keeper John might have lacked a little experience but he showed no signs of jitters from the first whistle to the last. The youngster pulled off a magnificent save from Silva's header despite being caught wrong-footed briefly.

The home fans, watching from a distance due to a running track around the pitch, thought their team had taken the lead after about 20 minutes but Mendes's shot in fact had brushed the side netting.

Alan Harrington gave away a free kick 25 yards out but Silva's effort cleared the crossbar and then, just after the half hour mark, Penarth-born Harrington breathed a sigh of relief again when he mis-kicked but was rescued by his colleagues.

Scoular, who had chosen to ignore FA advice by sitting on the touchline, would have been pleased – delighted, even – by what he had seen so far. But the tie took an unexpected twist on 31 minutes when City took the lead.

Farrell jinked his way forward, making 20 yards before passing out wide to Peter King. He bent in a cross for Tapscott, who controlled on his chest and laid the ball off for Farrell to smash a left-footed shot into the bottom corner from the edge of the area.

An eerie silence descended around the giant stadium, apart from the tiny band of jet-setting City fans.

John then made another fine save from Fernando Ferreira Pinto before Farrell had another good opening but this time he was off target. With half-time approaching Lewis, who had been up and down the pitch like a yo-yo, made a fine tackle to bring a Sporting attack to an abrupt end, the outside-left eventually emerging with the ball at his feet.

City did hold out to the interval. Director Vivian Dewey wiped the sweat from his brow and theatrically touched wood, according to the *Echo*. The same report added, "But he need not have worried as it was certainly not luck that had given City this 1-0 interval lead. It was sheer hard graft and persistence."

Sporting made frenzied efforts to get back on terms after the break and tore into tackles to try and unnerve the Bluebirds. Brian Stiles of the *Echo* said "many of the gorings would have been more suited to the bullring a mile down the road," and added, "Sporting tried to bludgeon a dirty path to victory in the second half."

Many City players were forced off the pitch temporarily with injuries, only to heroically return to the battlefield minutes later. Charles and Hole put in a series of crunching tackles and inspired their team-mates to do the same.

John made yet another fine save, this time from Mendes, while at the other end Farrell evaded three Sporting players in green and came close with his final effort. Though always dangerous on the break, the pressure was intensifying on Scoular's men and an equaliser looked inevitable when three forwards moved towards the City goal but somehow Don Murray, who was 18 at the time but would go on to be one of the club's greatest ever centre-halves, crucially scrambled to safety.

John had to be alert to beat out a surprise drive but then came a decent spell of City pressure. Carvalho came charging off his line to dispossess Tapscott and then City ought to have had a penalty for a foul on Lewis but the referee waved play on. The German official was reluctant to give City anything all night.

With about 25 minutes remaining Farrell picked up a thigh injury and limped his way through the rest of the match – but that didn't stop the tough Scot, who often frustrated supporters with his inconsistent performances, being involved in City's crucial second goal.

Farrell dodged his way past a couple of Sporting players and played to Tappy near the touchline. Fully 35 yards from goal, Tapscott tried to cross – though to who remains a mystery as there were no blue shirts in the area. It had little genuine pace yet somehow deceived Carvalho, who could only palm the ball pathetically against the post and into the net. Carvalho, who had played a key role in Sporting's European success the previous season, faced the wrath of his own supporters.

With all their recent problems and the crowd now growing anxious, the Portuguese club might have thrown in the towel but instead they pushed for a way back in. Figueiredo headed against the crossbar with John well beaten.

Sporting's tackles became harder and harder as desperation took hold. Peter Rodrigues, Williams, Lewis and Farrell were all forced off the pitch for short periods after picking up knocks but hobbled back on. Take note Premier League prima donnas of 2013.

Be had a good chance after cutting inside but he then shot straight down the throat of John.

City's defence was eventually breached with nine minutes to go. Figueiredo broke through the challenge of Murray and the ball sat up nicely for him to smash his volley into the bottom corner.

That seemed to be the jolt that Sporting needed and the home side pushed hard in the closing minutes with midnight approaching – but City held on to record an incredible victory – and to become the first Welsh team to win on foreign soil in European competition. "One cannot overestimate the performance of a single member of the City team," the *Western Mail* said.

The Sporting fans threw their seat cushions on to the track in disgust, while Scoular grinned from ear to ear. The emotional manager told the *Echo*, "I told each of them they were marvellous, and they certainly were. I am proud of them all. They flogged themselves so much that a number of them were in agony with cramp by the end of the game. I cannot praise them enough."

And there was praise, too, from Sporting skipper Mendes, who told the *Western Mail*, "I am bitterly disappointed but one must give Cardiff City full credit for their magnificent defence and the quick way in which they went into the tackle."

City celebrated with a champagne reception in their "plush hotel" – but only the most optimistic believed that the job was done. A tough test lay ahead at Ninian Park in the return leg two days before Christmas.

But Charles put in another Herculean performance to guide City to a 0-0 draw and progress to the quarter-finals of the competition against Spanish giants Real Zaragoza.

The Bluebirds were making waves right across the continent – and there was no stopping them now.

14 v **Real Zaragoza** 2-2

20 January 1965. Attendance: 35,000
European Cup Winners' Cup Quarter-Final.
Romareda Stadium

CARDIFF CITY:	REAL ZARAGOZA:
Bob Wilson	Enrique Yarza
Alan Harrington	Pepin
Peter Rodrigues	Francisco Santamaria
John Charles	Severino Reija
Don Murray	José Luis Violeta
Barrie Hole	Pais
Greg Farrell	D'arcy Canario
Gareth Williams	Santos
Derek Tapscott	Marcelino
Peter King	Carlos Lapetra
Bernie Lewis	Jose Maria Encontra

Referee: R. Huber (Switzerland)

"TREMENDOUS! MAGNIFICENT! Let the trumpets blow and the superlatives flow!" Those were the words of journalist Bryan Stiles in the *South Wales Echo* after probably City's greatest ever result away from home.

The Bluebirds had fallen two goals behind inside 12 minutes against Spanish giants Real Zaragoza in the first leg of this European Cup Winners' Cup quarter-final. Annihilation appeared a certainty. But somehow Jimmy Scoular's men recovered and first-half goals from Gareth Williams and Peter King, followed by a defensive display of epic proportions, earned City the unlikeliest of draws.

And the superlatives certainly did flow in the morning papers. *The Daily Mirror* described City's performance as "super human". *The Daily Express* lauded the "fabulous Second Division fighters of Wales". *The Times* praised City's "undying spirit and energy", while the *Western Mail* claimed a "tremendous boost to soccer in Wales and in Britain as a whole".

Nobody had given City a chance of achieving a result at Real Zaragoza's intimidating Estadio de La Romareda. Managed by former Real Madrid forward Roque Olsen, Zaragoza had become a genuine force in Spanish football. They were just one point behind leaders Real in the top Spanish league and had finished in the top five in their last four seasons.

And they had a formidable forward line, known as 'Los Cinco Magnificos', 'The Five Magnificents'. They had already rattled up more than 30 goals between them in the 1964/65 season and most were renowned internationals. Pundits purred at their supreme link-up play, but pick of the bunch was 24-year-old Marcelino, who had once studied for the priesthood but was now a national hero after scoring the winning goal in Spain's 2-1 victory over the Soviet Union in the 1964 European Nations' Cup Final. Another star was Carlos Lapetra, a 26-year-old who had recently made the transition from left-winger to inside-left. His pace made him a real handful.

Such was the seemingly impossible task facing City, the players were offered £15 a head if they could avoid losing by two goals or less! Speaking to *The Express*, Scoular hinted we would be quietly happy with a 2-0 defeat. "It would still give us a reasonable chance of winning through to the semi-finals if we can keep the score that low," he said.

And there was no lack of confidence from Zaragoza. Goalkeeper and captain Enrique Yarza told the *Echo* bluntly, "We are sure we will win by many goals, the more the better." The only man to give the Bluebirds a chance was director Vivian Dewey. "I am forever optimistic," he told the *Western Mail*, a little unconvincingly.

There was a little bad feeling between the clubs after Cardiff's players turned up for a welcome party an hour late. Scoular refused to call off a late night training session on the eve of the match, leaving Dewey the difficult job of entertaining Zaragoza's officials while they waited for the Bluebirds to arrive. Zaragoza were less than impressed, but Scoular ranted: "What do they think this is – a social jaunt? We have come here to play football not to go to drinking parties. My job is to get my players in shape for tomorrow's cup game and nothing they can do will stop me." Dewey added: "They were certainly very shirty about it all but they should have known better than to have called a reception so soon after we arrived." By the time Zaragoza made the trip to South Wales for the return leg a fortnight later there was gushing praise for the Spanish welcome from Scoular in the match programme.

The odds were undoubtedly stacked against City – but perhaps they should have been just a tad more confident in their abilities. They had pulled off a sensational 2-1 aggregate victory over cup holders Sporting Lisbon in the previous round and had five days earlier thumped Middlesbrough 6-1 at Ninian Park.

City named the same 11 which had battered Boro. There was just one change from the team which played both legs against Lisbon, goalkeeper Dilwyn John replaced by Bob Wilson, who was not eligible against the Portuguese.

City played a defensive 5-2-3 formation with man mountain John Charles – who scored two against Zaragoza when playing for Roma three years earlier – playing in a sweeper role.

But the quarter-final got off to the worst possible start as the home side zoomed into a two-goal lead. First skipper Williams needlessly fouled José Luis Violeta just outside the area and Lapetra fired the free kick into the top corner from 25 yards with less than two minutes on the clock. It was a pinpoint shot by a player considered the best outside-left in Europe but keeper Wilson was caught slightly unsighted and might have reacted quicker.

His disappointment was clear as he fished the ball from the net and slammed it against the floor. "The first goal caught me unawares," he told *The Express*. "I felt really choked. I thought I'd let the boys down."

The onslaught continued. Five minutes later D'arcy Canario unleashed a tremendous shot which Wilson would have got nowhere near but brave Charles threw his sizeable frame in front of it.

City looked to be finding their feet in the red hot La Romareda. Bernie Lewis curled a deft shot just under the crossbar but Yarza was equal to it. Then Greg Farrell forced a corner but Derek Tapscott was called offside before at the other end Wilson made a wonderful save from Lapetra after Williams had conceded a corner.

But then disaster for City as the home side, who had beaten Dundee United 4-3 on aggregate in the previous round, moved two ahead on 12 minutes. Wing-half Pais was allowed to dribble 30 yards before unleashing a rocket shot into the bottom corner which gave Wilson no chance. "Welsh hopes sank lower than a pit-shaft," the *Express* said.

Anywhere between 30 and 70 City fans had made the trip to Spain, depending on which newspaper you read, and they were now fearing the worst. If Scoular was willing to accept a 2-0 reverse before the game started, what would the tough Scot have dealt on now? Four? Five?

But somehow City found the character to respond and on 17 minutes they had a way back in through Williams. Barrie Hole dribbled forward before finding Williams, who in turn played the ball across to Farrell. The winger made good ground before crossing to Williams, who rose well to head an excellent goal.

"I must have jumped five feet when I saw my header going into the net," Williams told the *South Wales Echo*. "I knew then that we could hold them."

City visibly grew in confidence after the goal, but still Zaragoza piled on the pressure. Wilson showed good hands to collect a corner despite being heavily obstructed, while at the other end Tapscott burst through only to be halted just before he could get his shot away. Centre-forward Tappy, a prolific goalscorer in his seven years at the club, kept Zaragoza on their toes all evening by charging down goalkeeper Yarza when he was in possession, a tactic rarely used on the continent in the 1960s.

Williams went close with a header from a City corner before Wilson made a fine close-range save from Lapetra, the only man on the pitch born in Zaragoza.

Then, remarkably, ten minutes from half-time City found an equaliser. It came from a lightning-quick break after another period of intense pressure and again Farrell was the inspiration. The tricky 21-year-old darted down the wing and crossed for King to head beyond Yarza's desperate dive and just inside the post.

King, who spent 14 years at City, was in red hot goalscoring form having bagged a hat-trick in the drubbing of Middlesbrough. Madrid-based newspaper *MARCA* claimed that Farrell was offside when he picked up the ball initially, but this is not something alluded to in any other report. The 35,000-strong home crowd was stunned into silence.

Heavy rain fell at half-time which, according to *The Times* at least, had the effect of making the spectators look like "a field of mushrooms" in their capes and umbrellas.

City's defending in the second half was nothing short of sensational. Just as they did against Sporting Clube De Portugal in the previous round, City allowed their opponents to pass the ball around as they pleased – until they came within 30 yards of their goal and the shutters went up.

The example of Charles spread across the whole back-line and stirred them to throw their bodies in front of the ball. *The Times* said, "Charles, indeed, was king this night. He set the whole mood of the brave Welsh retort."

Charles may have been the inspiration, but every defender deserved a medal. Full-backs Alan Harrington and Peter Rodrigues didn't look out of their depth against wingers of world reputation while Don Murray did exceptionally well up against Marcelino.

With the words of Scoular still ringing in their ears, it was City who enjoyed the best early chances. Tapscott raced the length of the pitch to latch on to a Rodrigues pass and was only narrowly wide with his final shot. Farrell then terrorised the Zaragoza defence by beating five opponents before whipping over a cross which Tapscott nearly got on the end of.

But after that initial burst the home side really started to turn the screw and forced a succession of corners. Their fast, accurate passing had the journalists waxing lyrical. But with each foray forward repelled by determined Cardiff, Zaragoza grew more and more frustrated. Long shots rained in but Wilson was alert to them all.

Charles was penalised for a full-blooded tackle but the 25-yard free kick sailed over and then Hole got an important foot in to break up another attack.

Wilson might have been at fault for Zaragoza's first goal, but the shot-stopper more than made up for the error with two magnificent saves. First he flew across the goal to gather a fierce shot from Marcelino and then he tipped a Lapetra shot around the post.

When the final whistle did eventually sound, City's heroes were so exhausted that they barely had the energy to raise their arms in celebration. Zaragoza had had about 80 per cent of possession but after the first two goals never looked like breaching the solid blue wall in front of them.

The home fans had mocked City with cries of "Gamberros" throughout the game, meaning Teddy Boys, but in the end they offered a warm and sporting round of applause.

Delighted Scoular skipped on to the pitch and shook the hands of each of his players. The City boss was quoted in *The Daily Mirror*, "What can I say about the lads? I have never seen a team fight so hard in over 20 years in football. It was the proudest moment of my life to see the way the boys came back after such a disastrous start."

Charles, 33 by now and coming towards the end of a legendary career, told the *Echo*: "These continentals have got no stamina for hard battle. They were playing football well to start with, but after they had paced it we went in and they kept looking over their shoulder before passing so that suited us."

The City players were given a champagne reception to celebrate a champagne performance – and they each had £15 stuffed in their back pockets for good measure. Suddenly the Bluebirds were favourites to reach the semi-final of the competition by seeing off the Spaniards on 3 February.

City fought gallantly in the return leg but a single Canario goal in the 73rd minute gave Real Zaragoza a 3-2 win on aggregate in front of 38,458 fans. Scoular's men may not quite have finished the job by reaching the last four for the first time, but they had earned admirers across Europe with a performance of real courage.

15 v Middlesbrough 5-3

3 May 1966. Attendance: 12,935
Second Division. Ninian Park

CARDIFF CITY:	MIDDLESBROUGH:
Dilwyn John	Bob Appleby
Graham Coldrick	Alex Smith
David Carver	Billy Horner
Gareth Williams	Frank Spraggon
Don Murray	Gordon Jones
Barrie Hole	Dickie Rooks
Greg Farrell	Eric McMordie
Bobby Ferguson	Ian Gibson
George Andrews	Ian Davidson
Peter King	Jimmy Irvine
Bernie Lewis	Derrick Downing

Referee: P.R. Walters (Bridgwater)

CITY HAD been terrible all season. Abysmal for the most part, in fact. By the end of the campaign they had shipped an eye-watering 91 goals, the third worst tally in the club's history.

But when the chips were down, when only a win would do, somehow Jimmy Scoular's Bluebirds managed one almighty performance to cling on to their Second Division status.

There have been some heroic individual performances for City over the years, but few more so than Greg Farrell in this pulsating clash. The Scottish outside-right put in a virtuoso display of craft and guile to lead his team to a 5-3 victory.

The football cliché about games being 'six-pointers' – or even four-pointers as it was before the change of rules in 1981 – is often misused, but that certainly can't be said of this game. It was the final match of a difficult season for third-from-bottom Middlesbrough and they knew that defeat would take them down into the depths of the Third Division for the first time in their history. City, who were one place below Boro, still had two games to play after this one but were desperate to clinch the win which would safeguard their place in the division for another year.

It was a scenario which set the scene for a match bursting with guts and drama. For spells it looked like the Teessiders were more equipped for the fight, but the Bluebirds, driven by wing wizard Farrell, came back from 1-0 and 2-1 down to eventually win with something to spare. City were building a reputation as the Houdini of the Football League after leaving it late to pull clear of the relegation zone in recent seasons – but this was by far their greatest escape trick to date.

City had finished a disappointing 13th in 1964/65, only a late flurry of victories ensuring that they didn't get embroiled in a relegation scrap. So it was no shock when manager Jimmy Scoular embarked on a summer clear-out with several favourites heading for the exit. Ron Stitfall, 39, retired after making more than 400 appearances for the club while Ivor Allchurch returned to Swansea Town for £6,000. Alec Milne moved to New

Zealand, Steve Gammon and Alan McIntosh quit the game after leg-breaks, Mel Charles went into non-league football and 86-goal Derek Tapscott joined Newport County. Between them they had notched up 1,075 league appearances for Cardiff.

But rather than replace those departing, Scoular decided to put his faith in youngsters. Terry Harkin, £10,000 from Crewe Alexandra, was the only significant signing. Forward George Andrews was signed from Lower Gornal in October with City faltering and 16-year-old John Toshack burst on to the scene. He had scored twice on his full debut, a 4-3 win at Middlesbrough, but he had dropped out of the team by the time the reverse fixture came about.

On New Year's Eve Welsh international Peter Rodrigues was sold to Leicester City for £40,000 and Scoular responded by spending some of the cash on full-back Bobby Ferguson from Derby County and goalkeeper Lyn Davies. There was another setback, though, when long-serving Alan Harrington broke his leg for a second time so Scoular spent £11,000 on Rotherham's David Carver and two weeks later winger Ronnie Bird was bought from Bury for £5,000.

City were forced into making one change from the team which secured a crucial 1-0 win against Crystal Palace four days earlier, hard-tackling Ferguson taking the number eight shirt from injured David Houston. Middlesbrough player-manager Stan Anderson, who had taken over from Raich Carter just weeks earlier, was out injured, as was former England winger Eddie Holliday. But Ian Gibson, who later played for City, shook off a hamstring problem to start and left-back Gordon Jones was a surprise choice at outside-left.

The tension was almost unbearable as the winner-takes-all clash got under way. The crowd might have been shy of 13,000 but *The Northern Echo* described Ninian as "a cauldron of excitement". And the match set off at break-neck pace, Farrell signalling his intent by forcing a save from Bob Appleby within seconds. But the tension levels rocketed among City fans after just six minutes when Boro went ahead.

Jones swung over a corner from the right and centre-half Dickie Rooks rose unmarked to power a header over Dilwyn John's head.

City came back fighting and Gareth Williams might have found the back of the net but his piledriver cannoned off team-mate Ferguson. At the other end Jimmy Irvine went close for Boro. Peter King, who was bang in form with four goals in his last three, then fired just over the bar after a wonderful little move involving Williams, King and Barrie Hole.

The City fans sensed an equaliser – and it came after 24 minutes when Hole stroked the ball home confidently from Bernie Lewis's cross from the left. It was the wing-half's sixth goal of the season, and easily the most important.

But the Bluebirds were level for just two minutes. Williams handled to stop a Gibson through ball reaching Irvine and Rooks walked up and cracked in his seventh league goal of the season from the penalty spot to make it 2-1. It could have been a costly blunder by Williams. He told the *South Wales Echo* that he had thought he was well outside the area.

The pulsating pace continued and City were level at 2-2 just four minutes later with a penalty of their own. This time it was Gibson who handled a bouncing ball in the Boro area. It was an impulsive action by the Middlesbrough skipper, but a foolish one with little or no danger. He tried to tell the Bridgwater referee that the ball had hit him as he jumped but his efforts were in vain. Farrell, who was transfer-listed by City in February after a string of substandard performances, finished with a cocky swagger.

The battle for the lead raged furiously – and it was City who had it 11 minutes before half-time through Andrews, who out-jumped Rooks to glance a header home from a Lewis corner.

City had another corner before half-time but this time Andrews ballooned his effort over the bar. There was a standing ovation as the teams walked off for the interval.

The second half started at the same blistering pace. Andrews headed over the bar from a Carver free kick, while at the opposite end of the field an increasingly desperate Middlesbrough tried to put City under the cosh but the Bluebirds' defence, for once in this leaky season, was composed and organised.

The blood and thunder continued until City all but secured their survival with a crucial fourth goal 20 minutes into the second half. Williams passed to Hole and he intelligently found King, who lashed it home in fine fashion. The inside-forward had gone 24 games without a goal earlier in the season but had suddenly found his touch.

That goal lifted the Ninian tension and supporters began to sing. Farrell, who had to have a pain-killing injection at half-time, had them purring their approval when he weaved his way through and only a good save by Appleby denied the Motherwell magician a fantastic solo goal. Substitutions for injured players had been introduced at the start of the season, but Scoular was loath to take Farrell off.

Middlesbrough never gave up and threw Rooks up front for the final 15 minutes as they searched for their third goal. Williams saved the day for City when he hacked clear off the line with John beaten. But it was City who bagged the seventh goal of the game with five minutes left – and it was crafted by Farrell.

The 22-year-old burst between two defenders before putting across a low ball for Andrews to turn in. In a gushing appraisal of Farrell's performance, *Echo* reporter Peter Jackson pondered whether even Sir Stanley Matthews or Tom Finney could have done better. "He strode about like a soccer aristocrat," Jackson said.

Rooks completed his hat-trick with a 20-yard free kick with the last kick of the game, but his team were down and the mighty Bluebirds were safe. Relieved fans poured on to the pitch to celebrate.

It had been a fantastic game which made up for some of the disappointments throughout the season. As the distraught Boro players trudged off contemplating trips to dismal football backwaters like Swansea, Darlington and Workington, a City official came on the loudspeaker and declared that he hoped Middlesbrough would return to the Second Division quickly.

He had his wish – they went up at the first attempt the following season. But had they played with this intensity and grit throughout the season, they would have avoided the indignity of playing at The Vetch Field.

Scoular said afterwards, "That was one of the best matches I have seen at Ninian Park. On this form it is a tragedy that Middlesbrough have to crash into the Third Division."

In an interview with the *Sunday Sun* in 2010, Gordon Jones remembered the bitter disappointment. "We were sitting in the bath afterwards close to tears," he said. "And a lot of players that night were very, very angry. The things that happened on the pitch were unbelievable."

The victory saw City climb three places up to the heady heights of 18th. It is just as well City did the business against Boro though – four days later they were beaten 9-0 at Preston and then followed that by losing 2-0 at home to Norwich. The poor finish meant City survived by a solitary point and Scoular had plenty to ponder during the summer.

v Torpedo Moscow 1-0

16

3 April 1968. Attendance: 31,000
European Cup Winners' Cup, Quarter-Final Replay.
Rosenau Stadium, Augsburg, West Germany

CARDIFF CITY:

Bob Wilson
Graham Coldrick
Bobby Ferguson
Malcolm Clarke
Richie Morgan
Brian Harris
Barrie Jones
Norman Dean
Peter King
John Toshack
Ronnie Bird

TORPEDO MOSCOW:

Anzor Kavazashvili
Vladimir Nepomiluev
Leonid Pakhomov
Viktor Shustikov
Grigory Yanets
Aleksandr Lenev
Valery Voronin
Aleksandr Stenishchev
Mikhail Gershkovich
Eduard Streltsov
Vladimir Shcherbakov

Referee: Helmut Fritz (Germany)

MATCH-WINNING HERO Norman Dean was carried through Rhoose Airport by team-mates Steve Derrett, Ronnie Bird and Bryn Jones. Hundreds of City fans in blue and white had waited at the airport for the triumphant return of the odds-defying Bluebirds. Eventually at 9.55pm on Thursday, the day after Jimmy Scoular's men had sensationally beaten Torpedo Moscow 1-0 in West Germany, the team landed back on Welsh soil. Bells and rattles were shaken wildly as the players forced their way through the crowds. Second Division Cardiff City had reached the semi-finals of the European Cup Winners' Cup for the first time in their history.

It was Dean's 41st-minute strike that won the quarter-final replay in Augsburg and put City 180 minutes away from an unbelievable place in the final. The Corby-born forward had only played because of Bobby Brown's injury and Brian Clark's ineligibility – now he had etched his name into City folklore.

But this truly was a night of 11 heroes. Goalkeeper Bob Wilson produced a string of mind-blowing saves, including a full-stretch block in the second minute of injury time when Russian outfit Torpedo cranked up the pressure. Pipe-smoking skipper Brian Harris, too, was an unshakeable rock.

But perhaps most sensational of all was the performance of 21-year-old Richie Morgan on his first team debut. The Llanishen lad, who just two years earlier was playing in the Welsh League with Cardiff Corries, was thrust into the limelight at centre-half after Don Murray failed a late fitness test. Murray had played 84 consecutive first team games for City and was the cornerstone of the defence. Now Morgan had the unenviable task of plugging the gaping hole.

Speaking to the *Echo* afterwards, freckle-faced Morgan admitted he had been frightened at being plunged into action for such a momentous match. And Morgan, who went on to manage his home-town club, came in for some rough treatment. First he was belted in the kidneys by Eduard Streltsov but spat blood and played on. Then seven minutes later Morgan was kicked in the throat by the same player, causing him breathing problems for several minutes. A stretcher was called yet somehow he managed to clamber to his feet and continue.

"I honestly thought I was dying," he said afterwards. "I could not get my breath and my face must have gone blue." Scoular said, "I cannot say enough about his performance," while there was also gushing praise from Murray.

City had beaten Shamrock Rovers (3-1 on aggregate) and NAC Breda (5-2 on aggregate) before being paired with Russian juggernauts Torpedo Moscow in the quarter-finals. Aberdeen and Tottenham Hotspur had already fallen by the wayside, leaving Cardiff as Britain's sole survivors in the competition.

City were without Scoular's three newest signings – Leslie Lea, Fred Davies and Brian Clark – as they had been signed after the third round deadline, but City put in a stellar display to beat a defensive Torpedo side 1-0 at Ninian Park on 6 March, Barrie Jones the goalscorer two minutes before half-time.

The return leg on 16 March had to be switched to Tashkent near the Chinese-Afghanistan border due to sub-zero temperatures in Moscow, and City had to put in a stubborn performance to restrict their opponents to a 1-0 win and force a replay on neutral ground.

But the odds seemed stacked against Scoular's brave team. Murray would be a huge loss, Soviet midfield legend Valery Voronin was back for Torpedo after mysteriously missing the previous two games and the Russians had the backing of the German spectators. City's league form was anything but blistering, too. They were struggling in 15th position in the Second Division and had just lost four of their last five.

But fearsome Scoular had the ability to coax an extra ten per cent from his players when it really mattered – and on this famous night he managed to extract even more on top of that.

The previous three days in Augsburg, a peaceful Bavarian city, had seen beautiful weather, but that turned on the day of the big match with a snowstorm just before kick-off. Conditions were dangerous for the first 15 minutes as players on both teams struggled to stay on their feet, but the storm passed.

Perhaps the icy conditions better suited the Russians for it was Valentin Ivanov's team who started fastest. Morgan was immediately in action when he brought down Soviet player of the year Streltsov from behind but Harris was able to head the resulting free kick to safety. John Toshack had a half-chance for the Bluebirds, but Torpedo had the Welshmen under the cosh.

Outside-right Aleksandr Lenev fired just inches wide of the post before Wilson pulled off the first of a string of world-class saves. The £2,000 bargain buy from Aston Villa produced a brilliant leap to keep out a header from Voronin.

Just minutes later Wilson had to be on his toes once again when Streltsov burst through the City defence. The City keeper, who had lost the number one jersey for league games to new recruit Davies, came out intelligently to narrow the angle and save brilliantly.

It looked like being a long evening for City, but Scoular's men did weather the storm and gradually came more into the tie. Speedy Jones broke down the left wing before unleashing a surprise shot which Georgian goalkeeper Anzor Kavazashvili did well to grasp at the foot of the post.

Torpedo's defence looked nervy when under pressure. Viktor Shustikov managed to block a Dean effort – but there was no stopping the former Southampton man four minutes before half-time. Morgan began the move with a pass to Graham Coldrick on the right, who in turn played a high ball into the Torpedo area. Toshack, who had just turned 19, managed to out-jump 6ft 1in Leonid Pakhomov to flick the ball on for unmarked Dean. He brought it under his spell on his thigh, and let the ball bounce once before cracking his volley well away from the keeper from 12 yards.

"I have never been so thrilled in scoring a goal," he told the *South Wales Echo*. It was only his second goal of a frustrating campaign.

The Soviet cup-winners continued to throw everything at City after the break in a desperate attempt to haul themselves back into the tie. Heroic Morgan was in just the right place to clear off the line from a Lenev effort and then just a couple of minutes later 20-year-old Mikhail Gershkovich mis-kicked in front of goal when Wilson was helpless.

Swansea-born Jones, who played all but one of City's 59 games in the 1967/68 season, had a golden chance to give his side some breathing space in the 68th minute. He found himself with only Kavazashvili to beat but panicked and smashed straight at the keeper, the ball rebounding out for a corner.

Kavazashvili then did well to flick a great Dean header over the bar with his feet before it was Wilson's turn to make an heroic save on 75 minutes. Malcolm Clarke had a moment of madness when his misplaced pass sent Streltsov scurrying though on goal. Wilson rushed out to block the initial shot, but it fell to another Torpedo player who knocked it past the City keeper. It looked like it might roll in until Bobby Ferguson intercepted and turned it away for a corner.

The Russian bombardment continued in the closing minutes, but City's defence looked calm and composed. But with Ivanov bellowing instructions to his team from the edge of the athletics track, Torpedo almost forced extra time – and a possible coin toss decider – in the second of five added-on minutes.

Gershkovich, the man who had scored in Tashkent to bring the scores level on aggregate, unleashed a shot which appeared destined for the corner but Wilson sprung superbly to keep it out.

Eventually the German official did signal the end of a battle which had spanned four-and-a-half hours. The City players embraced one another while Morgan ran the full length of the field to hug Wilson. These were incredible scenes. Meanwhile, the Russians were unable to hide their upset.

City fanatic Gwilym Ballinger was one of only three Brits in the crowd that night. Gwilym was 23 at the time and had never been outside of Wales before being posted to Germany as a civilian attached to the British Army of the Rhine. The game came about one month after his arrival in the country, but with no car and no knowledge of the German trains, Gwilym was reluctant to make the trek from Düsseldorf to Augsburg. He had almost given up on the chance of seeing his Bluebirds in action when his wife's boss, a Reading fan, stepped in with an offer of a lift.

Gwilym said, "It's about an eight-hour drive by car, autobahn all the way, and we got there about an hour before kick-off. My memories of the match are being the only three Brits in a 30,000 crowd and me being the only one that was yelling and screaming. It was one of the bravest performances ever. For much of the game we were battered but Bob Wilson in goal was brilliant.

"Then against all odds we scored. Toshack headed down and a sweet strike by Norman Dean was enough. The rest was like *Rorke's Drift* but hold on we did. The journey home was so happy even though it was 6am when we arrived and we had to be in work at

8.30am. I didn't realise then it would be three years before I saw my beloved Bluebirds again – Düsseldorf to Cardiff was a long way in those days."

More than 45 years on and Gwilym is still City to the core – along with his two sons Julian and Ian and his grandsons Ellis and Archie.

"It's Wunderbar, Wunderbar," read the *Echo* headline the next day, along with a big picture of smiling European mastermind Scoular. "I almost feel lost for words," the City chief said. "I can only say that the lads were simply magnificent."

Hero Harris, meanwhile, the man who had anchored City's defence, said: "To have beaten Torpedo is a fantastic achievement. I feel as proud as when I was with Everton when they won the Cup Final."

City had to wait 21 days before facing West Germany giants Hamburg SV on their own patch in a fairytale semi-final.

v Hamburg SV 2-3
(3-4 on aggregate)
1 May 1968. Attendance: 43,070
European Cup Winners' Cup Semi-Final, Second Leg.
Ninian Park

CARDIFF CITY:	HAMBURG:
Ron Howells	Ankos Oezcan
Glyn Williams	Helmut Sandmann
Alf Sherwood	Juergen Kurbjuhn
Bobby McLaughlin	Klaus Hellfitz
Stan Montgomery	Egon Horst
Billy Baker	Hans Schulz
Roley Williams	Holger Dieckmann
Doug Blair	Werner Kraemer
Wilf Grant	Uwe Seeler
Ken Chisholm	Franz-Josef Hoenig
George Edwards	Gert Doerfel
Sub not used: Lyn Davies	Sub not used: Erhard Schwerin

Referee: L. Van Ravens (Netherlands)

THERE ARE plenty of candidates, but this surely has to go down as the most heart-breaking moment in Cardiff City history. Don't panic Anthony Gerrard, the prize for worst-timed blunder goes to poor old Bob Wilson.

It was the 92nd minute on a chilly May Day evening at Ninian Park and the Bluebirds were all square against West German powerhouse Hamburg SV. Jimmy Scoular's men had defended heroically to draw 1-1 in Hamburg in the first leg and had fought back from 2-1 down to level through Brian Harris with 12 minutes to go in the return fixture in Wales. A replay in Jutland appeared on the cards.

But then with the very last kick of the game – in time added on after excitable children invaded the pitch following Harris's equaliser – Franz-Josef Hoenig let fly with a tame effort from 25 yards. City goalkeeper Wilson, who until that crucial second had enjoyed a sparkling season in Europe, looked to have it covered but let it wriggle through his body and trickle agonisingly into the corner. For the 43,000 City fans in Ninian, it was the moment that time stood still.

The final whistle blew immediately after the kick-off and City's sensational European adventure was over, dreams of becoming the first Second Division team in all the nations to reach the final shattered. There was a stunned silence around the ground, soon followed by tears. City's exploits in the competition had been as unexpected as they had been brilliant, but they had fallen at the final hurdle – and in just about the worst circumstances imaginable.

Wilson had been lauded before the match for his breathtaking performance in the quarter-finals of the competition. The match programme talked about Wilson's ability to excel on the big occasions. Now the 24-year-old from Birmingham was a broken man.

He told the *South Wales Echo,* "I feel sick – and I'm sick of people coming up to me and saying bad luck. I know the other lads in the team have told me to forget my last minute mistake but I can't forget it just like that." And to the *Western Mail* the honest keeper said,

"It was a perfectly innocent-looking shot. The ball slithered off my jersey and twisted slowly into the net."

City's run in the cup had been tremendous and unlikely to ever be repeated. It had started with a 3-1 aggregate win over Shamrock Rovers, followed by a 5-2 aggregate win over Dutch side NAC Breda. Scoular's heroes then needed a replay in Augsburg, West Germany, to eventually beat Torpedo Moscow 1-0 after the two-legged quarter-final had finished 1-1 overall.

Hamburg, though, posed a sterner test again. The giants of European football and three-times German champions included seven internationals and were famed for their fast-moving play. Their stars included 59-times capped Uwe Seeler, who led Germany's forward line in the 1966 World Cup Final against England, and midfield maestro Werner Kraemer. Other dangers included flying winger Gert Doerfel and 27-year-old full-back Juergen Kurbjuhn. The only non-German in their ranks was Turkish international goalkeeper Ankos Oezcan, who had been in outstanding form since making the move from Austria Wien.

Hamburg's coach was 63-year-old Georg Knopfle, who won 23 caps for Germany. He was supported ably by trainer-assistant Kurt Koch.

The first leg at the magnificent 71,000-capacity Hamburg City Stadium had gone superbly for the Bluebirds. Norman Dean, who had scored the winner in the Moscow play-off, got City off to a dream start when he bagged the opener on ten minutes. The Germans hammered away at the City defence but Wilson was in incredible form. Full-back Sandemann equalised in the 69th minute but City held out for an historic 1-1 draw.

Confidence was high in South Wales that City could finish the job seven days later in front of their excitable fans. A place in the final in Rotterdam against either AC Milan or Bayern Munich was within touching distance.

Hamburg had had a disappointing season in the main, slipping to third from bottom of the league at one stage before eventually turning the corner towards the end of 1967. They were safely positioned in mid-table by the time this replay came along and free to concentrate on Europe.

There was no such luxury for Cardiff, though. Success overseas and the demands of travelling thousands of miles had contributed to a disappointing league campaign and the Bluebirds were 17th in the table and just seven points above the relegation zone.

City knew that there was still much work to be done in the second leg, particularly as Seeler was back from injury for the visitors. Seeler, though perhaps past his best, was regarded as one of West Germany's all-time greats. There was some relief, however, that Willi Schulz, a defender of world-class ability, failed a late fitness test and watched from the stands.

Scoular told the *Echo*, "This match is going to be every bit as tough as it was in Hamburg. They are the best side we have played in the tournament. The only difference between tonight and before we played the first leg is that the pressure is now on Hamburg and that we will have our supporters behind us." Knopfle said simply, "One goal will decide it. We think we will get it."

The match was billed Cardiff's biggest since 1927 by the press and one of the most important nights in club history by chairman Fred Dewey. The eyes of Europe were on the Bluebirds – and for once the bulk of public support was with them. The *Echo* reported that since City's home-coming they had been shaken by the hand everywhere they went – not only in Cardiff but in Blackburn too, while in Lancashire for a 1-1 league draw.

Cardiff City's Greatest Games

Scoular named the same side that performed so well in Germany, resisting the temptation to include the skilful yet inconsistent Graham Coldrick ahead of David Carver.

It was the home side who did the early pressing and after ten minutes, ironically while John Toshack was lying injured on the floor, European ace Dean put City seemingly on the road to a famous success. Malcolm Clarke broke down the left wing and pulled the ball back for Dean to sweep home his third goal in as many games in the competition.

Dean, 23, had scored just once in all other competitions that season and had only forced his way into City's 'European team' because of an injury to Bobby Brown and Brian Clark's ineligibility.

But amid scenes of mass hysteria on the terraces, City could only hold on to their advantage for seven minutes. Doerfel passed across for Hoenig to thrash a rocket of a shot into the roof of the net.

For the rest of the half it was all City as they piled on the pressure to try and regain the lead. Great build-up play by Toshack ended with Oezcan pulling off a fine save from Barrie Jones before Egon Horst bravely charged down a Dean shot which was set to break the net.

With so much at stake, it was a remarkably open game. At the other end Kraemer saw a shot curl the wrong side of the post and then Toshack got his head on to a free kick after a foul on Leslie Lea but there was no team-mate to get on the end of it.

City came close on the half-hour when Jones produced a fine bit of skill to send a cross in. Lea was there to meet it but rushed his shot and missed the target.

The Bluebirds were playing good football and deserved to be ahead. Fifteen-goal Peter King was next to go close from just four yards after a good cross by Jones but he dallied for a second too long, allowing the Hamburg keeper to come out and smother.

Hamburg were dangerous on the counter-attack and hit the crossbar from a Kraemer free kick but City were well on top and on the stroke of half-time Toshack capitalised on a mix-up in the visitors' defence but it was dramatically cleared at the last moment.

But just 11 minutes into the second half came Wilson's first blunder which gifted the Germans the lead for the first time in the tie. Don Murray had done a fine job in silencing Seeler but for once the limping forward found an inch and sent a hopeful lob on the turn in the general direction of the goal. It looked to be drifting over and Wilson let it go, only to see it drop underneath the crossbar. There was a stony silence but for the faint cry of "Uwe, Uwe".

That was the catalyst for five minutes of Hamburg pressure – but City soon regained their composure. King and Clarke both tried to force the ball over the line after a good old-fashioned goalmouth scramble. Then in the 66th minute King should have made it all-square from 12 yards but ballooned his shot badly over.

As the pressure mounted on the Bluebirds, gaps inevitably started to appear at the back. Hans Schulz struck the post after being set up by an explosive Kraemer run while Seeler found the net but was correctly ruled offside.

But it was City who grabbed the crucial fourth goal of the night on 78 minutes to make it 2-2 and set up an unbelievable finish. Jones was hacked down on the right and skipper Harris charged through a crowded box to head home his free kick. It was Harris's first goal in 88 games for City and capped a supreme display.

Ninian Park burst into sound as the dream was re-ignited. Some fans made it on to the pitch but were quickly bundled back into the stands. There was no need for banning orders in 1968.

The momentum now was with City. Toshack was hacked down on the edge of the area and the resulting free kick by Dean was kneed off the line by Kurbjuhn. Moments later Tosh was inches away from getting on the end of a Dean cross.

But then with the very last kick came the heartbreak as Wilson allowed the ball to squirm through his hands. "Nothing could have been more calculated to break a person's heart," said *The Times*.

King grabbed the ball and raced it back to the centre circle – but the game was up.

Scoular, though visibly upset, tried to remain upbeat. He told the *Western Mail*, "Of course I'm disappointed. But it was one of those streaks of fate which robbed us of at least a replay. I was very proud of the boys, particularly in the first half when with any luck at all we would have had what would have proved to be a winning lead." And there was an honest appraisal from Seeler, too, "I thought we were very lucky to get away with a win. Soccer is a 90 minutes game and we won it in the last second. What more can I say?"

Hamburg went on to lose the final 2-0 against AC Milan while City stuttered to finish 13th in the league. Wilson was released at the start of 1970 and went on to make 205 appearances for Exeter City after a brief loan spell at Bristol City.

How things could have been so different.

v Pezoporikos Larnaca 8-0

16 September 1970. Attendance: 12,984
European Cup Winners' Cup Round One, First Leg.
Ninian Park

CARDIFF CITY:	PEZOPORIKOS LARNACA:
Frank Parsons	Takis Palmiris (Kiriakides 46)
David Carver	Giannis Petrou
Gary Bell	Giannis Paridis
Mel Sutton	Kallis Konstantinou
Don Murray	Stelios Kyriacou
Brian Harris	Dinos Chatzistillis
Ian Gibson	Giorgos Kounnidis
Brian Clark	Antonis Karapittas
Bobby Woodruff	Christos Loizou
John Toshack	Grigoris Filiastides
Peter King	Stavrinos Konstantinou
Sub not used: Leighton Phillips	
Referee: Jacques Colling (Luxembourg)	

"THE MOST absurd one-sided farce I have ever seen," was how *South Wales Echo* reporter Peter Jackson described this 8-0 win over Cypriot minnows Pezoporikos Larnaca, City's biggest scoreline in European football.

All the pre-match talk had been about not underestimating the European Cup Winners' Cup debutants but the amateurs were lambs to the slaughter as Jimmy Scoular's team scored at will. John Toshack and Brian Clark helped themselves to two each, while there were also goals for Mel Sutton, Ian Gibson, Peter King and Bobby Woodruff.

The only surprise at the end of 90 minutes of target practice was that City's tally had not reached double figures. According to reporter Jackson, City had 47 attempts on goal, Toshack leading the way with 11, while Frank Parsons had just one save to make from a bobbling 30-yard punt. Jackson likened it to putting Jack 'the Galveston Giant' in the same boxing ring as flyweight Benny Lynch – except in football the referee cannot step in to bring an end to the duel.

Second Division City had qualified for the European Cup Winners' Cup for the sixth time in seven years after beating Chester City 5-0 over two legs in the final of the Welsh Cup. City would have represented Wales overseas even if they had lost given that Chester were an English club. Larnaca, meanwhile, won the Cypriot Cup for the first time in their 43-year history but had missed out on their domestic championship on goal difference.

Cypriot clubs did not have a good record in Europe, but even so City boss Scoular warned against complacency and pointed to mighty Leeds United's slim 1-0 Fairs Cup win at Norwegian club Sarpsborg 24 hours earlier as proof that no game is easy.

"There is no such thing as a racing certainty in football," Scoular said. "Football is full of upsets and you can take it from me that our cup tie will be no formality. I will tell my players to treat this match as if they were playing one of the top teams in the world."

And there was plenty of fighting talk from Larnaca's coach, former Hungarian World Cup star Gyula Zsengellér. The 55-year-old, most famous for his part in firing Hungary to the 1938 World Cup Final against Italy, announced his team would be adopting an Italian-style defensive system.

Zsengellér had played for AS Roma and AC Ancona during his glittering career, both of which used the notorious 'catenaccio' system. Literally translating to door-bolt from Italian, the system was hyper-defensive and became popular during the 1960s when Argentinion coach Helenio Herrera used it to lead Serie A club Inter Milan to several championships. It normally meant two lines of defenders with a sweeper sitting behind.

Zsengellér said, "Maybe we defend with a small catenaccio." Zsengellér hoped that his team could take City back to the Mediterranean island with a small deficit and then the rock hard, bare pitch could prove a leveller.

Scoular showed Larnaca some respect by naming the same starting 11 for the ninth consecutive game in all competitions. City's league campaign had got off to a flying start, four wins and two draws enough to see them top of the table after seven games. On the weekend they had beaten Bolton Wanderers 2-0 with goals from Clark and Gibson.

And City had their opponents under the cosh right from the off, spurning a clutch of chances before eventually taking the lead on 18 minutes. Sutton got it when he hammered into the top corner after the ball had eventually reached him from a short corner routine. It was the second of just three goals that season for the hard-tackling midfielder from Birmingham.

The chances continued to come thick and fast. King scooped over the bar from little more than a yard after Gibson had hit the base of the post before Toshack placed his header wide after Gibson had carved his way through the Cypriot defence with startling ease.

But then came the predicted goal avalanche as City bagged four inside 11 minutes to effectively kill the tie before it had really began. On 33 minutes Gibson thumped home after Clark had unselfishly headed down into his path from a cross by solid full-back David Carver. Two minutes later King picked his spot for 3-0 after Larnaca keeper Takis Palmiris had panicked under pressure from Tosh and punched a Sutton cross straight to the City forward.

Woodruff got in on the act on 42 minutes when he sent a half-volley into the bottom corner after Sutton had pulled the ball back to Gibson, whose neat little clipped cross was nodded down invitingly by Toshack. And Clark made it 5-0 at half-time with a wonderful header at the far post from an expertly delivered Gary Bell cross.

Larnaca, playing with two orthodox wingers who saw little of the ball, were shattered with Gibson running the show. Palmiris, a 24-year-old electrician, had a reputation as one of the best goalkeepers in his country but was hauled off at half-time, despite receiving generous applause from the City fans. In terms of abysmal goalkeeping performances at Ninian Park, Palmiris's efforts have to be right up there with the legendary Peter Zois, the Aussie who was about as much use as an inflatable dartboard in City's 2-2 draw with Rotherham United in 1998.

Larnaca's star player, Cyprus international forward Christos Loizou, was barely involved under the close attentions of rock Don Murray. In fact Parsons did not have to take a goal kick until seven minutes before half-time in what must surely rank as his easiest game in three turbulent years at Cardiff.

Kiriakides faired marginally better than his predecessor between the sticks and made two good saves from Toshack. The *Echo* report said he went about his job with "the relish of someone trying to repair the crumbling Walls of Jericho". But he was merely stemming

Cardiff City's Greatest Games

the tide as ten minutes in, 21-year-old Tosh had his first of the game, and his fourth of the season. The Welshman, who was sold to Liverpool just two months later, smashed confidently past the visiting keeper after a good pass by Sutton.

Clark made it seventh heaven for City with 20 minutes left with a smart flick header from Bell's drilled cross. And with 79 minutes on the clock Toshack wrapped things up as he drilled home number eight.

Eight was apparently enough for City and against all the odds the visitors did venture into City's half twice in the dying moments – only for Loizou to get caught offside on both occasions.

Pezoporikos Larnaca's club emblem before merging with EPA Larnaca to form AEK Larnaca in 1994 was a camel. It was supposed to represent the club's history as a long distance walking club rather than its questionable footballing ability, but it seemed a very apt logo on an easy evening for the Bluebirds. And for all Zsengellér's confident talk before the match, he admitted afterwards, "We expected six Cardiff goals but not eight."

Kiriakides was mobbed by a handful of City fans at the final whistle as they celebrated a European haul which eclipsed the 7-1 win against Mjondalen in Norway the previous season.

The threadbare Larnaca pitch did even things out in the return leg two weeks later as the teams played out a drab 0-0 draw. Little did Cardiff know at the time, but they had taken the first step towards one of the club's most famous nights – a home tie against Spain's mighty Real Madrid in the quarter-finals.

v Real Madrid 1-0

10 March 1971. Attendance: 47,500
European Cup Winners' Cup Quarter-Final, First Leg.
Ninian Park

CARDIFF CITY:	REAL MADRID:
Jim Eadie	Jose Luis Borja
David Carver	Fernando Zunzunegui
Don Murray	Manuel Sanchis
Leighton Phillips	Jose Antonio Grande
Gary Bell	Gregorio Benito
Mel Sutton	Ignacio Zoco
Ian Gibson	Amancio Amaro
Bobby Woodruff	Pirri
Peter King	Raymon Grosso
Brian Clark	Manuel Velazquez
Nigel Rees	Miguel Perez

Referee: Vital Loraux (Belgium)

THIS IS the game which has gone down in the history books as City's most famous victory. Those Bluebirds fans crammed into Ninian Park will never forget the fairytale moment Brian Clark rose majestically to head in the goal which beat Spanish giants Real Madrid. And those not old enough to be there have heard countless tales of how little Cardiff City toppled the Emperors of European football on a moist spring evening under floodlight.

After breezing past Larnaca in the first round (8-0 on aggregate) and FC Nantes (7-2 on aggregate) in the second round, this was the quarter-final draw that everyone at the club longed for. In his programme notes, chairman Fred Dewey described it as "the most attractive club game ever held in this country".

Real Madrid arrived on Welsh soil for the first time having already been crowned kings of Europe six times. Included in their alumni were Ferenc Puskás, Alfredo Di Stéfano, Francisco Gento, and Raymond Kopa of the all-conquering teams of the late 1950s and early 1960s. They had thrilled millions with their modern, attacking philosophy and won an unrivalled five consecutive European Cups between 1955 and 1960. Now they were looking to lift the European Cup Winners' Cup at the first attempt. In truth, the Real class of 1970/71 was not a patch on those great teams. They had slipped as low as sixth in the league during the season, but had climbed back up to third by the time they came to Cardiff. But the famous name was enough create a terrific air of excitement around the city – and Miguel Munoz's team were certainly no mugs. Among their ranks were Pirri and Ignacio Zoco, who comfortably fell into the world-class category. Six of their starting 11 – Manuel Sanchis, Zoco, Amancio Amaro, Pirri, Raymon Grosso and Manuel Velazquez – had been at Real the last time they won the European Cup in 1966. City themselves were flying high and brimming with confidence. Goal machine John Toshack may have been sold to Liverpool four months earlier, but Jimmy Scoular's men went into the game top of the Second Division, tied with Hull City on 40 points. Alan

Cardiff City's Greatest Games

Warboys had smashed four goals as the promotion chase remained right on course with a 4-0 win over Carlisle United just four days earlier. But Warboys was not eligible against Real as he had not been registered in time following a £42,000 move from Sheffield Wednesday.

Step forward Bristolian Clark, who had been benched against the Cumbrians. Clark was in his fourth season with City having made an £8,000 move from Huddersfield during the 1967/68 campaign. He had already scored 11 league goals that season and three in European competition. Seventeen-year-old outside-left Nigel Rees, meanwhile, had to beg for his release from the Wales youth squad to take his place.

Officially 47,500 had packed into Ninian Park to see what the commentator announced as "Cardiff's City's greatest fixture ever" – but most people believed it to be more like 55,000. City fans used to dodge the entrance fee by climbing over a wall at one end of the ground, making it impossible to know exactly how many were there for the big games.

City made a settled start but could have found themselves a goal down early on when David Carver was too casual in possession. He tried to play a short pass across the box for Mel Sutton but only succeeded in finding Miguel Perez. Fortunately for the Bluebirds Jim Eadie was quick off his line and was able to save low down to his left. Carver was quite rightly given an ear-bashing from Sutton.

It was a decent open start to the game with excitement at both ends to rouse the huge crowd. Football songs were still in their infancy, but sporadic chants of "Cardiff, Cardiff" filled the air.

Grosso tried his luck from 30 yards after ghosting past Bobby Woodruff, but his effort trickled harmlessly through to Eadie.

Madrid had the ball in the net after about ten minutes when Leighton Phillips tried to head back to his keeper after a hopeful punt upfield. Perez nipped in but the referee spotted the use of his arm to put the ball past Eadie.

But it was far from one-way traffic and soon after City had their best chance so far. Woodruff's header from Peter King's cross was cleared by Zoco, who was enjoying his second visit to Ninian having played for Spain against Wales in 1961. But it only went as far as Ian Gibson 25 yards out, who fired his volley just wide of the post.

City were finding their straps as early nerves settled. A Gary Bell cross-field ball was headed out to the wing by Clark to Rees, who skinned Fernando Zunzunegui as if he wasn't there and delivered an enticing ball in the area. Gregorio Benito managed to head clear with King steaming in at the back post.

A decent Gibson free kick was then headed into the keeper's arms by King before immediately at the other end sloppy defending by Sutton gifted the visitors their first corner. Perez took it, almost standing in among a section of the City fans in the corner of the Grandstand. City failed to clear their lines properly and it eventually came to Velazquez, who could only curl his effort from the edge of the area wide.

Clark was winning everything in the air and from a high up-and-under Eadie kick he powered a header out to King on the wing. He whipped in a fine cross which was cleared by the diving head of Zoco, only as far as Clark who hit a first-time volley just wide. City were driving the "prancing, darting Spaniards back into their own half", *The Daily Mirror* reported.

Midway through the half King was hacked down by Zungunegui yet managed to earn a yellow card from the Belgian referee for his protestations. "Quite honestly I don't know what he did," said the commentator, after explaining the new yellow card system which had only been introduced less than a year earlier at the 1970 World Cup finals. From the free kick Gibson found Clark, who rose way above his defender and was close to finding the back of the net.

The game was getting a bit tasty in the centre of the park on the bobbly Ninian surface. Solid centre-half Don Murray twice rose highest to deal with consecutive Perez corners. But at the end other, attacking the old Canton Stand, City were looking dangerous from deep crosses and the huge long throws of Woodruff.

And it was inevitably a cross and a header which created the only goal of the game on 31 minutes. Woodruff played a nicely weighted ball down the line for Rees, who broke through two Real players and sent in a perfect cross from the byline for the unmarked Clark to power a header into the top corner.

Clark's immortality was secured in that one historic moment. It is a goal which has been replayed umpteen times over the years – but it is impossible to ever tire of seeing it. Ninian Park erupted and scarves were swung above heads. Many supporters have said it was the single loudest cheer ever witnessed at the old ground. The commentator said it was simply "deafening". Scoular did not move from his seat in the tiny dugout.

After the game and after a series of television interviews, Clark told the *South Wales Echo*, "No goal has ever given me greater pleasure and I don't suppose I'll ever get one to please me as much again. Not surprisingly most of the reports before the game were pointing out that Alan Warboys was not eligible to play. It's very hard to fill the boots of someone like Alan, who whacked four goals against Carlisle the Saturday before.

"I wouldn't say I was on a hiding to nothing, but I knew what was expected of me and I knew that I hadn't been playing very well recently. But to score the only goal in any match is pleasing. To score it against Real Madrid, that is something I only dreamed about."

Clark died in August 2010 and the tributes poured in from far and wide. Neil Kinnock, former Labour Party leader and keen City fan, said he was "unequalled as a man". Toshack praised his generosity in the game. Clark remained close to the club long after retiring and even co-commentated on a number of games for the official website. He must have been asked about that goal a million times or more. That moment was the shimmering pinnacle of a successful career and remains an iconic flashpoint in Cardiff City's mixed history.

Real Madrid, wearing dark red, were cautious in the second half, confident in their ability of turning the tie around at the 125,000-capacity Bernabeu Stadium in Madrid a fortnight later. After the game Real boss Munoz admitted he had ordered a defensive approach after being surprised by the City performance.

"Cardiff played a lot better than when I saw them in the league and they are a difficult side to beat," he said. They had reason to back themselves at home. In 46 home cup ties in Europe stretching back to 1955, Real had been beaten only three times – by Inter Milan, Standard Liege and Wacker Innsbruck.

City fans suspected that a second goal was needed to stand a real chance of progressing to the semi-finals. Their side started well enough with Gibson probing for the ball over the top and a Rees cross was just too short for Clark, but it was Real who had the first opening. The visitors counter-attacked through Jose Antonio Grande but his though ball for Amancio was snuffed out by Eadie.

At the other end, Bell did well to find Clark with a cross from the byline, but the City striker was further out this time and powered his header wide. Then seven minutes after the break Cardiff had a huge chance to make it 2-0. Tenacious Gibson intercepted in the middle of the park and played down the line for Clark, who headed infield for Sutton. His first effort was blocked, it came back to him inside the area but he could only send his half-volley into the arms of Jose Luis Borja. A second goal would have raised the roof.

Soon after a Bell free kick found Murray in space deep inside the area but the centre-half's effort lacked any real conviction and Benito was able to hook clear off the line. Real were struggling to get a hold of the game and, uncharacteristically, were resorting to thumping long, hopeful balls into City's half.

Gibson was having the game of his life. Midway through the second period he left Grosso for dead and his side-footed cross nearly found the head of Clark. Later a huge punt by the excellent Phillips, a 21-year-old playing for the injured Brian Harris, was punched clear by Borja with Clark ready to pounce on any slip.

Scoular was looking anxious on the sidelines as the game grew old. City were clearly the better side in the second half but just could not force the all-important second goal. The final five minutes saw a shortage of goalmouth action with both teams relatively happy with the scoreline.

Jubilant fans poured on to the pitch at the final whistle. The commentator remarked that it would do the muddy Ninian surface no favours, but who could blame them.

Clark is the name that will forever be synonymous with this great victory. He had a fantastic game, but City's shining light was Gibson. The midfielder was here, there and everywhere for the entire 90 minutes. He told the *South Wales Echo*, "Another goal and we would have clinched it. But what a result to beat Real Madrid anyway. Let's go on and win the Second Division now."

On a night when Manchester City and Chelsea, the only other British teams left in the competition, both lost, Scoular hailed the win as a triumph for Wales – and predicted success in the Spanish capital.

"I believe now we can win the tie, although we deserved to have won last night by at least two clear goals," he said. "Whatever happens nobody can take anything away from the players for their wonderful show. For me they were great, just great." *The Daily Mirror* proclaimed that "on this form Cardiff have nothing to fear in the second leg", though feeling among supporters was more realistic.

City did eventually crash out of the competition, losing 2-0 in Madrid after two defensive blunders. And there was heartbreak in the league, too, as late-season defeats by Watford and Sheffield United ended dreams of promotion into the top flight.

But nothing could tarnish the memories of the night Cardiff City got one over on Spain's Royal Club.

Peter Jackson, the *Echo*'s Cardiff City reporter at the time, mused 40 years later, "That's Cardiff City for you, the only club to beat Real Madrid and lose to Maidstone United."

20 v Crystal Palace 1-1

30 April 1974. Attendance: 26,781
Second Division. Ninian Park

CARDIFF CITY:	CRYSTAL PALACE:
Ron Healey	Paul Hammond
Phil Dwyer	Paddy Mulligan
Freddie Pethard	Stewart Jump
Clive Charles	Jeff Johnson
Richie Morgan	Roy Barry
Tony Villars	Mel Blyth
Gil Reece	Derek Jeffries
Johnny Vincent	Derek Possee
Leighton Phillips	Alan Whittle
Willie Carlin (Derek Showers)	Don Rogers
Willie Anderson	Peter Taylor

Referee: Jack Taylor (Wolverhampton)

THIS WAS a night when 12 men in blue fought and scrapped their way to league safety – and became heroes. There have been few nights of such tension and emotion in City's history. The mathematics was simple on City's final game of the league season: a draw would keep the Bluebirds in the Second Division, defeat would send them down and opponents Crystal Palace would survive instead. The immediate future of two proud clubs was on a knife-edge. It all came down to 90 minutes of thrilling blood and thunder football in the drizzle at Ninian Park.

City looked doomed after 28 minutes when Stewart Jump put the visitors ahead. Suddenly the huge crowd fell silent as they contemplated life in the third tier for the first time in 27 years. But how Jimmy Andrews's men responded.

On 39 minutes Cwmbran lad Tony Villars scored a stunning equaliser that would still be talked about 30 years later. And somehow, by the skin of their teeth, the blue wall held firm for 51 more agonising minutes.

Supporters swarmed on to the pitch as if promotion had been achieved. Cardiff City, the perennial strugglers, were safe for another year.

Every man was a hero, but none showed more bravery than wee Scot Willie Carlin. The 33-year-old, one of the game's great personalities, had announced that his 427th league appearance would be his last before retirement. The motivational master arrived at City in November 1973 to try and add some steel to the midfield. He had brought much more than that.

Boss Andrews said in one interview that Carlin was the only man he had met who had a heart that could be seen to be beating as well as heard. He delivered one final performance just when City needed it most, despite being forced off at half-time after being kicked from pillar to post.

Also worthy of praise were Clive Charles, who had been drafted in from West Ham on transfer deadline day in March, and Gil Reece, who ran himself into the ground. Goalkeeper Ron Healey, too, received plaudits for some good saves in wet conditions.

But the man of the hour was Villars, the winger plucked from obscurity by Jimmy Scoular three years earlier. The 22-year-old may have frustrated fans at times with his inconsistency – but here he showed why Scoular had believed he would one day be worth £100,000.

Six minutes before half-time Villars intercepted Peter Taylor's square pass ten yards inside his own half, beat one tackle and skipped in between two more Palace players. After dashing 50 yards Villars, under pressure from Mel Blyth, slipped the ball to Reece. The Cardiff lad shielded the ball well and found Villars again in his new position, who hammered right footed into the bottom corner. Goalkeeper Paul Hammond did well to get a hand to it, but there was no way he was keeping it out. *Western Mail* reporter Clive Phillips rated it the best goal at Ninian Park that season.

"He (Villars) was marvellous and revealed the greatness we all knew to be in him," said Andrews afterwards.

The fact that Palace found themselves in such a perilous position was a shock to many. The South Londoners, playing their first season in red and dark blue after switching from claret and sky blue, had been relegated from the First Division just 12 months earlier and were many people's tip for an immediate promotion. The squad had seen a huge change in personnel but they still had big name players including strikers Don Rogers and Derek Possee.

And in manager Malcolm Allison, Palace had one of the brightest and most extravagant men in British football. Cigar-puffing Allison had masterminded Manchester City's four major trophies in three seasons just a few years earlier. He had taken over at Selhurst Park in March 1973 but could not save them from the drop.

Palace started the 1973/74 season in horrendous fashion and remained rooted to the foot of the table until a good Easter period gave them some hope. They were playing good football and most thought they would go on to secure survival with something to spare – but three successive defeats in April saw them heading to Cardiff knowing only a win would do.

As fate would have it, the game was originally due to be played in February but was postponed because of a waterlogged pitch. There were just a handful of games left to be played in the division – but no others which could affect the relegation shake-up. Swindon and Preston were already goners and normally that would have been that but at the start of the campaign league bosses had decided to add a third promotion and relegation place to increase excitement.

Pulling the City strings on a colossus night was caretaker boss Andrews, the third manager of a typically chaotic season. Scoular had started off in the hot-seat but was dismissed in November after nine years at the club. Former Manchester United boss Frank O'Farrell was drafted in as his replacement within days, and he hired Andrews as his coach.

But O'Farrell lasted just 158 days before agreeing to take on a position as manager of the Iran national side. Andrews took over as acting manager with the unenviable job of saving the Bluebirds from relegation. O'Farrell did, however, stay at the club in an assistant capacity until the end of the campaign. To add a little more spice, Allison, O'Farrell and Andrews – an Englishman, an Irishman and a Scotsman – had all played in the same West Ham team in their 20s.

As if there was not enough riding on the do-or-die Palace clash, Cardiff Council not for the first time displayed its disdain for the club by delivering a truly bizarre ultimatum – stay in the division or lose Ninian Park. The threat, if that's was it was intended to be, came from councillors Bill Herbert and Phillip Norton. The pair claimed that the land, which was leased to the football club, could be put to better use for housing. City chairman David Goldstone laughed it off, particularly as the council had lent the club £225,000 at the start of the season to build the new 3,300-seat Grandstand.

Both managers tried to instil confidence with their pre-match comments. Andrews insisted that he had felt no fear or apprehension about the game, while Allison went a step further. "A Second Division side we are – a Second Division side we will remain," he had said without a quiver of doubt.

A crowd of 26,781, City's biggest gate in the league for almost five years, packed into Ninian for the Tuesday evening fixture – far more than the 15,000 that had been expected.

But it was Palace, backed by their 6,000 fans, who started best. Healey had to be sharp to save a header from 21-year-old Taylor, who 32 years later would go on to manage the Eagles. Minutes later Phil Dwyer, in his second of 13 seasons at City, headed a Jeff Johnson cross over his own crossbar with Healey at sixes and sevens.

Diminutive Carlin was the subject of bully-boy tactics from Palace and twice needed treatment after crunching tackles by Blyth. But Palace also had the flair to back up the muscle and Blyth enjoyed some neat interchanges with Rogers and Alan Whittle.

The visitors were looking the more dangerous and they had their breakthrough 17 minutes before half-time from a set-piece. Healey was surrounded by a scrum of players and misjudged an in-swinging corner, allowing defender Jump to hammer the ball in from just a couple of yards out. Healey claimed that he had been fouled, but there was no way for the referee to tell through the ruck of activity.

That was enough to send a new wave of nervousness swirling around the home supporters. Chants of "come on you super blues, come on the cream of Europe" were just a little less convincing than they had been.

For ten terrifying minutes, the Eagles took over, passing the ball around with a confidence that belied their league standing. Taylor's corners were wreaking havoc – Carlin heading off the line from one – and the rowdy Palace fans sensed that the great escape could be on. Yet remarkably, almost out of nothing, Villars's wonder goal put City on level terms to set up six minutes of mayhem before half-time. Another dazzling run by Villars then gave Reece a great chance for 2-1 but the 19-cap Wales international fluffed his shot straight at Hammond.

But this end-of-season cliffhanger was far from over and with the last kick of the half Palace hit the post through Taylor after Johnny Vincent failed to clear a corner.

Derek Showers replaced Carlin at the start of the second half, Carlin having ruptured a tendon. Palace threw men forward at every opportunity – centre-half Roy Barry playing virtually as a striker for long spells – as they searched desperately for a second goal.

Much of the game was played deep in the City half but as Palace committed more and more to the cause, Villars was able to exploit the space on the counter-attack. On one occasion he steam-rolled his way 50 yards up the pitch before running out of puff and letting off a tame final shot.

Palace continued to have too much possession for comfort, but the excellent Leighton Phillips marshalled his defence expertly. The 26-year-old Welshman was forced to head clear from an unguarded net on one occasion.

Blyth fired over the crossbar when he really should have scored and then Healey swallowed up a long shot by the same player. Possee also headed wide from close-range and Paddy Mulligan missed from a good position.

The Palace fans sang "we'll support you ever more" as the final whistle blew to start an outpouring of joy and relief from the City faithful. Their team had put them through the mire once again. In the previous two seasons City had secured their place in the division with a game to spare – this time they had taken it right to the wire.

The City players enjoyed champagne from china teacups as they toasted their success, while *The Express* reported that Allison could be found head down outside the silent Palace dressing room. "I never thought they'd break us once we scored that first goal," he told the paper in a whisper.

Andrews was officially named as the new permanent City manager within hours of the final whistle. He warned of the need for City to improve "50 per cent" if they were to compete in the Second Division the following season against the likes of Manchester United and Southampton, who had both come down from the top flight.

But for all the optimism of that unforgettable night under Ninian floodlights, it came as no great shock when City finally were relegated to the Third Division the following season. There are only so many times you can dodge the bullet playing Russian roulette.

21 v Hereford United 2-0

14 April 1976. Attendance: 35,549
Third Division. Ninian Park

CARDIFF CITY:	HEREFORD UNITED:
Ron Healey	Kevin Charlton
Phil Dwyer	Steve Emery
Freddie Pethard	Steve Ritchie
Alan Campbell	John Layton
Mike England	John Galley
Albert Larmour	Jimmy Lindsay
Peter Sayer (Gil Reece 62)	Terry Paine (Eric Redrobe 56)
Doug Livermore	Dudley Tyler
Tony Evans	Steve Davey
Adrian Alston	Dixie McNeil
Willie Anderson	Roy Carter

Referee: Trevor D. Spencer (Wootton Bassett)

C IGAR SMOKER Malcolm Allison opened his delivery of six bottles of champagne and looked at the little card inside. You can imagine his wry smile as he read its message, "With love, from Cardiff City."

City vice-chairman Tony Clemo had sent the gift to the larger-than-life Crystal Palace manager after he had claimed that his club were bigger than the Bluebirds. "Cardiff are not in the same league as us when it comes to support," Big Mal had said after watching his side lose against City on the weekend in front of 25,863 at Selhurst Park. Little Cardiff could never manage such a gate, he had claimed. Not for the first time, flamboyant Allison was forced to eat his words after more than 35,000 emerged from the woodwork to see City take a monumental step towards promotion at Ninian Park.

Allison, football's first playboy manager, would have felt confident that his comments would not come back to haunt him. After all, City's last three home gates had been 12,185 v Millwall, 9,622 v Grimsby and 12,408 v Preston. But the Wednesday night visit of table-toppers Hereford had captured the imagination with City fans desperate to see their team take a decisive step towards the Second Division. It turned out to be City's biggest league crowd since 1961 when 45,463 saw a 3-2 win over Tottenham Hotspur.

"Malcolm Allison did us a favour by saying we could not match Palace for support," said Clemo, who had joined the board of directors in the summer. "Our fans were determined to prove him wrong."

It might have been an even bigger crowd as many would-be supporters who ignored the repeated advice to arrive early turned around and went home after seeing the chaos on Sloper Road caused by turnstile jams.

As third tier games go, the visit of Hereford couldn't have been much bigger. John Sillett's Bulls were perfectly equipped for the Third Division and had topped the table since trouncing City 4-1 at Edgar Street in February. With five games to go they were just three points short of being confirmed champions. They had the best away record in the Football League with 12 victories and 41 goals. All told they had rattled up 77 league goals with hot-shots Dixie McNeil and Steve Davey sharing 49 of them.

But Jimmy Andrews's Cardiff, five points behind their close English rivals in second, were also in decent form and looking good for an immediate return to the Second Division after relegation 12 months earlier. The Bluebirds had won their last four – including that crucial success at Palace – and in Tony Evans and Adrian Alston had a prolific strike force of their own, with 34 goals between them to date. But despite City's good form, they went into the game just a point clear of third and fourth place Brighton and Millwall.

Former Chelsea and Coventry full-back Sillett was tipping City to crumple under the pressure and to drop out of the promotion places. He told the *Western Mail,* "All the pressure will be on Cardiff. They are only now beginning to experience the terrific tension involved in a promotion race and are still glancing back at their close rivals."

Veteran Terry Paine had tormented City with his pinpoint free kicks in the match at Edgar Street and was a surprise inclusion in the United starting line-up ahead of Eric Redrobe. Sillett predicted that City would have formulated a plan to deal with dead balls and promised that his team had a few surprises up their sleeves – but Andrews was keen to maintain an air of confidence. "We are putting our game together with considerable skill and running into form at the right time," he said. "But it is going to need an outstanding display from 11 players to rattle Hereford."

John Buchanan and Clive Charles had returned to training after injury but Andrews stuck with the same team which had done so well at Palace four days earlier. Doug Livermore played with four stitches in his head after a collision at Selhurst Park and in-form 21-year-old Peter Sayer kept his place in midfield.

Repeated calls went out over the loudspeaker for supporters to bunch closer together as thousands continued to pour in long after the game began. It is believed up to 3,000 fans missed the first half-hour of the game and there were five arrests as frustrated fans tried to force their way in.

But they would have been more annoyed had Sayer put City ahead after just five minutes. Liverpudlian Evans showed great control in the middle of the park and burst through Hereford's defence with a trademark run. The visitors' defence froze still waiting for an offside flag which never came and 21-goal Evans found Sayer on the left wing with a wonderful pass. Welsh winger Sayer cut inside but his angled drive was so wild that it went out for a throw-in.

Six minutes later Phil Dwyer was booked by pernickety referee Trevor Spencer for a foul on 37-year-old former England cap Paine as Hereford counter-attacked.

City, spurred on by their vociferous supporters, continued to attack but struggled to find a way through against a Hereford defence which hustled and harried and often looked for the back-pass to goalkeeper Kevin Charlton.

And increasingly, despite good City possession, there were nail-biting moments as chances began to fall Hereford's way. Ron Healey, 23 and City's number one for the bulk of the campaign, nearly gifted the leaders a goal when he let a long-range lob from John Layton slip through his grasp and McNeil looked ready to pounce. Fortunately for the Bluebirds his shot rebounded to safety off brilliant centre-half Mike England, who had emerged from retirement to play one solitary season for City.

Hereford did have the ball in the net midway through the half when Layton powered home a Paine free kick but the joy of the 3,000-or-so travelling fans was short-lived as the linesman raised his flag. Newspaper reports claim an offside call, but the referee later told Sillett that he had spotted a push by Davey.

And Cardiff had another escape when Healey came charging off his line to clear but completely mis-kicked. Predators McNeil and Davey moved in for the kill but Albert Larmour, a £12,000 Jimmy Scoular signing from Linfield, belted clear.

Healey, who today runs goalkeeping courses in his home city of Manchester, did settle down as the half went on and redeemed himself somewhat by turning a Roy Carter drive round the post.

It had been a difficult first half for City and a neutral could have argued that Hereford should have been in front. But City came out for the second half at breakneck pace and completely took control of their destiny with Willie Anderson playing just behind Evans and Alston. First Alston headed just narrowly wide from Anderson's neat cross and then soon after Australian Alston stung Charlton's hands with a thunderous 30-yard drive.

The crucial goal came on 54 minutes. The excellent Freddie Pethard picked up a throw from Healey and he sent Evans away with a ball down the left. The former electrician curled a perfect ball into the box with the outside of his right boot and Livermore was there to connect with a great diving header from eight yards. Ninian Park went bonkers as the former Liverpool man jogged back to the centre circle grinning from ear to ear. It was Livermore's first headed goal since he bagged the equaliser for Norwich against Spurs in 1973. "I met it just right with my head," he said afterwards. "And what a roar when the ball went in. Fantastic."

The goal was a catalyst for ten minutes of the best football City had played that season. Evans ought to have made it 2-0 but fired his shot straight at Charlton and then Alston smashed a close-range effort over the crossbar.

Hereford threw on big striker Redrobe for Paine before John Galley was booked for a rash tackle on Alston. Then in the 69th minute Gil Reece came on for the injured Sayer to make his first appearance in more than two months in his second stint with the club.

It wasn't often that Hereford failed to score so City were grateful to wrap the precious points up with a second with five minutes remaining – and what a super goal it was.

Evans collected the ball on the left and slipped a pass to Livermore. The future Swansea manager sent a delightful chip forward to find Alan Campbell, who nipped in, knocked it past Charlton and rolled it into the empty Canton Stand net to send the City fans into raptures. Campbell, a £20,000 March signing from Birmingham, told the Echo, "I glanced at the linesman to see if I was onside. He kept his flag down and I reached for the cross and turned the ball past Kevin Charlton who had left his line. I think it would have rolled in but I followed up just to make sure."

The signing of Campbell was a shrewd move. The Scot settled City down defensively and could create something out of nothing with the ball at his feet. He appeared in all of City's final 14 games of the season after making the move from St Andrew's, and in that time City were beaten just once and conceded just eight.

The magnificent victory moved City to within three points of the Bulls with three games remaining. There was still some work to be done – but this was an almighty step towards glory. Andrews, acknowledging the importance of the result, strode to the Grandstand and delivered a fist pump that Malky Mackay would be proud of. "This was the night we regained our pride as a football club, the pride that Jimmy Scoular built up in the 1960s," he said. "What a fantastic occasion, one of the proudest of my life." And the popular Scot could not resist a little dig at Allison: "We proved that the club has greater

Cardiff City's Greatest Games

potential than Crystal Palace." Whether that assertion has been borne out in the 37 years that have followed is open to debate.

And there was praise too from Sillett: "They (Cardiff) must be a good side to beat us as well as they did. They were the better side on the night and I can think of only two or three times during the season when we have not created chances for our strikers."

City went on to record back-to-back 0-0 draws against Swindon Town and Peterborough United over the next five days. That gave Palace a chance, but the South Londoners drew their two games in hand and City made absolute certain of promotion on the final day with a 1-0 away win at Bury, Alston the scorer. City finished in second place with Hereford worthy champions and Millwall in third.

City have not come close to matching that huge crowd since. Unless the ground is expanded in the future, it will never be bettered. The first home game in the Second Division was a local derby of sorts against Bristol Rovers yet just 12,665 rolled through the turnstiles. Quite where the missing 22,884 were is anybody's guess!

22 v Tottenham Hotspur 1-0

8 January 1977. Attendance: 27,868
FA Cup Third Round. Ninian Park

CARDIFF CITY:	TOTTENHAM HOTSPUR:
Ron Healey	Pat Jennings
Phil Dwyer	Keith Osgood
Brian Attley	Terry Naylor
John Buchanan	Steve Perryman
Paul Went	John Gorman
Albert Larmour	John Pratt
Steve Grapes	Glenn Hoddle
Doug Livermore	Alfie Conn
Tony Evans	Peter Taylor
Peter Sayer	Ralph Coates (Don McAllister)
David Giles	John Duncan
Sub not used: Keith Pontin	
Referee: Alex Lees (Bridgwater)	

JIMMY ANDREWS had every right to feel a little bit smug after this FA Cup victory over First Division Tottenham. Before the game the City boss had boldly predicted that the pace of his front men Peter Sayer and Tony Evans would be too much for Spurs – and he was bang on the money.

"These are two of the fastest front runners in football," Andrews had warned. "Their speed will make up for our lack of height and we should cause Tottenham's suspect defence many problems with our quick breaks."

The prophecy came true after just six minutes when a bad back-header fell to Steve Grapes, who played in Sayer for the only goal of the tie. The City forward raced through and fired a bouncing half-volley past Pat Jennings from way outside the area.

The Cardiff-born 21-year-old was more comfortable on the wing but had been thrown up top alongside marksman Evans as Robin Friday, the striker who had scored twice on his debut seven days earlier after signing from Reading, was cup-tied and Derek Showers was injured. Andrews admitted afterwards that he had considered playing John Buchanan in attack with Evans but was loath to lose him from the midfield.

As the game was shown on *Match of the Day* later that evening, the goal catapulted Sayer to national stardom. He was presented with a TR7 sports car emblazoned with his name, invited to open new shops, was capped by Wales and was even linked with a move to Liverpool as a replacement for Kevin Keegan. It is amazing what one goal can do sometimes. "What happened against Tottenham was dream stuff," said Sayer years later.

The result fell comfortably within the parameters of being a major cup shock. In an interview with the *South Wales Echo* in 2007, Spurs defender John Gorman recounted how a cloud of gloom had descended on the away dressing room after the defeat. But actually it shouldn't have been such a surprise, not by today's Cup standards anyway.

City were 14th in the Second Division after being promoted the previous season and had started 1977 with two important home wins against Hereford United and Fulham.

Spurs, meanwhile, despite boasting players like Jennings, Steve Perryman, Glenn Hoddle and Peter Taylor, were struggling in 19th position in the First Division having won just five of their first 20. They had also conceded an appalling 41 goals in the league – by far the worst record in the division – including eight at Derby in October.

Nevertheless, Keith Burkinshaw's million-pound Spurs side still should have been able to see off City, whose most expensive player was £30,000 Paul Went. Andrews had also opted to give youngsters David Giles and Brian Attley a rare start. Giles, who was transfer-listed at his own request, had made just one substitute appearance in the league against Hereford on Boxing Day. Attley, meanwhile, played left-back for only the second time that season as Clive Charles failed a late fitness test on a groin injury.

Peter Sayer – nicknamed Leo after the pop star of the time – was told by Andrews to shoot on sight, and that's exactly what he did after just six minutes. The Spurs defence was slow to clear its lines and Ralph Coates directed a header straight to Grapes. The £7,000 signing from Norwich City spotted Sayer's burst through the centre and found him with a header over the Spurs back-line. Sayer had four yellow shirts in pursuit, but managed to nod it down before unleashing a right foot drive into the bottom corner from all of 25 yards. Jennings, one of the best goalkeepers of his day, couldn't get anywhere near it. "I thought I was dreaming when I saw the ball bulge the back of the net," said softly-spoken Sayer.

Four-times England cap Coates held his hands up for his part in the goal – but blamed his all-round poor performance on a high temperature. "I had made a wrong decision to declare myself fit," the winger told *The Tottenham & Edmonton Weekly Herald*. "Certainly it wasn't a very pleasant trip to Wales for me." He was taken off in the second half.

Once City had the lead, Spurs searched frantically for a way back into the game. The Londoners had the vast bulk of possession but stuttered when they got to the penalty area and were crowded out by determined City defenders. Spurs wanted to play sophisticated football and were always looking for the square ball, but that required space and time and Andrews's pumped-up boys were drilled to snap away at everything in front of them.

Ron Healey had a decent game but the majority of his work was cutting out simple crosses. Frustrations started to show among the Spurs team and in the 29th minute John Pratt cynically clattered into Evans off the ball. Two minutes later skipper Perryman was booked for tripping Buchanan after the two players had been involved in a crunching tackle. Referee Alex Lees did well to keep control of the tie.

Such was the frustration of some of the 1,000 Spurs fans sat in front of the Ninian directors' box that they turned and threw rubbish at their club's money men! But that was nothing compared with the ugly scenes when the two teams last met in the FA Cup in 1923. According to a press report, cheating Spurs players kept kicking the ball into the crowd to waste time and on one occasion a Tottenham fan caught it in the Grandstand.

The reporter said, "He tucked it up his jumper and held up two fingers to indicate how much time there was left to play. Instantly there was a howl of rage and a shower of oranges, programmes and anything else the City fans could lay their hands on."

As the game wore on, chances inevitably fell to Spurs. Healey was almost caught out by a deflected shot by Taylor but managed to recover in time. Then a smart one-two between John Duncan and Hoddle produced an opening but Hoddle's effort flew over the bar. Hoddle was just 19 years old but already his talent was obvious and he was being tipped to reach the very top.

When Healey did slip up and dropped a Pratt cross, man of the match Went moved in to make a crucial block from Perryman's shot. Went's determination eventually made him a huge favourite with the City fans. Phil Dwyer, too, produced clearances of the quality of a "bionic man", as the *Western Mail* put it, Albert Larmour battled hard and Attley barely let England's Taylor out of his sights.

But City, wearing the classic retro blue shirt with a yellow and white stripe down the left side, did not completely give up on attacking and the pace of the front three, Grapes, Evans and Sayer, continued to cause Tottenham problems. *The Times* said, "Sayers and Evans played to a simple old-fashioned formula – push the ball forward and run like hell after it." Jennings had to pull off two good saves to prevent City running clear.

For all their possession and fruitless corners, the real nail-biting for City fans did not come until the last six minutes when Taylor almost scored in spectacular fashion. The 24-year-old's terrific overhead kick hit the inside of the post, trickled agonisingly across the goal-line and into baffled Healey's hands.

That was the visitors' last assault and the Bluebirds had done it. They had beaten a First Division side in the cup at home for the first time since knocking Charlton out in 1950. And they had done it through sheer desire and hard work.

Times reporter Tom Freeman concluded, "The lesson of this game is that even in these days of sophisticated football, the simple approach, rather than the elaborate one, is more likely to win matches."

The solemn faces of the Spurs players told the story. Their reputation as a cup team was in tatters – the five-times winners had not negotiated their way past the third round for five long years. "I remember vividly after the game sitting in the away dressing room trying to come to terms with what had happened," said Gorman 30 years later. Distraught Burkinshaw's words were few. "I'm deadly disappointed," he muttered to the journos as he brushed past their notepads.

But if Spurs thought things couldn't get any worse they were wrong, for four months later they finished rock bottom of the First Division and were relegated into the second tier for the first time since 1950.

But for City, 50 years on from 1927 and all that means to the club, it was a joyous moment. "This is the happiest day since I took over," said beaming Scot Andrews, who died in 2012. "We beat Spurs because we had the bigger heart and more graft."

City were into the fourth round of the world-famous competition and when the draw pitted them against either Wrexham or Sunderland at home, absolutely anything seemed possible.

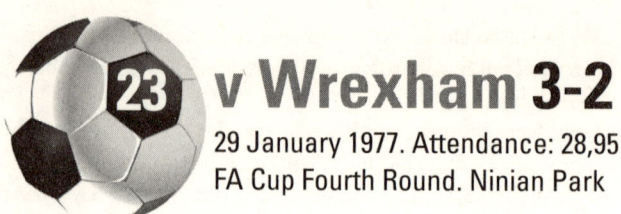

23 v Wrexham 3-2

29 January 1977. Attendance: 28,951
FA Cup Fourth Round. Ninian Park

CARDIFF CITY:	WREXHAM:
Ron Healey	Brian Lloyd
Phil Dwyer	Gareth Davis
Brian Attley	Mickey Evans
John Buchanan	Wayne Cegielski
Paul Went	John Roberts
Albert Larmour	Mike Thomas
Steve Grapes	Bobby Shinton
Doug Livermore	Mel Sutton
Tony Evans	Billy Ashcroft
Peter Sayer	Graham Whittle
David Giles	Arfon Griffiths
Sub not used: Willie Anderson	Sub not used: Stuart Lee
Referee: John Hunting (Leicester)	

IT WAS billed as "The Battle of Wales" as Third Division high-flyers Wrexham visited Ninian Park in the fourth round of the FA Cup. It was the first FA Cup match between two Welsh sides since Swansea faced Wrexham in 1928. The north versus south showdown caught the imagination of the nation – and it produced a final 60 seconds never to be forgotten.

Prolific striker Billy Ashcroft had scored a deserved equaliser for Wrexham with less than a minute left on the referee's watch. It was 2-2 and a replay at the famous Racecourse ground loomed large. But City had other ideas.

With the visiting fans still going wild, Steve Grapes set off on a mazy run down the right flank. The 23-year-old slipped in between two Wrexham players, and darted towards the byline before cutting back to John Buchanan. The midfielder was famed for his thunderbolt shooting, but this time he kept his cool and passed into the bottom corner from the penalty spot. Ninian exploded into joy – Cardiff were the undisputed kings of Wales.

The final whistle blew just ten seconds later to bring an end to a thrilling cup tie. The City heroes enjoyed two crates of champagne while the stunned North Walians sat in silence. "We were still thinking about Billy Ashcroft's equaliser and sat back to allow Cardiff to pinch a winner," admitted Wrexham boss John Neal, speaking to the *Western Mail.* "We lacked professionalism in that final minute." The stupendous cup tie had been captured by the *Match of the Day* cameras, prompting City manager Jimmy Andrews to say, "We are now on the football map."

Despite City plying their trade in the division above Wrexham and enjoying home advantage, pundits had predicted a tight encounter. The Robins were third in the Third Division and pushing for a place in the second tier for the first time in their history. They were playing an entertaining brand of attacking football – and scoring goals for fun. Bobby Shinton, Ashcroft, and Graham Whittle had scored 45 between them while midfielder Arfon Griffiths was still pulling the strings in midfield. The 35-year-old Welsh international, known as 'The General', had just been awarded an MBE and had also taken on the job as assistant manager-coach at his home-town club.

Also among the Robins' ranks was defender Wayne Cegielski, the lad from Blackwood who asked for a trial at the club at the start of the season and was a now a Wales Under-21 international. He had forged a good partnership with former Swansea man John Roberts, who became Wrexham's record transfer buy at £30,000 when he joined from Birmingham City at the start of the season. Hard tackling midfielder Mel Sutton, by now 30, returned to face Cardiff, the club he had left four seasons earlier after making himself a favourite in 165 appearances.

Wrexham had impressed in cup competitions that season. In the League Cup they had beaten First Division big boys Leicester City at the Racecourse and then earned a spectacular 3-2 win against Spurs at White Hart Lane before eventually losing against Aston Villa at Villa Park. In the FA Cup they had thumped Gateshead United 6-0 before beating Goole Town after a replay and then causing an upset by sending First Division Sunderland crashing out of the competition.

But City were doing well in their first season at the higher level and went into the match in 14th position and on the back of a four-game unbeaten run. Andrews's men owed much to the thrilling attacking pace of Tony Evans and Peter Sayer. Former electrician Evans had topped the club's league scoring charts with 21 goals during City's promotion season in 1975/76 – and he had been at it again in this season, netting on 17 occasions up to this game to make him the Second Division's joint top marksman. Cardiff-born winger Sayer, meanwhile, had scored the spectacular winner against Spurs in the third round of the FA Cup three weeks earlier.

But just as important as the attack in this all-Wales humdinger would be the defence. Phil Dwyer, Albert Larmour, Brian Attley and Paul Went, a former England youth who signed for the Bluebirds for £30,000 from cash-strapped Portsmouth, knew they would have their hands full with the tremendous three, Shinton, Ashcroft and Whittle.

There was a blow for City, though, as bad boy Robin Friday, who had scored twice on his debut on New Year's Day, was cup-tied – and had suffered a fractured cheekbone. Nonetheless, there was certainly no shortage of confidence from the City ranks 50 years on from that famous cup success of 1927.

"Wrexham's back four will be frightened of our attacking pace," said City skipper Doug Livermore. "I believe we can turn our dream of reaching the Cup Final into a reality," said confident/deluded chairman Stefan Terlezki. And Andrews added, "You could say we are all looking forward to winning the tie."

The rain had poured for days before the game but constant attention from ground staff ensured it went ahead. And there was a boost for City with goalscoring midfielder Buchanan given the nod to start after missing the last two games with a thigh problem. His inclusion meant Andrews could name the same 11 that beat Spurs so impressively. Willie Anderson, who the day before had negotiated a move to Portland Timbers in the USA, remained on the bench.

Both teams lined up with their familiar 4-3-3 formations in front of a bubbling crowd of almost 29,000. And on a heavy pitch it was the visitors who started best. Thirteen-goal Whittle saw his effort well saved by Ron Healey, who was enjoying a run in the team after starting second fiddle to Bill Irwin. Sixteen-goal Shinton also went close twice.

But it was the Bluebirds who stormed ahead on 20 minutes through 20-year-old David Giles, who had put himself on the transfer list at the start of the season. Grapes pinged over a corner. Dwyer and Roberts jumped for it on the penalty spot but it sailed over their heads and all the way out to Giles on the edge of the area. The long-haired winger had made his FA Cup debut against Spurs and had been a bit-part player in the league. He did his reputation no harm by smashing a fierce left foot volley through a thicket of legs and into the bottom corner before dropping to his knees in front of the Canton Stand in celebration.

Giles told the *South Wales Echo* after the match that Dwyer had told him to lurk behind him in anticipation of the corner coming over his head. "It was the most perfect shot I have ever hit," said Giles, who is these days better known as a radio and newspaper pundit.

City continued to boss the midfield with Livermore, 29, pulling the strings. Wrexham's Welsh international keeper Brian Lloyd – who on this day set a new record with 286 consecutive first team appearances – was called upon to make a string of steady blocks.

The visitors thought they had drawn level on 38 minutes when Roberts headed home, but referee John Hunting ruled that Healey had been fouled. It was a soft decision.

But things were about to get a lot worse for Roberts 11 minutes into the second half when a shocking lapse of concentration gifted City a 2-0 advantage. A free kick was played from deep inside City's half in the general direction of livewire Evans. Roberts intercepted well initially but then instead of thumping the ball clear, he inexplicably turned and played a poor backwards pass to Cegielski. Stand-in front man Sayer nipped in and easily chipped into the corner past Lloyd for his second goal in as many cup ties.

That looked like it was game over and the blue and white scarves were swung over the heads of City fans behind the Bob Bank netting. But 2-0 is a dangerous score as the old adage goes and four minutes later the Robins were back in it when Whittle expertly hooked an overhead volley past Healey from 15 yards from Shinton's cross.

That set up a frantic last hour. City had two confident penalty appeals turned down and Sutton and Grapes were both yellow-carded after a coming together. Both keepers were called into action, most notably Lloyd when he made two fine saves from the heads of Dwyer and Evans described simply as "out-of-this-world" by the *Echo*.

When Griffiths – who had once again defied his age with an energetic performance – hit a crafty 20-yard free kick against the inside of the post with two minutes to go, it looked like City had held out.

But then, with seconds of normal time remaining, the visiting fans were bouncing after Ashcroft somehow found just enough space to force home a near-post header from Shinton's corner. By the *Echo*'s reckoning there were 34 seconds of the match left.

Wrexham celebrated like they had won the Cup rather than forced a fourth round replay, but there was to be one last twist to the unofficial Welsh Cup Final. The visiting players were still slapping each other's backs when Evans battled for the ball in the middle of the park and eventually scrambled it out wide to Buchanan, who played a smart first-time ball down the line for Grapes.

The 23-year-old, a £7,000 signing from Norwich, had produced a number of encouraging performances since his promotion to the first team at the end of December, and it was his flick-on that created the winner against Spurs. This time Grapes jinked and twisted past Whittle and Roberts before finding Buchanan, who had continued his run into the area. The cool side-footed finish from ten yards brought huge cheers as Buchanan ran towards the fans. Buchanan told the *Western Mail* afterwards that he was in two minds whether to attempt a trademark thumper but instead went for placement.

Buchanan, in fact, almost didn't play at all. Andrews revealed that he had taken a big gamble in naming the Dingwall-born ace in the starting line-up after his thigh inflamed "like a balloon".

There were contrasting emotions from the managers after the game. Neal, a quiet but straight-talking man, told the *Echo*, "I thought justice had been done when we drew level. But then we went overboard. We were still congratulating each other when Cardiff scored the winner. We forgot that games are not over until the final whistle."

Andrews, meanwhile, was perhaps getting over-excited when he exclaimed in the *Western Mail*, "We are now on the football map and are in the position to get the pick of the best schoolboy talent in the area. But this is only the start. Within the next five years we will have a great club, and I mean great."

City's reward was a fifth round tie against Everton, which attracted a crowd of 35,582. Evans put City ahead early on but the First Division outfit fought back to win 2-1 and end pipe-dreams of a Wembley appearance.

Wrexham, meanwhile, suffered a poor end to the season and missed out on promotion, finishing fifth. They did, however, romp to the title the following season under Griffiths with what Bill Shankly called "the best Third Division team" he had seen.

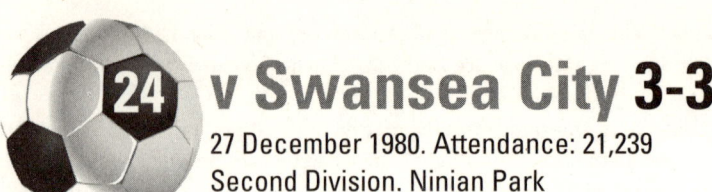

24 v Swansea City 3-3

27 December 1980. Attendance: 21,239
Second Division. Ninian Park

CARDIFF CITY:	SWANSEA CITY:
Ron Healey	David Stewart
Linden Jones	Brian Attley
John Lewis	Dzemal Hadziabdic
Wayne Hughes	John Mahoney
Paul Maddy	Nigel Stevenson
Phil Dwyer (Paul Giles 46)	Leighton Phillips
Ray Bishop	Alan Curtis
Peter Kitchen	Robbie James
Gary Stevens	Leighton James
Billy Ronson	Jeremy Charles
John Buchanan	Neil Robinson
	Sub not used: Dave Rushbury

Referee: Jeff Bray (Hinckley)

A FLASH OF genius can define a footballer. Midfielder John Buchanan is well remembered for spectacular goals during 231 appearances for Cardiff, but his 35-yard last-gasp thunderbolt against Swansea City in 1980 was surely his finest.

Classy Swansea were second in the old Second Division for this Christmas cracker at Ninian Park. They had captured the nation's hearts by climbing the divisions at break-neck pace. And the Jacks, managed by former City hero John Toshack, were deservedly 3-1 ahead with just four minutes remaining.

Peter Kitchen gave City some hope by pulling a goal back before just 60 seconds later Buchanan produced one of the most sensational strikes in Ninian history.

Wayne Hughes nudged the free kick an inch to the side and the slightly-built Buchanan lashed the ball with incredible ferocity into the top corner to rescue a point for the struggling Bluebirds. The distance was so great that Swansea keeper David Stewart had more than a second to react from the time Buchanan made contact, but the power and accuracy were just too much for him.

Toshack admitted that he had hoped the 29-year-old would shoot as he thought a goal was impossible. "I have never seen a goal like it," he told the *Western Mail*. "I was hoping Buchanan would shoot because you cannot score from that range. I couldn't believe it when he did."

Buchanan, originally from the small Scottish town of Dingwall, put together a fine portfolio of goals from set-pieces during his seven years with City, but this is the one savoured by supporters fortunate enough to have witnessed a special moment.

Speaking to the *South Wales Echo* 25 years on, Buchanan said, "I was poised to hit the ball from about 35 yards and I heard Toshack say 'let him shoot'. And I did, and fortunately I caught the ball right and it just flew into the corner of the net. Ninian Park just erupted. It was just one of those shots that came right – I nearly climbed the fence!" Most players wouldn't have even started the match. Buchanan, who was transfer-listed at

Walter Bartley Wilson, a key mover in the formation of Cardiff City Football Club.

City's all-time greatest manager? Stewart was in charge at City for 22 years between 1911 and 1933, winning the FA Cup and taking the club into the top flight.

The Cardiff City heroes of 1920/21. Fred Stewart's men won promotion to the First Division.

(Far left) Forward Fred Pagnam, part of City's 1920/21 promotion-winning team.

(Left) Irish goalkeeper Tom Farquharson made more than 400 appearances for the Bluebirds between 1922 and 1935. He became known as the Penalty King for his many fine saves from spot kicks.

Cardiff players being introduced to the Duke of York (later King George VI), at the Sheffield United v Cardiff City FA Cup Final, Wembley, 25 April 1925.

The 1924/25 Bluebirds who came so close to glory but were beaten in the FA Cup Final by Sheffield United.

Billy Hardy drinks champagne out of the FA Cup after City's heroics. Holding the cup, cigarette in hand, is Fred Keenor, who now boasts a statue outside the Cardiff City Stadium.

Fred Keenor, Cardiff captain, shaking hands with Charles Buchan, Arsenal captain.

Hughie Ferguson gets the ball past Dan Lewis to score the goal which took the FA Cup out of England for the first – and possibly last – time.

The players take the cup back to the dressing room.

Born and bred: Colin Baker (left) was proud to pull on the Cardiff shirt as a local lad. Baker played for City between 1953 and 1966, making almost 300 appearances. (Huw Evans Picture Agency)

Defender Danny Malloy was a real fans' favourite and made more than 200 appearances for Cardiff between 1955 and 1961.

Cardiff City v Real Madrid. European Cup Winners' Cup quarter-final, first leg. One of the most famous moments in Cardiff City history – Brian Clark leaps high to power a header past Real keeper Jose Luis Borja. Clark now has a road named after him near the Cardiff City Stadium. (Huw Evans Picture Agency)

January 29th 1994. Cardiff City v Manchester City. FA Cup fourth round. Cardiff City's Nathan Blake takes on Terry Phelan. Blake secured legend status with the club by cracking home the winner. (Huw Evans Picture Agency)

May 1st 1999. Cardiff City v Scunthorpe United. Division Three. City's Kevin Nugent holds off Richard Logan. The Bluebirds earned the point they needed to secure promotion. (Huw Evans Picture Agency)

January 6th 2002. Cardiff City v Leeds United. FA Cup third round. Leeds star Jonathan Woodgate gets to grips with Danny Gabbidon with keeper Nigel Martyn in close attendance. Scott Young went on to score a famous goal as the Bluebirds dumped the Premiership team out of the competition. (Huw Evans Picture Agency)

May 25th 2003. Cardiff City v QPR. Division Two Play-Off Final, Millennium Stadium. City's Andy Campbell fires home the winning goal in the 114th minute. (Huw Evans Picture Agency)

March 9th 2008. Cardiff City v Middlesbrough. FA Cup quarter final - Defender Roger Johnson wins the ball from Middlesbrough's Afonso Alves. Johnson scored one of City's two goals on a memorable afternoon up north. (Huw Evans Picture Agency)

May 17th 2008. Cardiff City v Portsmouth. FA Cup Final. Portsmouth's Kanu gets past Cardiff keeper Peter Enckelman but fails to find the back of the net. But the Nigerian did break City hearts by scoring the winner for Pompey, ending City's dreams of replicating the 1927 heroes. (Huw Evans Picture Agency)

April 3rd 2010. Cardiff City v Swansea City. The Championship. Swansea's Leon Britton and Cardiff's Peter Whittingham compete. Michael Chopra hit a last gasp winner for the Bluebirds. (Huw Evans Picture Agency)

February 26th 2012. Cardiff City v Liverpool. Carling Cup Final, Wembley. Joe Mason slides the ball past Pepe Reina to give the Bluebirds an astonishing lead against the Premiership giants. Liverpool went on to win the game on penalties. (Huw Evans Picture Agency)

April 16th 2013. Cardiff City v Charlton Athletic. Hero Kevin McNaughton is held aloft by the crowd as the pitch is invaded following City's 0-0 draw with Charlton. The point saw City back in the top flight for the first time in 51 years. (Huw Evans Picture Agency)

What a sight! Every blade of grass is covered by supporters after City secured promotion to the Premier League with a 0-0 draw against Charlton. (Jon Candy)

The players enjoy their moment after earning promotion to the top flight. Aron Gunnarsson is seen grinning into the camera, flanked by Craig Noone, Kevin McNaughton, Andrew Taylor and Fraizer Campbell. (Jon Candy)

Craig Noone holds the Championship trophy aloft on City's triumphant bus tour through Cardiff. Also seen are Craig Conway and Craig Bellamy. (Jon Candy)

Thousands of fans at Roald Dahl Plass at Cardiff Bay during the incredible open top bus tour after City's promotion to the Premier League. (Jon Candy) his own request the previous month, needed seven stitches to his dynamite right foot after sustaining a nasty cut in a bruising Boxing Day clash at Bristol City just 24 hours earlier.

His bravery earned the praise of City boss Richie Morgan, who told the *South Wales Echo*, "There's no disputing John's courage. He had a nasty cut in his ankle and a lot of players wouldn't have played but he just went out and got on with the game."

Two games in such a short period would be tough for anyone, but it posed a particular challenge for City after 20 days out of action following two postponements. That spell did City's league position no favours, slumping to 18th in the table before the Swansea game.

Swansea, meanwhile, had spent more than £1m in assembling a squad littered with international talent. They had climbed from the old Fourth Division with two promotions in three years and were now behind only West Ham in the second tier.

For long spells the match seemed to be going to form – but the South Wales derby has a habit of throwing up the unpredictable. Indeed, both clashes in the previous season were decided in the closing minutes.

The biggest crowd in over four years, 21,239, shook off the excesses of Christmas to pack into Ninian Park for the highly-anticipated clash. Tosh had his men fired up. Swansea legend Alan Curtis was beginning his second spell at the club after a disappointing season with Leeds.

In the excellent book *Derby Days* by Neil Palmer, Curtis recalled, "Tosh said to us in the dressing room before the game, 'We need to win this match and Cardiff are in our way en route to promotion. They're taking the bread from our mouths and we need to beat them'. It really fired us up."

Swansea, wearing red and black, started well with the cultured play they had become known for. But despite their possession, it was City who took the lead on 13 minutes – and from an unlikely source. Billy Ronson's cross was headed out of the box by the Swansea defence. Buchanan picked it up on the left and delivered a delicious 40-yard cross for Gary Stevens to stretch and volley into the corner from just outside the six yard box. It was the number nine's first goal in 21 games.

The visitors pushed forward for an equaliser but found Ron Healey, an understudy of England international Joe Corrigan at Manchester City, in good form.

City looked to have done enough for an important half-time lead – but a rare moment of madness from Mr Cardiff City, Phil Dwyer, saw the Jacks level on 40 minutes. The defender played an atrocious square pass which caused the initial problem and then John Lewis failed to make amends when he lost a tackle he was favourite to win. Neil Robinson, a £70,000 signing from Everton, broke clear and confidently smashed into the bottom corner from the edge of the area. Thousands of Jacks in the Grange End celebrated.

And things got worse for the Bluebirds on 43 minutes when Swansea went ahead through Curtis. Healey made a complete mess of a long-range shot by Robbie James, managing only to palm it a yard to his right. Leighton James nipped in ahead of the panicking City keeper and knocked it across to Curtis for a simple finish, despite Pontin's best efforts. "It was only a tap in but it was great to score, especially as I thought it was no more than we deserved," Curtis told *Derby Days*.

Dwyer, City's all-time record appearance maker, did not come out for the second half. The official line was a recurrence of a thigh injury, but in his autobiography Dwyer suggests it was more of a tactical move. Morgan reorganised with Hughes switching to partner Pontin at the back and Ray Bishop dropping deeper and substitute Paul Giles playing wide on the right. There was much talk before the match about the possibility of

City's Giles coming up against his older brother David, who was plying his trade at the Vetch Field at the time. But a South Wales derby first never materialised as David failed to recover from injury.

Though Swansea always looked the classier outfit, the Bluebirds didn't look out of the contest. Buchanan squeezed through three red shirts before letting off a decent shot. Stewart could only push the effort to one side and Kitchen looked destined to level the scores from close-range but Stewart managed to scamper across and save the follow-up.

But City's challenge did appear over when Curtis dinked over a neat cross and Leighton James, the man Cardiff fans now love to hate, looped a clever 73rd minute header over Healey and into the corner. The Welsh international had had a subdued game by his standards but had still played a big part in two of Swansea's goals. He told *Derby Days* years later, "It was great to score especially as I did not get many with my head and I remember running to the fans and thinking, 'this is game over now'."

But City, despite their lowly position, were unbeaten in their last six league games and refused to give in. Four minutes from time a bad back-pass by Nigel Stevenson sent Kitchen through and the forward, a £100,000 summer signing from Fulham, calmly chipped home with Stewart racing off his line. It was the 28-year-old's 14th goal in 24 games.

According to the *South Wales Echo*, hundreds, possibly thousands, of City fans had given up the ghost and had already taken to Sloper Road. They would be kicking themselves a minute later when they heard the roar from the home supporters following Buchanan's goal of a lifetime. Leighton James described the noise as "unbelievable".

Both teams had chances to bag the most dramatic of winners in the dying embers of the game. Bishop and Buchanan fired shots off target. Bishop shot tamely when Kitchen was better placed and in the last minute Healey made an important save from Robbie James.

But even without a winning goal, this dramatic derby day will always be remembered as one of the best between the fierce rivals. Joe Lovejoy, one of the best journalists to ever cover City games, wrote in the *Echo*, "It should not be forgotten that the match was full of good things – even before those dramatic last few moments. For the purist there may have been too many unforced errors, but in every other respect it was a classic, brimful of excitement, entertainment and, best of all, goals."

Dwyer recalls that the atmosphere in the dressing room was "buzzing" after the game. "Ritchie told us we could build our season on a comeback like that," he said in his book. The atmosphere in the visitors' dressing room was at the other end of the spectrum. According to Swans defender Stevenson, furious Tosh launched a cup of tea against the floor as the players sat with their heads bowed.

But City could not build on the comeback. It was a fourth consecutive draw in the league and that run would stretch to six before four successive defeats saw City lingering ominously one point above the relegation zone. Tensions among the squad became fraught and things came to a head when Lewis and Bishop came to blows in a nightclub.

A goalless draw at home to West Ham on the final day of the season saved City from relegation on goal difference, but it had been a mediocre season at best emphasised by average home gates of just 6,700.

Swansea, meanwhile, earned a third promotion in four seasons to take their place among England's elite.

v Leyton Orient 2-0

7 May 1983. Attendance: 11,758
Third Division. Ninian Park

CARDIFF CITY:	LEYTON ORIENT:
Andy Dibble	Mervyn Day
Linden Jones	Bill Roffey
Jimmy Mullen	David Peach
David Tong	Colin Foster
Phil Dwyer	Nigel Gray
Gary Bennett	Barry Silkman
David Bennett	Peter Smith (Kevin Godfrey)
Roger Gibbins	John Cornwell
Bob Hatton	Keith Houchen
Jeff Hemmerman	Peter Kitchen
John Lewis	Mark McNeil
Sub not used: Paul Bodin	
Referee: Ron Bridges (Deeside)	

SOME 356 days earlier Cardiff City had suffered the indignity of relegation after six years in the old Second Division. Now Len Ashurst's exciting team cobbled together from free transfers had bounced back to the second tier at the first time of asking.

Ashurst replaced Graham Williams towards the end of the previous season for the first of two stints in the Ninian Park hot-seat but could not save a poor side from relegation. With the club £1.5m in the red and harbouring an overdraft of almost £500,000, Ashurst, who led Newport County to the Third Division in 1979/80, knew that he would have to wheel and deal to turn City's fortunes around.

And he did so brilliantly. A number of players moved on, including Gary Stevens to Shrewsbury Town for £20,000 and Steve Grapes, who went to Torquay. That gave Ashurst the room to raid the free transfer market. The only fee paid was a modest £10,000 for skipper Jimmy Mullen, who had impressed on loan at the end of the previous season.

In came Jeff Hemmerman from Portsmouth, who would turn out to be an inspired signing, midfielder David Tong from Shrewsbury, Roger Gibbins from Cambridge United and full-back Paul Bodin from Newport.

And the Bluebirds hit the ground running, five wins from their first seven league games taking them to third position. City briefly topped the pile during February before a bad patch saw them slip to fourth – but a late surge had seen them move to within touching distance of promotion.

A home win against struggling Leyton Orient – who came down with City in 1981/82 – would finish the job. And City would also go up, regardless of their own result, if Newport failed to beat Huddersfield at Leeds Road.

Before the game Ashurst pleaded with the fans to put their apathy of recent years behind them and back the club. Ashurst said: "I'm asking the crowd, just this once, not to have a go at us if we're not playing well." A crowd of about 16,000 was anticipated but just 11,758 materialised.

On paper, beating Orient looked a straightforward task. City had not lost at home in the league since the opening day of the season. But Ashurst recalled his team's dismal 4-0 defeat at Orient at the start of the season to warn against any complacency. "Orient are a hard side who are fighting like mad to stay up," he told the *South Wales Echo*. "Games against that sort of opposition are always dangerous and anyway, I don't think they are as bad as their league position suggests."

There was a big boost for City as leader Mullen shook off a calf strain to line up in defence. The 30-year-old had been a huge player for City and was out to complete an impressive treble by captaining his third club to promotion from the Third Division after recent successes at Sheffield Wednesday and Rotherham.

City made hard work of their 2-0 win over a stubborn Orient – but what promotion day would be complete without a few jitters?

One man out to spoil the party was Peter Kitchen. The striker, who scored 22 goals for City in 72 appearances, was barracked by the Bob Bank with cries of "Cardiff reject". He had made it clear before the game that he was still aggrieved about being benched against Luton on the final day of the last season.

And Kitchen felt he should have had a penalty in the opening minutes after a strong tackle by Phil Dwyer. Referee Ron Bridges saw nothing in it – but Kitchen's bloody mouth suggested otherwise.

The Bluebirds' task was made easier when Orient full-back David Peach was foolishly sent off midway through the first half for a second yellow card. The 32-year-old, an FA Cup winner with Southampton in 1976, was booked for deliberate handball after 19 minutes and then just four minutes later hacked down Linden Jones.

City spurned a great chance to go ahead minutes later after a series of mis-kicks and bobbles. Bob Hatton teed up John Lewis but his cross was flat. It should have been easily dealt with by the O's defence but instead the visitors' centre-back succeeded only in fluffing it into the path of Hatton, who side-footed wide of the target from 12 yards. The moustached forward, who managed nine goals in his only season for City, claimed a corner to try and spare his blushes.

The important opening goal came two minutes into first half injury time – and in controversial circumstances. It started with an Orient corner in front of the Grange End. An in-swinger caused all sorts of problems and eventually Peter Smith's goal-bound header was cleared off the line by Gibbins, City's only ever-present player that season. The Orient players claimed that it had hit him on the arm – Gibbins later confirmed that they were right – but while they complained in vain, City broke.

Dave Bennett did well to win the ball and found Tong in the centre. Tong instinctively slid a killer ball forward to Hemmerman who, despite the appeals, was clearly a yard onside. Hemmerman knocked it across the box for Hatton, but he was closed out by a desperate defender and the chance seemed gone.

Not so, though, as Dave Bennett cut the ball back for Lewis to sweep home his third goal in four games into the bottom corner. John Cornwell and Keith Houchen were both booked for their over the top protests while Orient boss Ken Knighton had to be restrained after making his feelings crystal clear to both the referee and the linesman.

"Going up, going up", chanted the home supporters, and the half-time whistle blew seconds later.

The game could have been put beyond doubt early in the second half when Gary Bennett collected the ball from the excellent Mullen not far outside his own area, opened his stride and moved at pace to the halfway line. The Orient defence parted like the Red Sea and Bennett knocked a perfect ball through for Tong. He had Hatton waiting in the middle but just couldn't find him with his dinked cross.

Then it was the brilliance of the older Bennett brother Dave which nearly eased any remaining nerves around Ninian. The winger skipped past one man before nutmegging another and suddenly he was through. Dave Bennett picked out Hemmerman just eight yards out but he lacked his usual composure and side-footed his shot wide of the post.

Orient fought hard despite their numerical disadvantage and there was one heart-in-mouth moment for fans of a Bluebirds persuasion when Mark McNeil crossed in and Andy Dibble's palm out fell to Houchen. He looked destined to score but Gary Bennett came charging out bravely to take the sting off the effort and Dibble, on the eve of his 18th birthday, was able to collect.

The decisive second goal came with 15 minutes remaining – and it was another lightning quick break to turn defence into attack. A poor Orient free kick was picked up by Mullen, who sent Hemmerman racing down the left at lightning pace. With the O's defence in disarray, the Yorkshireman found Dave Bennett. He still had a lot to do but made it look easy, cutting inside before smashing left footed into the bottom corner, his 13th goal of a great season.

Dave Bennett jogged over to claim the praise of the adoring Bob Bank while most of the players congratulated top scorer Hemmerman for his unselfishness.

And now there was no doubt that City were on their way back to the Second Division at the first attempt – and on the same day that Swansea's relegation from the top tier was confirmed. Cardiff were the number one team in Wales once more.

Orient's Colin Foster sent a diving header over the bar from McNeil's cross with the last move of the game before the final whistle blew and thousands ran on to the pitch.

Ashurst, watching from the stands in a fetching blue tracksuit and brown shades, applauded the team which he had assembled on a shoestring along with his assistant Jimmy Goodfellow. "Our next target must be Division One," he said bullishly.

As fans celebrated on the hallowed turf, the City heroes reaped the rewards of nine months of labour – with four bottles of cheap champagne to share between them! "It was hardly a mouthful," said Lewis in John Crooks's book, *The Bluebirds*.

The party was extra special for City stalwart Dwyer, who at the end of the last season had been released after ten years at the club. In a remarkable turn of events, however, while on trial at Torquay United, Ashurst got wind that 'Joe' was back to his best and offered him a new contract at Ninian Park.

In his autobiography, Dwyer said, "Precisely a year earlier I had been told that my career was over and that never again would I play for my beloved team. Never in my wildest dreams did I think that I would play an integral part in a promotion-winning Cardiff City team."

Hopes of clinching the championship were ended by Portsmouth's win against Walsall three days later in their game in hand, but second place would do just nicely.

The Monday papers made for all-too-familiar reading after a Cardiff promotion. In among the photos of beaming teenagers with scarves aloft was the warning that the club could not continue to survive on meagre crowds. The average for the season had been just 7,036. Chairman Bob Grogan told the *Western Mail*, "There isn't much of a future at all for Cardiff City unless we get more people through the turnstiles. We are living on a knife-edge. If the bank insisted we reduce our overdraft by, say, £200,000 we would be out of business. The club is in a very, very precarious position." Cheery stuff indeed.

No surprise, then, that Ashurst had no money to spend to build a team for the challenge ahead. In fact the squad got weaker with Hatton and crocked Hemmerman retiring and Dave Bennett being sold to Coventry City for £120,000.

But City were at least mixing with the big boys once again – though the average attendance rose by a measly 30!

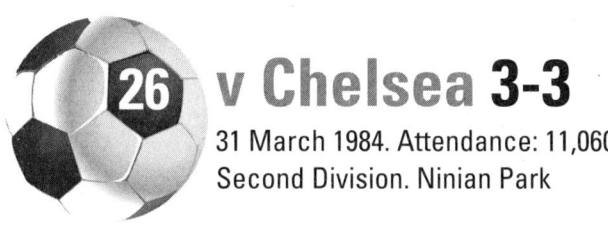

26 v Chelsea 3-3

31 March 1984. Attendance: 11,060
Second Division. Ninian Park

CARDIFF CITY:
Andrew Dibble
Karl Elsey
David Grant
Phil Dwyer
Colin Smith
David Tong
Gordon Owen
Roger Gibbins
Nigel Vaughan
Jeff Hemmerman (Martin Goldsmith)
Trevor Lee

Referee: R.F. Nixon (West Kirby)

CHELSEA:
Eddie Niedzwiecki
Colin Lee
Joey Jones
Colin Pates
Dale Jasper
Tony McAndrew (John Bumstead)
Pat Nevin
Nigel Spackman
Kerry Dixon
David Speedie
Mickey Thomas

CARDIFF CITY have made spectacular collapses an art form. Perhaps it all started when the Bluebirds missed out on the First Division title by a goal average difference of 0.024 in 1924 despite going into the final game of the season as firm favourites. In more recent years City fans stood open-mouthed as they watched their team throw away a four-goal lead to draw 4-4 at Peterborough.

But maybe the most extravagant crumple came in 1984 when John Neal's table-topping Chelsea came to Ninian Park. Mid-table City had stormed into a 3-0 lead and, despite a few scares along the way, they looked home and dry with just six minutes to go. Three goals by the visitors in just 360 seconds had the home fans shaking their heads in disbelief once again.

This is a game which is often reminisced by City fans – and not just because of the dramatic swing in the scoreline.

The 1980s had been a bad time for football attendances with crowds down across the board. In City's last game just 3,870 had turned out at Ninian for a second tier game against Shrewsbury. But against the grain Chelsea's away support had exploded in 1983/84 – and they came in their thousands to South Wales. The overall attendance was 11,060 and best estimates are that about half had come from London. They flooded the Grandstand while others gained entrance to the Family and Grange End Enclosures and climbed over the walls to join their fellow Blues fans. City season ticket holders were consequently forced to sit elsewhere, much to their annoyance.

In an apology printed in the programme a fortnight later, managing director Ron Jones said, "I admit, frankly, that we under-estimated the ingenuity, ferocity and sheer violence of these so-called supporters, but, in our defence, we have never experienced scenes like this before."

Football violence was also rife in the mid 1980s and this proved to be an ugly afternoon with reports of brick throwing and train station ambushes.

Jones added, "The Chelsea nightmare heralds a new phase of stadium security – and the extent to which we must go to protect innocent supporters. We are determined that they can come here to enjoy their football in safety. The only other trouble at Ninian Park this season came from Portsmouth supporters … and today Chelsea are at Fratton Park. I'm glad I'm not organising security for that match!"

The stage was set for a feisty afternoon – and the football didn't disappoint.

It had been a turbulent season for City. A lot of money had been spent on the Cardiff City Blue Dragons rugby league side but it was now attracting crowds of just 600 at Ninian. The failed project meant City boss Len Ashurst had little cash to play with. He also lost winger Dave Bennett to Coventry for £120,000, Paul Maddy departed and forward Bob Hatton retired. In another shock, Bob Grogan, the man who had saved City from bankruptcy, stepped down as chairman and in early September died from cancer.

Results were mixed with decent wins against the likes of Manchester City and Swansea City offset by too many poor performances. On 4 March Ashurst resigned as manager to take up the top job at First Division Sunderland. Assistant Jimmy Goodfellow was appointed caretaker manager until the end of the season with Jimmy Mullen named his right hand man. The two Jimmys managed wins against Cambridge United and Shrewsbury Town in their first two games, both 2-0, and were unlucky to lose 2-1 at Manchester City. Chelsea, though, posed a sterner test.

It had already been a record-breaking season for Chelsea who had won more points (65) than in any other campaign. That had a lot to do with the three-points-for-a-win rule brought in two seasons earlier, of course, but this was a strong and exciting Chelsea side.

Three former Wrexham players were at the heart of the Chelsea surge: young goalkeeper Eddie Niedzwiecki, defender Joey Jones and attacker Mickey Thomas. And Neal, who had himself enjoyed 11 successful seasons at Wrexham, proved himself to be a shrewd judge of talent by bringing in Nigel Spackman, David Speedie, Kerry Dixon and Pat Nevin for a combined total of just £390,000.

The Blues were bang on course to win the Second Division championship at last after five second-place finishes in the last 77 years. Sheffield Wednesday were keeping pace and were level on points while Newcastle, too, were just two points shy.

It looked a tough ask for City and Chelsea were on the front foot from the off when Speedie found himself one-on-one with Andy Dibble but shot wide after five minutes.

And that miss proved costly. In the 18th minute Trevor Lee picked up a Gordon Owen flick-on and dodged past two Chelsea defenders before cutting a sublime left foot pass right through the heart of the visitors' defence. Roger Gibbins slid in and superbly finished in the corner past Bangor-born Niedzwiecki. It was the fifth goal of the season for Gibbins, who signed for City on a free transfer in 1982 and was ever-present in back-to-back seasons, playing in 91 consecutive league games. In the eyes of many, it was City's goal of the season.

City were looking lively and came close to a second minutes later. As the City fans taunted their visitors with chants of "one-nil, one-nil, one-nil", Karl Elsey played a looping ball forward which bounced right in front of a Chelsea defender and was won strongly in the air by Trevor Lee. Hemmerman put a tempting low cross into the danger area but Chelsea hacked clear.

Unusually Dixon and Speedie were then not quite on the same wavelength and the ball ran harmlessly through to Dibble. The visitors looked to be forcing their way back into the game but four minutes later City were in dreamland with a second goal.

Jeff Hemmerman flicked on a long ball which caused havoc in the Chelsea area. Colin Lee tried to dribble his way to safety but lost out to Hemmerman and foolishly lunged in on the far edge of the area. Referee Nixon had no hesitation in pointing to the spot, despite protests from half the Chelsea team. Niedzwiecki guessed the right way but Owen's shot low into the bottom left hand corner had enough power. It was the fan-favourite's 16th goal of the campaign after signing on a free from Sheffield Wednesday at the start of the season. The moustached winger saluted the Bob Bank.

Soon after an Owen cross was far too deep but was picked up on the opposite side of the pitch by David Grant. His flat cross came out to Trevor Lee, who was clipped on the heels by a Chelsea man. In typical 1980s fashion, the referee had waved off several more meaty tackles yet gifted City a free kick in a decent position for something far softer. Colin Smith wandered up from the back and made a late curled run into the area. It was simple but completely missed by Chelsea and the big man was just an inch away from getting on the end of Owen's quick set-piece.

Incredibly, a third goal was just around the corner for City on the counter-attack on 25 minutes. Swansea-born Elsey made a sterling run from deep inside his own half and a ball over the top breached the Chelsea back-line. He took one touch to take him to the edge of the area and sent a bobbling cross over with his second. Dale Jasper should have got it clear but only succeeded in poking it to Nigel Vaughan, who squeezed a shot in off the post from the edge of the six-yard box.

Vaughan, by his own admission, had not been playing at his potential and had been taking some stick from City fans, who are often quick to stick the boot in, but he was in the right place this time. The City fans could not believe what they were seeing. Chelsea, meanwhile, were slumped on the floor and looked a beaten team.

Tony McAndrew blazed a shot over before Wales ace Thomas looked like causing problems but was eventually stopped mid-flow by Owen.

Chelsea were vastly improved in the second half but 18-year-old Dibble, who had been brilliant in City's promotion season in 1982/83, was in fine form. Spackman, a £35,000 signing from Bournemouth, thought he had pulled one back when he lashed home in the 61st minute from a free kick but the referee disallowed it for a dubious offside.

Minutes later Dibble got a crucial fingertip to a low cross while at the other end Grant's ball in was too close to Niedzwiecki.

City then surrendered possession easily and Chelsea broke. Nevin played a long ball forward and Dixon fired a ball across the area which Dibble gathered at the second attempt. A scuffle in the area ensued with City players claiming Speedie had tried to reach the loose ball a little too rashly.

But it was not one-way traffic. After about 70 minutes Owen cut inside Colin Lee but over hit with Trevor Lee lurking at the back post.

Then came one of the worst capitulations in Cardiff City's history. Just six minutes were left on the clock when Dixon brought the ball down on the edge of the box, turned eloquently and volleyed into the bottom corner. There was barely a celebration from the striker, who would later go on to win eight caps for England. Speedie felt differently, though. He raced to get the ball and carried it back to halfway while his team-mates strolled.

"We showed great determination and great character in that team and once we got one back, we believed we could get more," remembered Mickey Thomas, speaking to the official Chelsea website before City's FA Cup game against Chelsea in 2010. "We knew we had a chance because the Chelsea fans had come down in their thousands to get behind the team. They followed us everywhere that season."

Chelsea felt they should have had a penalty immediately from kick-off for a fairly innocuous collision – and another less than a minute later when Dixon took a tumble.

City were rattled and Chelsea didn't have to wait long for their second. Colin Lee eventually bundled in from all of three yards after a series of mis-kicks among the City defence. The travelling fans celebrated as if they had bagged the winner.

Then in injury time and with the temperature rising inside Ninian, Spackman thumped the ball goalwards and it was blocked by the midriff of David Tong – but a penalty was awarded. There is no way he could have got out of the way. In the days that followed Tong was asked on countless occasions to reveal the bruising which proved that the fierce drive had not been stopped with the arms.

"In the circumstances, I was almost glad that the bruising stayed around for a week," joked Tong. "It wasn't at all funny at the time."

Normal penalty taker McAndrew had been substituted and Dixon clearly didn't fancy it after a succession of misses earlier in the season, so responsibility fell to Spackman. Dibble got a good hand to it but it nestled in the top corner regardless.

The only mercy was there was not another two minutes left as Chelsea would likely have gone on to win it.

Thomas added, "In the dressing room afterwards it was incredible. John Neal gave us plenty of credit for coming back from that. I was going back to North Wales by car and there were coaches and coaches of happy Chelsea fans. I passed a lot of them the way I was driving!"

Chelsea did go on to win the league on goal difference from Sheffield Wednesday. City, meanwhile, finished an incoherent season in 15th position.

27 v Scunthorpe 3-0

8 May 1993. Attendance: 7,407
Third Division. Glanford Park

CARDIFF CITY:	SCUNTHORPE:
Gavin Ward	Mark Samways
Robbie James	Joe Joyce
Damon Searle	Nicky Platnauer
Derek Brazil	Dean Martin
Jason Perry	Matthew Elliott
Paul Millar	Glenn Humphries (Jason Maxwell 47)
Paul Ramsey	Graham Alexander
Nicky Richardson	Jason White
Phil Stant	Ian Helliwell
Nathan Blake	Ian Thompstone
Cohen Griffith	David Hill
Subs not used: Chris Pike, Carl Dale	Sub not used: David Foy
Referee: John Key (Sheffield)	

THE POPE, a pantomime horse and dozens of middle-aged men in drag – they were all at Glanford Park to see City end a 46-year wait for a league title. The good people of Scunthorpe were in for a shock as more than 4,500 City fans – many enjoying the long tradition of wearing fancy dress to the last away game of the season – descended on their town. Afterwards striker Phil Stant said, "When we were coming to the ground all we could see was blue and white. It made your hair stand on the back of your neck."

The famous Ayatollah salute – the patting of one's head with both hands – was only three years old and City fans had really taken it to heart. Many took it a step further by wearing Arabic head-dress and fake beards to Scunny. The *South Wales Echo* likened the terraces to a "Middle Eastern bazaar".

Demand for tickets had been so high that City had been allocated both stands behind the goals, ousting the locals unceremoniously from their favourite Rod Mill Stand. In a crowd of just over 7,407, the Scunny fans were heavily outnumbered on their own patch. And when the final whistle blew after two goals from Cohen Griffith and one from Stant had given City a 3-0 win to clinch the Third Division title, the colourful masses were over the walls and on to the pitch to celebrate.

The players sprinted for the tunnel as burly Welshmen in floral dresses came at them from all directions – but for some there was no escape. Star striker Stant, who had smashed 15 goals in all competitions since his £100,000 December transfer from Mansfield, had been caught stranded at the end of the pitch. The tough City legend headed for the main stand in the hope of jumping down into the tunnel but was stripped of his shirt and shorts before he could make it, leaving him just in his underpants and socks.

In Stant's autobiography *Ooh Ah Stantona* the City legend said the incident raised the eyebrows of kitman Harry Parsons. 'H', who died in 2006 after a life devoted to the club in every position from coach to coach driver, told Stant to go back and retrieve his kit. "You ****ing go and get them," Stant replied – and the pair rolled about laughing.

Modern-day City supporters have been treated to big games and technically excellent players. Older supporters can remember the great European nights of the 1960s and 1970s. But many still refer to 1992/93 as their favourite season as a Bluebird.

It was the late, great Eddie May's second season at Ninian Park after narrowly missing out on the play-offs in 1991/92. There was suddenly a feel-good factor at the club and the crowds had returned with average home attendances up from a paltry 2,946 in 1990/91 to 8,560 in 1992/93. And there were some real characters in the side.

There was defender Jason Perry, nicknamed 'Psycho' by fans for his uncompromising style, Northern Ireland midfielder Paul Millar, flamboyant Nicky Richardson and goalscoring winger Griffith. Up front was 21-year-old Nathan Blake who was being tipped for greatness, and soldier-turned-goal ace Stant. Carl Dale, City's joint-third highest ever goalscorer, had found the net on 17 occasions in all competitions but missed the game in Scunthorpe due to a knee injury.

There were goals and excitement right through the team. The treble in this game meant May's Darling Buds finished the campaign as the league's highest scorers with 77 in a season when goals for counted instead of goal average. Between 24 October 1992 and 20 March 1993 City managed at least one goal in 23 consecutive games, which is still a club record at the time of print. Blake finished with 11 league goals, Griffith 10, Chris Pike 12 and Stant 11.

After a fairly mediocre start to the season, City turned on the style at the turn of the year, putting together a sensational run of 12 wins and a draw to climb into pole position. There followed a brief stutter, during which the Bluebirds slipped into second position, but promotion was assured with a 2-1 home win over Shrewsbury Town on May Day in front of more than 17,000 fans.

Now City needed to pull off one final win against the mid-table Iron to guarantee their first championship since 1947. Only Barnet could realistically pip City to the trophy with Wrexham still mathematically in the chase but needing to make up a three-goal deficit.

With the chance to become history-makers and the droves making the four-hour journey to North Lincolnshire (or Humberside as it was at the time), the City players could have been forgiven for feeling the pressure – but there was never any sign of that on a sublime day for the club. Indeed, *Echo* scribe Robert Phillips said, "Considering the occasion and pressure this was their best display of the campaign."

Scunthorpe, who included former City midfielder Nicky Platnauer, would have loved to have played the party poopers. Richard Money's United, who had lost three of their last four, started well enough as they forced three corners in the first five minutes. Just momentarily it seemed City might miss the experience of former Wales skipper Kevin Ratcliffe, who was out with a knee problem. Ratcliffe might have lost some of the electric pace which earned him stardom at Everton but his arrival at City in January 1993 had coincided with the Bluebirds' great run of form – and that was no fluke.

But the party was in full swing after just 11 minutes when Guyana-born Griffith put the champions-elect 1-0 ahead. Up-and-coming Welsh star Blake latched on to a Robbie James free kick and controlled with his head, knee and chest before charging into the six-yard box and finding the long-haired Richardson at the back post. His effort struck Iron's David Hill on the line but Griffith was on hand to scramble home and settle any nerves.

From that point on there was little doubt that the sparse trophy cabinet at Ninian Park was about to have a new addition. And the hordes of City fans were in ecstasy on

35 minutes when Stantona, back in the fray after missing the Shrewsbury game through suspension, made it 2-0.

Bargain buy Richardson picked up the ball midway inside the Scunny half and some shoddy defending saw the ball break to Stant. He forced his way to the edge of the area before slotting a left foot shot past Mark Samways. The striker fell to his knees in delight.

Iron had plenty of possession but rarely looked like breaching City's defensive wall. Graham Alexander, 21 years old, fired one shot over the bar while Gavin Ward made a decent stop from the same player.

But Scunny's best chance fell to Jason White just before half-time. A clever pass from Hill played him in and for once the City back-line was compromised. White saw Ward approaching and went for the lob but got it completely wrong, fluffing both wide and over. Cue ironic cheers from the City fans.

The job was nearly done; nine months of hard work and the top prize almost secure. May would likely have told his troops to keep it tight for the first quarter of the second half – but instead they removed any doubts by making it 3-0 inside two minutes.

Full-back Damon Searle, who was named in the PFA Third Division Team of the Year, charged down the left and crossed low for Stant. His diving header was tucked in neatly by the lurking Griffith. The *Echo* said, "Workaholics Stant and Griffith totally undermined the home defence."

By now there was a carnival atmosphere inside Glanford Park – and even the referee got involved. Sheffield's John Key, who let the game flow well, responded to banter from the home supporters with a wink and a blown kiss.

Scunthorpe immediately made a change by bringing on young striker Jason Maxwell for defender Glenn Humphries.

It was then just a question of playing out time for City as supporters waited impatiently for the celebrations to start.

Scunny had two chances to get on the score sheet. Ward made an excellent reflex save to stop Ian Thompstone's header and in the closing minutes Maxwell froze at the crucial moment and his poor shot was blocked by the legs of the City keeper. City fans swayed back and forth saving imaginary goals while chanting Ward's name.

Key closed the season with the final whistle and 22 players dashed for the tunnel faster than greyhounds released from the traps. It was Cardiff's 12th win on the road of an unforgettable season, a record bettered only in all four divisions by Newcastle United and equalled just by Port Vale.

With the pitch a sea of blue and white, grinning May eventually led his players back out of the changing rooms to lap up the praise. It was a fantastic moment for a special group of players, not least as a bonus of up to £40,000 per player based on appearances had been banked. But more importantly it was the first time any of the City players had won a championship medal, with the exception of Ratcliffe. In the end City had a three point cushion at the summit as Barnet were thumped 4-1 at Crewe while Wrexham beat Colchester 4-3.

No one had waited for this feeling longer than James. The 36-year-old had scored 99 goals in 394 league games for his home-town club Swansea City and had been an integral member of the team that took the First Division by storm in 1981/82. But, despite his questionable past, the defender had been accepted by City fans and had played in all 56 games this season in five different competitions, bar the first leg of the European Cup Winners' Cup against Admira Wacker.

Cardiff City's Greatest Games

Sipping champagne, player of the year James told the *Western Mail*, "I've waited 21 years for a winner's medal so it feels really good. That is why this season has been as satisfying and enjoyable – if not more so – as any in my career including the glory days with Swansea City."

James sadly died at the age of 40 while playing in a Welsh League game for Llanelli.

And there was plenty of excitement from the rest of the squad, too. "This is the best day of my life," Derek Brazil said. "This is the highlight of my career," said Griffith, whose painful memories of being part of the City side which suffered relegation in 1989/90 were beginning to fade.

But of course the plaudits really belonged to May, the Epping-born mastermind with an endearing grin. "I don't think anything could beat today, it's been unbelievable," he told the *Western Mail*. "The success is down to the players. I've asked them to play in different positions to solve injury problems and they've come through with flying colours. I just hope the club goes on from here."

Eight days later, against a familiar backdrop of financial worries with chairman Rick Wright threatening to pull his support, City completed a unique championship and Welsh Cup double by beating Rhyl 5-0 at Cardiff Arms Park in front of 16,443 spectators. Stant smashed a hat-trick and Griffith scored another two to make for a comfortable afternoon.

City were back in the third tier after three seasons journeying to the likes of Darlington, Halifax and Hereford – and the bonus of a ticket into Europe had been achieved as well. Cardiff City had a new hero. As the cry regularly echoed around the Bob Bank went, "What's his name? Eddie May!"

v **Middlesbrough** 2-1

19 January 1994. Attendance: 10,769
FA Cup Third Round Replay. Ayresome Park

CARDIFF CITY:
Mark Grew
Derek Brazil
Damon Searle
Mark Aizlewood
Jason Perry
Paul Millar
Garry Thompson
Nicky Richardson
Phil Stant (Cohen Griffith 14)
Nathan Blake
Tony Bird
Subs not used: Nathan Wigg, Phil Kite
Referee: David Elleray

MIDDLESBROUGH:
Steve Pears
Curtis Fleming
Richard Liburd (Derek Whyte)
Steve Vickers
Nicky Mohan
Graham Kavanagh
Robbie Mustoe
Jamie Pollock
Andy Peake
Craig Hignett
Paul Wilkinson
Subs not used: Andy Collett, Michael Barron

T HE MERE mention of the words Middlesbrough and FA Cup conjure up sweet memories of Peter Whittingham and Roger Johnson firing City into the semi-finals in 2008.

But wind the clock back 14 years and the North-East was the location again as Eddie May's Cardiff pulled off a Cup shock good enough to rival that wonderful day.

Second Division City had twice come from behind to draw 2-2 and force a replay against First Division Middlesbrough in the third round of the famous competition. The goalscorers at Ninian Park were Phil Stant and Garry Thompson in a rip-roaring contest in front of 13,750 fans.

City piled on the pressure in the final minutes but when golden boy Nathan Blake mis-kicked from two yards with only the keeper to beat, most thought the chance of making a rare foray into the fourth round had passed.

But May's Darling Buds shrugged off their poor league form to give fans a Cup giant-killing to celebrate.

May's popular team had struggled at the higher level since winning the Third Division title the season previous. Back-to-back wins had been few and far between and going into this Cup fixture on the south bank of the River Tees the Bluebirds were precariously positioned in 17th, just two points above the relegation zone.

As well as their league commitments, City were also competing in five cup competitions: the FA Cup, the Coca Cola Cup, the Autoglass Trophy, the European Cup Winners' Cup and the Welsh Cup. But despite the intensity of the schedule, the knock-out competitions had offered a welcome reprieve from the struggles of the bread and butter.

The FA Cup campaign had started with a whimper. The Bluebirds needed a replay to eventually see off non-league Enfield 1-0 at Ninian, Blake's goal sparing the blushes. It was the first time City had successfully navigated past the first round since 1989/90. But City then made light work of Second Division rivals Brentford, winning 3-1 at Griffin Park, and a Cup run of sorts was under way.

A 2-2 draw against Middlesbrough had lifted supporters who were just beginning to ask questions of the management – but a convincing defeat at Ayresome Park looked almost a formality. Keep the score down, bow out gracefully and concentrate on the league, surely. Boro, managed by future City boss Lennie Lawrence, had aspirations of an immediate return to the top flight after suffering relegation in their previous season and were big favourites to progress.

The odds might not have looked good for City, but with a plum tie against Premier League big boys Manchester City awaiting the winners, about 600 Bluebirds made the 285-mile trek up north. And what a treat they were in for.

Things appeared bleak for City, though, when star striker Stant tripped over Boro keeper Steve Pears and injured his knee with seven minutes played. In his autobiography *Ooh Ah Stantona,* Stant describes the pain as "unbearable" – but still the former SAS hero was reluctant to come off. Three minutes later the tough 31-year-old hobbled into the right position to put City ahead.

It was a typically quick City breakaway. Wild-haired Nicky Richardson slid a wonderful ball down the channel for ex-Manchester United man Derek Brazil, who dodged a rash Boro slide tackle and crossed a perfect ball for Stant. The forward was completely unmarked and managed to jump on his one good leg to head easily into the corner.

In his book, Benson & Hedges smoker Stant said, "The lads came running over to me to celebrate but all I could scream was '**** off, keep off me, keep off me.'" He lasted just another four minutes before being helped off the pitch to be replaced by Cohen Griffith. It would later transpire that Stant had scored while suffering from a partial tear in his medial ligament.

Chances continued to fall for City, who were wearing the classic blue *Echo* shirt with dark splashes. Blake curled a shot straight at the keeper and Brazil was wide from the edge of the area but at the other end there were heart-in-mouth moments aplenty as the Bluebirds defence backed up against the ropes.

In his programme notes Lawrence had called on his misfiring team to be more clinical in front of goal – in the league they had managed just 33 goals – but his words fell on deaf ears. Robbie Mustoe, 25 at the time, was woefully wide in the 15th minute before Mark Grew had to think fast to head clear a poor back-pass from Jason Perry. It was a rare moment of uncertainly from the skipper, who otherwise had a brilliant night.

City had a reputation as a tough, no-nonsense side and were upsetting the home team with a string of crunching tackles. Thompson, Perry and Damon Searle were all booked for what could generously be called 'wholehearted' tackles. Others might call them dirty fouls. Paul Millar could consider himself lucky to stay on the pitch after a bad tackle not long after picking up a yellow card from Premier League ref David Elleray for dissent.

Despite the pressure, though, sturdy City defending saw Boro limited to just a handful of serious chances and 600 Welsh voices cheered their team down the tunnel with a surprise one-goal advantage.

May would have warned his troops against a second half onslaught. It did come but Boro's finishing was woeful.

Three minutes in, the otherwise excellent Grew hit a weak clearance straight to Graham Kavanagh. Irish midfielder Kavanagh, who seven years later would go on to become a Cardiff legend, ran through unchallenged but Grew redeemed himself with a low save at full stretch.

Seconds later Craig Hignett had two horrendous moments he would rather forget. First the Scouser, who had a very respectable goalscoring record throughout his 19-year playing career, smashed his shot wide with an open goal begging. There was worse to come as Kavanagh's shot rebounded to Hignett off Grew's leg and Hignett could only hit the post from just a few yards. Shivering City fans began to believe this was their night.

Teenager Tony Bird could have made those hardy supporters feel a little bit more comfortable when he was set up by Griffith down the left on 74 minutes but the striker side-footed wide from 12 yards.

Grew's handling was faultless throughout. He made two decent saves in quick succession, first from a low shot from Hignett and then from the same player from a 25-yard free kick.

City looked to have weathered everything Boro could throw at them but then, just a minute later, Kavanagh struck his third goal of the season to make it 1-1. Kav, almost unrecognisable with jet black hair, flicked the ball up an inch and volleyed into the corner on the spin.

The momentum ought to have been with Middlesbrough but City maintained their composure in extra time and continued to threaten on the break. Boro thought they had stolen a winner, though, when Mark Aizlewood scrambled off the line after Grew had saved with one hand from Paul Wilkinson's header. Red arms shot up in the air claiming that it had crossed the line – replays showed they were probably right – but Elleray, after a quick look towards his linesman, was having none of it.

And just seconds later City rubbed salt into Boro's wounds by bagging the winner. Thompson's clever lofted ball was nodded on by Richardson and Blake was ready to pounce. There were tired legs all round but the highly-rated Welshman won the race against Steve Vickers and his stabbed shot squirmed through the body of Pears.

There were just five minutes remaining but still time for two red cards. Thompson got involved in an altercation with Boro's Jamie Pollock. The Boro midfielder, sporting a ridiculous 'bowl' haircut, looked to be the aggressor but both had been booked and it was no surprise when yellow became red. The argument continued as the pair headed down the tunnel. Thommo told the *South Wales Echo*, "He had been giving out a bit of stick to the lads. I was trying to get up off the floor and he put the head in."

But that was a mere footnote on a fantastic night for Cardiff City. A money-spinning last 32 clash against Manchester City was in the bag.

There was a sense that Middlesbrough had been a tad over-confident about getting the victory. They had, after all, looked the better side at Ninian Park 11 days earlier. Speaking to the *Echo* after the game, Blake revealed that Boro's attitude spurred the Bluebirds to success. "They were really full of themselves on the pitch," said the 21-year-old. "And when they scored so late our heads really dropped. But they were really starting to rub it in – and the more they did that, the more determined it made us to beat them."

For May, the result was particularly sweet. Eddie had worked under Lawrence as his assistant at Charlton Athletic – now the student had turned teacher. He told the *Echo*, "When the equaliser came I was concerned their heads might go down. But in fact we looked the stronger in extra time. I had told them we had to show heart and battle away. They did just that and I was very proud of them."

Lawrence, who only lasted another four months at Ayresome Park before being ousted from the hot-seat, said, "I cannot think of a game where the manner of defeat has been so devastating to the players, to me and to the club as well."

The next day the *Echo*, in its final few days as a broadsheet, carried a front page picture of half-naked City players celebrating in the changing rooms. Chairman Rick Wright, who had listened to the game while on holiday in Australia, was rubbing his hands with glee at the thought of a £50,000 gate receipt.

The following Saturday City played out a 0-0 bore draw against Barnet in front of 5,698 fans but everyone was waiting for the visit of Manchester City seven days later – a match which would prove to be even more exciting than this classic.

v Manchester City **1-0**

29 January 1994. Attendance: 20,486
FA Cup Fourth Round. Ninian Park

CARDIFF CITY:
Mark Grew
Derek Brazil
Lee Baddeley
Jason Perry
Damon Searle
Cohen Griffith
Paul Millar
Nicky Richardson
Mark Aizlewood
Garry Thompson
Nathan Blake

Referee: Michael Reed (Birmingham)

MANCHESTER CITY:
Tony Coton (Andy Dibble 70)
Richard Edghill
Alan Kernaghan
Keith Curle
Terry Phelan
David Rocastle
Garry Flitcroft
Kaare Ingebrigtsen (Mike Sheron 70)
Alfons Groenendijk
Michel Vonk
Carl Griffiths

THIS WAS a classic Cup giant-killing which earned Cardiff City – and some chap called Nathan Blake – national acclaim. It was Blakey's magnificent 63rd-minute goal after beating three defenders which earned the Bluebirds a place in the fifth round of the competition for first time in 17 years and assured City legend status for the bulky Welsh striker.

But all 11 City players should be remembered as heroes on one of the club's greatest FA Cup days, from goalkeeper Mark Grew, who saved an 80th-minute penalty, right through to striker Garry Thompson, who relished the occasion.

A capacity crowd of 20,486 packed into Ninian Park for the Second Division v Premier League clash with all home tickets snapped up within four hours. An estimated 250,000 more watched on the BBC. Eddie May's team had captured the imagination of the city's population the previous season by being crowned Third Division champions – but they were finding life in the Second Division rather more difficult. They were 18th and just three points above the drop zone.

But in a season competing on six fronts (the league, the League Cup, the Football League Trophy, the FA Cup, Welsh Cup and the European Cup Winners' Cup), City had saved their best performances for the FA Cup. They had needed extra-time to get past non-league Enfield in the first round but then breezed past Brentford (3-1) before memorably seeing off First Division Middlesbrough 2-1 in an Ayresome Park replay.

Hopes were high that City could add another scalp to the list against Brian Horton's under-fire Manchester City. Defeat at Liverpool the previous weekend had seen them drop into the Premier League's relegation zone for the first time since late August. Their season had been badly disrupted by a deluge of injuries and they had not won a league game since early December. In a sure sign that the football gods had turned against them, even when they did look like gaining maximum points in January against Ipswich the match was abandoned.

Even so, most pundits tipped Man City with the likes of Keith Curle, Terry Phelan and Tony Coton to have enough to at the very least force a replay against the Bluebirds.

And Cardiff could have been behind in the opening minutes. Derek Brazil misjudged the pace of the ball as he tried to let it run for a goal kick, allowing Michel Vonk to nip in. He hooked it back into the middle and Grew grasped the ball just a fraction of a second ahead of Carl Griffiths.

There was more pressure from the visitors to come. A free kick was whipped in from the right but the referee blew for a foul on Grew and then Jason 'Psycho' Perry made a crucial, last-ditch interception.

But Cardiff, backed by the vociferous home supporters, soon found their feet. With marksman Phil Stant ruled out with a knee ligament problem, Thompson was given the nod up front alongside 22-year-old Blake. And the pair combined soon after. Blake flicked on and Thompson forced his way between Curle and Lomas before curling his shot just wide from the edge of the area.

Manchester City were then awarded a soft free kick by referee Mike Reed after what appeared to be a fair tackle by Perry on Griffiths, much to the anger of the locals behind the Ninian cages. Alfons Groenendijk got his effort over the wall and towards the bottom left corner, but Grew flew across his line to make the save.

At the other end, some fantastic football nearly earned the Bluebirds the opening goal. Mark Aizlewood knocked it out wide for Damon Searle, who drove in-field and found an inch-perfect pass between Curle and Lomas for Paul Millar deep inside the area. He spun well but his low left-footed effort lacked the power to beat Coton, who was considered one of the best keepers in Britain at the time.

Cardiff were in inspired form and pushed forward with gusto. Coton had to make a decent catch after Searle had burst into the penalty area. It was a team growing in confidence by the minute that trotted off down the tunnel for half-time with the scores locked at 0-0.

Manchester City had a gilt-edged opportunity early in the second half thanks largely to a tremendous run by Curle, who was back in the mix after a month out through injury. The defender picked up a loose ball practically on the halfway line and steamed past Brazil like a juggernaut. He kept it in on the byline and crossed it in to the back post for Vonk, who beat Lee Baddeley in the air and knocked it down for unmarked Garry Flitcroft on the edge of the six-yard box. Grew stood motionless as the midfielder's volley cannoned off the foot of the post and to safety.

From that point, it was Cardiff who were the classier team. After about 50 minutes a Brazil throw-in went to wild-haired Nicky Richardson, who hooked into the box for Thompson. The former QPR man might have looked for a team-mate in a better position but instead tried an ambitious lob from an acute angle which Tony Coton did well just to fingertip over the bar.

Now the belief was growing among Cardiff fans young and old. And just past the hour Blake, the man whose fruit machine misdemeanour will never be forgotten, hit the jackpot with a moment of sheer brilliance. Blake, a free signing from Chelsea, controlled the thrown-in with his chest towards the edge of the area. With his back to goal, he looked as if he was harmlessly shielding the ball, waiting for a team-mate, but in the blink of an eye he had changed direction and powered past Curle and Phelan and into space. There was one more delightful touch past Flitcroft before Blake, the jewel in City's crown, curled a sublime left-footer into the top corner.

There is an iconic photograph of Coton in mid-air looking over his shoulder just as the ball is about the cross the line, the Bob Bank terrace ready to erupt.

The Manchester City fans standing on the Grange End thought their team had hit back within a minute. City were under pressure from a corner and only half-cleared to Alan Kernaghan. He curled one in and Curle managed to get a toe on it to beat Grew – but he hadn't beaten the offside flag. Cardiff heads were in hands and Curle was posturing in front of his supporters but the celebrations were brought to an abrupt end. It must have been close.

Soon after City went close to doubling their lead after one of the best moves of the match. Searle played a long ball forward to Blake, whose well-directed header found Thompson. He teed up Richardson but his thundering shot from the edge of the area was tipped over the crossbar by Coton.

But then, just as City fans were beginning to discuss who they fancied in round five, the visitors were awarded a dubious penalty with 11 minutes remaining. David Rocastle twisted his way into the area, leaving Baddeley on his backside in the process. He must have felt the faintest of touches to the back of his heel from Searle and fell to the ground. May's incredulous expression in the dug-out told its story.

Curle looked confident despite the piercing whistles from the home fans but 35-year-old Grew, who had been in out of the side all season, saved magnificently to his left-hand corner. The moustached hero was mobbed by relieved City players. It was Grew's second penalty save of the season and he was particularly pleased as it was his wayward kick that sent Rocastle going forward at the very start of the move.

"I was disappointed with my kick out which had originally put us in trouble anyway," he told the *South Wales Echo*. "So it was more important for me to save that penalty because it would have been all my fault. After all the hard work we had put in, to give it away like that would have been a crime."

Blake could have sealed the win in style minutes later as Manchester City committed more men forward. He picked the ball up in his own half and played inside for Thompson. He returned the ball to Blake, who skipped inside Phelan with a perfect first touch to move goalwards. A second touch took it past the sliding tackle of Curle but Blake pulled his shot wide of the post. The City striker lay prostrate on the ground for several seconds, contemplating how two goals against a Premier League side might have helped his on-going contract negotiations.

There was to be one last heart-in-mouth chance for the visitors in the dying seconds. Lomas played a good ball down the line for Flitcroft who pulled it back for Curle, but the defender's header was expertly saved by Grew at his feet. Anywhere else and Manchester City would have had the equaliser to spare their blushes.

Cardiff held out and May charged on to the pitch with his arms high in the air. Ecstatic supporters were over the fences and on to the pitch in their droves – despite repeated requests for them not to. The shell-shocked visiting players trudged off dejected, anticipating the media battering that awaited them in the morning.

There were nerve-racking moments for the City fans but in the end May's team fully deserved their famous victory. There may have been an element of luck in City's third round replay win against Middlesbrough but Cardiff had been the better side for long periods against a Manchester City side on the downward spiral.

Eddie May beamed in the *Wales on Sunday*, "To pull off a giant-killing is one thing – to do it in the style we did is even better. We thoroughly deserved the win.

"We had a long team meeting before the game but I deliberately didn't discuss Man City at any length. I had them watched against Liverpool the previous week so I was able to give my players a general view of how they play, but that was it.

"The most important thing was to get our own house in order so I just told my players to go out there, enjoy the game and remember the day."

A downbeat Horton could not deny that City were good value for their win. "I don't think anything else can go wrong," he told *The Times*. "The whole club is flat; you can see it, feel it. Cardiff fought harder than us and that's difficult for me to take. You can't do anything without fighting for it."

Holiday camp magnate Rick Wright, who had bought Cardiff two years earlier from Tony Clemo, used the rare interest of the national media to appeal for new backers. Despite a disappointing average home league attendance of just 6,731 that season before the Manchester City game, Wright was adamant that the club had the potential to attract regular crowds of at least 40,000.

With words strikingly similar to those used by Sam Hammam years later, he said, "We showed today that this club is ready for the Premier League – all we have to do is get there. We could build new stands at both the Canton End and the Grange End which would give us a 40,000 capacity rather than the 20,000 we were limited to today."

The win secured City a plum home tie against either First Division Luton Town or Premier League title-chasers Newcastle United. A sell-out crowd was guaranteed whichever way the replay went, but most fans, and Eddie May, were hoping, and expecting, for a shot against the Magpies. As it was, Luton edged past Kevin Keegan's side 2-0 and went on to beat City 2-1 in the next round. City were left with just the Welsh Cup and the league to compete for – but it had been an exciting FA Cup journey.

As for Blake, City fans hoped beyond hope that there was some way the club could keep hold of their star man. But inevitably, as had been the case with so many players before, the striker was sold less than a month later to Sheffield United for £300,000 having scored 40 goals in 164 outings for the Bluebirds. He went on to have a decent career, scoring regularly for Bolton, Blackburn, Wolves and Wales, though his latter years were dogged by injuries.

v Fulham 4-1

31 January 1997. Attendance: 6,459
Third Division. Craven Cottage

CARDIFF CITY:
Tony Elliott
Lee Jarman
Kevin Lloyd
Jeff Eckhardt
Jason Fowler
Scott Young
Craig Middleton (Ian Rodgerson 75)
Gareth Stoker
Steve White
Simon Haworth (Tony Philliskirk 87)
Paul Ware (Jimmy Rollo 87)

Referee: M. Fletcher (West Midlands)

FULHAM:
Tony Lange
Paul Parker (Martin Thomas 49)
Mickey Adams
Nick Cusack
Danny Cullip (Paul Brooker 53)
Mark Blake
Darren Freeman
Richard Carpenter (Rod McAree 61)
Mike Conroy
Simon Morgan
Rob Scott

BEFORE THE internet and saturation television coverage, football fans across the land sat glued to Teletext to discover the fortunes of their team. There was little more exciting than staring at a black screen when your team was 1-0 up away from home with a minute to go, desperately waiting for the little 'FT' to appear next to the scoreline.

By 1997 the Sky Sports revolution was in full swing, but with City languishing in the Third Division it was still considered a rare treat when the camera vans rolled up to bring the Bluebirds into thousands of homes across the country.

On the last day of January the media circus arrived in West London for Fulham v City at Craven Cottage, a match shown live on the new Sky Sports 3. In recognition of the rarity of the occasion, *The Guardian* said, "Fulham must be making progress if live television deems them worthy of a Friday night call."

It was Fulham the cameras had come to see. Twelve months earlier the Cottagers, a top tier mainstay during the 1960s, were beaten by Torquay, the only team below them in the entire Football League. Under the guidance of player-manager Mickey Adams and coach Alan Cork they had been rejuvenated and were now sitting proudly at the top of the table. They had occupied top spot since the middle of October and went into this game knowing that a win would take them nine points clear of second place Wigan Athletic.

These were not glory days in the history of Cardiff City. The previous season they had finished 22nd in the Third Division, their lowest ever league position. City boss Phil Neal, a former Liverpool legend, promised better at the start of the 1996/97 season but only lasted until October when he left to become assistant manager to Steve Coppell at Manchester City.

Kenny Hibbitt initially took charge but in November he was moved upstairs to director of football and former England international Russell Osman took over the reins. Results had been encouraging at first but then hit a dire run of seven defeats in eight league games. However, a 2-0 home win against Hull City on the previous weekend had ended a run of four consecutive defeats and kept City in touch with the play-off positions in 11th.

The poor form had caused City to take the remarkable step of slapping the entire squad on the transfer list. Whether it was a gimmick, an attempt to shake the players into action or a genuine attempt to shift some dead wood remains a mystery. Whatever the motive, it came as no real surprise that there were no offers for any of the squad.

City's problem had been their away form. Osman's men had lost six from 13 on their travels and had scored a pitiful eight goals. They had failed to score a single goal in their last four away games.

Those were worrying statistics going into a game against a Fulham side who were fresh off the back of a 4-1 win at Scunthorpe and who had murdered Darlington 6-0 in their last home match. "The doubters and the cynics will have to bite their tongues for now," snapped Adams in his programme notes.

To add to City's woes, marksman Carl Dale, who had scored in both defeats against Fulham the previous season, was out with a knee injury. Skipper Jason Perry was also suspended and winger Jimmy Gardner missed the match with a groin strain.

There was, however, some rare positive news from Ninian Park in the days before the clash. The owners of the city's ice hockey team Cardiff Devils, Celtic Leisure Company, had announced new investment in the club. That had led to the immediate arrival of tough-tackling Gareth Stoker for £80,000 from Hereford United and fellow midfielder Paul Ware, on loan from Stockport.

Fulham's midfield – which included future City player Richard Carpenter – was considered the best in the division and regularly steam-rolled their opponents. But with Stoker and Ware snapping away in midfield alongside Craig Middleton and Jason Fowler, City took control and were good value for their stunning result.

Adams, 35 years old, named himself as left-back as two of the season's defensive mainstays were out with long-term injuries. Also in the Fulham side was 32-year-old right-back Paul Parker making his third appearance for the Cottagers after signing on non-contract terms, returning to the club where he started his career 15 years earlier. Top scorer for the home side was Mike Conroy who had banged in 18 goals in 28 league games.

It was City who were out of the blocks faster and they might have gone ahead early on when Steve White, who was still a handful despite his 38 years, beat keeper Tony Lange to Stoker's long diagonal ball but steered his header wide of the goal. White, who was the Third Division's top scorer in 1995/96 with 32 goals for Hereford, had scored 12 so far this season – though he had failed to find the net in his last eight appearances.

The ease with which City carved their opponents open appeared to unnerve Fulham and the visitors hadn't fully recovered when the Bluebirds went ahead on 29 minutes. Skilful Fowler played a neat one-two with Ware, moved forward and hammered a left-footed drive into the roof of the net. It looked like the finish of a man in complete control – but his comments to the *Echo* afterwards suggested otherwise.

It was only Fowler's third goal of the season. "The ball ricocheted off a couple of players before it came to me and when I saw the goal I panicked," said Sky Sports' man of the match. "Then I thought I had shot too high and it was a great relief to see it go in."

City were well worth their 1-0 lead at the interval – the only concern was that it should have been more.

But less than a minute into the second half City doubled their lead, and in magnificent fashion. Snappy Middleton was fouled as he played Simon Haworth into space but the referee smartly allowed play to continue. Nineteen-year-old Haworth played in a perfect cross which White was able to head into an empty net at the far post.

Adams tried to change the tide by bringing on Martin Thomas for Parker – but rampant City had a third after 51 minutes. Danny Cullip's back-pass was short and White went strongly into the challenge with Lange outside the area. White was briefly floored but managed to get back on to his feet quicker than most men half his age and rolled the ball across to Haworth for a simple finish. It was Bambi's second goal of the season having opened his account against Hull in City's previous game.

Fulham chairman Jimmy Hill rubbed his famous chin in shock.

City were cruising to an unlikely victory, but there were some jitters when solid centre-back Jeff Eckhardt put through his own net against his former club after 55 minutes to make it 3-1. There was little former England youth goalkeeper Tony Elliott could have done about it.

Speaking to the *South Wales Echo*, Eckhardt, who played more than 250 games for Fulham between 1987 and 1994, said, "The ball flew across and two players in front of me ducked. I just didn't see the ball coming and it bounced off my chest and into the goal. I wanted to score, but not like that!"

Rod McAree came on for Fulham as they threw everything at City in search of a way back into the contest, but City were compact, committed and not afraid to show their muscle. The Bluebirds were completely unrecognisable from the team that served up such tripe just weeks earlier.

Osman brought on defender Ian Rodgerson, enjoying his second stint with City, to tighten things up. The temperature rose briefly and Scott Young was booked while Osman was sent to the stands for a comment made to the linesman when he felt his team should have had a penalty. "It turned out to be a good move," smirked Osman afterwards. "The view was better from there."

But any Fulham hopes of a late comeback evaporated when White ran direct at the home defence with three minutes remaining and fired an unstoppable drive which went in off the post.

With the three-goal breathing space restored, City were able to bring on the much-maligned forward Tony Philliskirk for *Echo* man of the match Haworth, while 20-year-old Jimmy Rollo came on to make his debut for the impressive Ware.

The small band of City fans inside Craven Cottage celebrated a fantastic result which reignited the season. Thousands more raised a Friday night jar from the comfort of their armchairs in front of Sky. And hundreds more stared at Teletext in disbelief.

It was the second victory since Hibbitt took the dramatic decision of putting the entire squad on the transfer list. But despite this victory which moved City to within two points of the play-offs, the 'for sale' signs remained up. "One swallow doesn't make a summer," said the director of football. The only player not up for grabs in the Ninian bazaar was Stoker.

The post-match comments from the managers were at the opposite ends of the spectrum. Osman beamed, "When you've scored just eight away goals, few people would expect to get half that number in one game. The fact it was against Fulham makes it even more pleasing." Shell-shocked Adams said, "I've seen things in my players that worry me. I won't tolerate it."

City's sporadic form continued for the rest of the campaign but they did manage to squeeze into seventh position, the final play-off place. Unfortunately they were outclassed in the semi-finals against Northampton, eventually going down 4-2 on aggregate, and a third consecutive season in the basement division loomed.

Fulham earned promotion as runners-up to Wigan. Egyptian businessman Mohamed Al-Fayed bought the club in the summer of 1997 and guided the club into the Premier League in just four seasons, where they have since established themselves.

31 v Chester City 6-0

14 November 1998. Attendance: 4,220
FA Cup First Round. Ninian Park

H E PICKED the ball up 20 yards inside his own half and just ran and ran. Past two players and then in between two more with devastating pace. Suddenly he had covered 80 yards but still had the energy to squeeze his shot into the far corner. It might have been Mark Delaney's only goal for City – but what a goal it was.

It took Delaney, the man known as 'Forrest Gump' to his team-mates, just nine seconds to cover the length of the pitch from first touch to last. Striker John Williams launched his 6ft 2in frame on to his back in celebration while Wayne O'Sullivan and Mike Ford dropped to their knees to bow in adoration in front of him. That was the fifth goal in a scintillating 6-0 drubbing of Chester City in the first round of the FA Cup, City's biggest post-war victory in the competition. Such big victories tend to live long in the memory. Delaney's explosive contribution made sure this one was unforgettable.

"My first touch wasn't great and I thought the goalkeeper would reach the ball first but I just kept running," Delaney told the *South Wales Echo* afterwards. "I just managed to poke the ball in before he could reach it and the feeling was great. I've scored goals before but this was my first for Cardiff City and I'll treasure the moment."

There had been a few raised eyebrows when Frank Burrows signed Haverfordwest-born Delaney from Carmarthen Town. Burrows had promised supporters that City would be competing for promotion out of the Third Division. An unknown 22-year-old on a free transfer from the League of Wales was not what fans had had in mind.

But the right-back soon won them over with a string of eye-catching performances and it wasn't long before scouts from the top clubs in Britain were keeping tabs on the Welshman. This has to go down as one of his best games in the blue and white of Cardiff.

City had not expected an easy ride against Chester City. Lee Jarman and Matt Brazier earned City a point at the Deva Stadium in a competitive 2-2 league draw just two months earlier.

But Chester, managed by former Everton, Wales and City defender Kevin Ratcliffe, were a club in turmoil. They were £500,000 in the red and were put into administration a few weeks before this game with some creditors calling for a winding up order. Striker Rod Thomas, who scored against the Bluebirds in September, had moved on to Brighton for a paltry £17,500 and defender Spencer Whelan was shipped out to Shrewsbury Town.

Ratcliffe, who had been manager of the Blues since 1995, had done his best to keep morale up – and with limited success. They were unbeaten in six before losing their last two games, albeit five of those were draws.

City, meanwhile, under the guidance of Burrows for a second time, were third in the Third Division after 17 games. From their last 12 league games they had won eight, drawn three and lost one. This was a team built around defence. City had scored 19 goals in the league – just four more than Hull City at the very foot of the table. They had kept four consecutive clean sheets (not including the FAW Premier Cup) but had scored just two in their last five. All of which made this demolition display all the more surprising.

There was just one change for City from the team that beat Scarborough 1-0 four days earlier, skinhead O'Sullivan coming in for loanee Chris Allen. Loan players were ineligible to play in the cup at the time. The competition did, however, allow for two extra places on the substitutes' bench, giving 19-year-old Christian Roberts and 17-year-old Robert Earnshaw a chance.

Chester, meanwhile, included former City favourite Nicky Richardson in their starting line-up. The midfielder played a key role in City's championship and Welsh Cup double winning team of 1992/93.

A crowd of just 4,220 trickled into Ninian for the first ever FA Cup meeting between the clubs. It might have been higher had it not been for the Wales v South Africa rugby match on TV at the same time. Cardiff had thought about moving the game to Friday evening or even Sunday afternoon but in the end opted to stick with Saturday 3pm. Those who choose the egg-shaped ball over round missed what the *Echo*'s Terry Phillips described as "the closest to the complete performance I've seen from a Third Division side".

City had Chester on the back foot from the off. Jason Fowler, often referred to as one of the classiest midfielders to have played for the club, had a decent chance early on after keeper Neil Cutler had come charging out of his area to head clear a through ball. It fell to Bristol-born Fowler at chest height but his first-time shot lacked accuracy. That was the first of 19 shots to pepper the visitors' goal.

Two minutes later with ten on the clock Fowler was on target to put the Bluebirds ahead with only his second goal of the season. Williams won a ball out of defence by O'Sullivan and Kevin Nugent was able to send a pass through for Fowler. With the coolness of a top striker, Fowler took the ball around Cutler and passed into the empty net.

Fowler later revealed that a conversation with his father had inspired his finish. "My dad and I have been talking about how players don't often dribble past goalkeepers these days," said the 24-year-old.

City fans had hardly time to draw breath before seeing their side double their lead. Again it was Williams, not renowned for his aerial abilities, who won the crucial first header. O'Sullivan picked it up and slid the ball through for Craig Middleton, who lunged in to poke in his third goal in five games.

Burrows had sent his team out with a clear game plan to exploit Chester's high pressing up the pitch. Fowler told the *Western Mail* that the team had worked in training on getting the ball over the top for the midfielders to run on to. Less than a sixth of the game gone and it had already worked twice.

Chester were beginning to look like a team in disarray. With 18 minutes played the Bob Bank rose to its feet when Middleton ran towards goal – but this time Cutler made an excellent save with his feet. Seven minutes later Delaney set off on a good run down the right and pulled the ball back for Williams but he saw his shot saved.

Williams fired another shot at Cutler before Fowler did eventually make it 3-0 five minutes before half-time. Fowler started the move with a beautiful diagonal ball to Williams. He showed a glimpse of the pace which earned him the coveted Rumbelows Sprint Contest crown in 1992 with a 100m time of 11.49 seconds to leave Chester's defenders for dead. Williams's shot beat Cutler this time but it was blocked on the line by Ross Davidson – but he could only push it into the path of Fowler for a simple finish. Fowler took a bow… literally.

It was raining chances. On 43 minutes only a desperate tackle by Andy Crosby stopped Williams from adding to Chester's embarrassment.

"Ratcliffe, what's the score?" enquired the home supporters as the teams headed for the changing rooms at half-time. It was long before the days of the big screen at Ninian Park and it would seem some fans had already lost count.

There was a brief Chester flourish at the start of the second half. Two minutes in and Scott Young had to clear off the line from Chris Priest's shot after a goalmouth scramble. At the other end Richard Carpenter's shot looked to be heading in after striking a defender but wrong-footed Cutler was pleased to see it fly past the post.

It was merely a matter of time though as the visitors' back-line edged ever further up the pitch – and on 55 minutes Williams finally did hit the target. Middleton flashed over a low cross and Williams nipped in front of Cutler to guide it into the net.

Chester had brought a small but hardy bunch of supporters to South Wales and their two drummers had drummed relentlessly throughout the game – until now.

Another Williams shot was blocked before along came goal number five just after the hour. Jon Hallworth rolled the ball out to Delaney well within his own half and off he went, striding from one end of the pitch to the other like a racehorse before lashing into the corner from a tightening angle.

There were still 20 minutes left when the scoreline entered the realms of the ridiculous as City made it six. This time Fowler placed a sumptuous curling ball to Middleton on the other side of the pitch. His first touch was perfect, playing back across into Williams's path for a simple finish from 12 yards, his sixth of the season. Chester, apparently not yet au fait with the new rules, appealed for offside against Delaney but he was not interfering with play.

Burrows, one of the sport's last cheerleaders for the humble flat cap, took off man of the match Fowler and Williams for the last nine minutes to give Nathan Cadette and Roberts their chance. Cadette had impressed for the youth and reserve teams during the previous season while Roberts appeared destined for great things.

Fowler received the standing ovation his performance deserved. At the time it was regularly mooted by the *Echo* and supporters that Fowler would one day grace the Premier League. Perhaps that was a stretch of the imagination and unfortunately Fowler was diagnosed with an over-active thyroid in 2000. He left City to join Torquay United in 2001 and spent four years at Plainmoor before retiring in 2005 because of arthritis in his hips.

Young went close with a couple of headers but City seemed more than happy with their six goals. It was the first time they had scored half a dozen in the FA Cup since an Adrian Alston hat-trick helped beat Exeter 6-2 in 1975 – and their biggest win in the competition since demolishing Enfield 8-0 in 1931.

"We've been playing as well as that all season but when you're not scoring people get edgy," Burrows told the *Western Mail*. "We've been making chances but we're not taking them. The difference here was that we took our chances and the ball went in the net."

Ratcliffe, in his day one of the greatest centre-backs in the world, was not so impressed with his team's efforts. "We've played well in recent games and kept the ball well," he said. "But Cardiff got the ball forward a lot quicker with midfield players making good runs."

City's reward for beating Chester was a home match against old Welsh Cup foe Hednesford Town, which they won 3-1 to set up a third round tie against Conference outfit Yeovil Town. City drew 1-1 at Ninian but eventually avoided embarrassment by winning 2-1 at Huish Park after extra time in the replay. Dreams of cup glory evaporated with a 4-1 tonking at Sheffield United in the fourth round.

In the league, the result could not spur City on to success at The Vetch Field eight days later, the Bluebirds falling to a 2-1 defeat. But Burrows's team did achieve ultimate success by earning promotion into the Second Division in third position.

As for Delaney, he lasted just four more moths at Ninian Park before being sold to Aston Villa for £250,000. City fans were furious – but not surprised. The club's stature and finances at the time meant they were at the mercy of the big boys. Delaney went on to make 193 first team appearances for Villa in all competitions but his career was hampered by knee injuries and he retired in 2007.

v Scunthorpe United 0-0

1 May 1999. Attendance: 12,455
Third Division. Ninian Park

CARDIFF CITY:	SCUNTHORPE UNITED:
Seamus Kelly	Tommy Evans
Wayne O'Sullivan	Tony Witter (Russ Wilcox 11)
Jeff Eckhardt	Chris Hope
Mike Ford	Andy Dawson
Graham Mitchell	Richard Logan
Mark Bonner	Paul Harsley
Craig Middleton (Danny Hill 63)	Justin Walker
Jason Fowler	Alex Calvo-Garcia
Andy Legg	Gareth Sheldon (John Gayle 65)
Kevin Nugent	John Eyre
John Williams (Jason Bowen 52)	Jamie Forrester (Gary Bull 80)
Sub not used: Richard Carpenter	

Referee: Andy D'Urso (Billericay)

T HE CLASS of 1998/99 might not have created the same fervour among supporters as Eddie May's superstars of 1992/93. It was lacking the creativity and passion of that great side of Cohen Griffith, Carl Dale and Phil Stant et al. Yet it managed something that just a small number of City teams have achieved since 1910: promotion. As thousands of success-starved Bluebirds fans poured on to the Ninian Park turf and attempted to rip the clothes off their heroes' backs after elevation from the Third Division was assured with a point against Scunthorpe, how the feat was achieved mattered not a jot.

The team was by and large made up of workhorses seasoned with a sprinkling of players with a track record for delivering the goods. There was dogged midfielder Richard Carpenter who had won two promotions in his previous three campaigns, skipper Mike Ford, who had tasted promotion with City in 1987/88, and striker Kevin Nugent, though this was his first promotion in 15 years in the game, had a decent scoring record.

But that is not to say there was no flair in this team. In fact, City had three players in the PFA Team of the Year: elegant midfielder Jason Fowler, goalkeeper Jon Hallworth and Mark Delaney, who was sold before the season's end in March 1999 for £250,000 to Aston Villa. Robert Earnshaw had also announced himself to the world with his first goal for the club on the opening day of the season – an overhead kick against Hartlepool – while super fast John Williams had earned cult status with his huge heart.

The season had begun with little or no optimism among the City fans. The previous campaign had been appalling with the Bluebirds eventually finishing 21st out of 24 in the Third Division. Only Hull City, Brighton & Hove Albion and Doncaster Rovers were below them in the entire Football League. Just 5,629 fans had turned out for the first home game of the new season, a 3-1 defeat against Peterborough United.

But the arrival of Frank Burrows as manager had at least brought just the faintest flicker of hope. Burrows was called 'bonkers' by Harry Redknapp when he quit his job as a coach at West Ham to take over from Kenny Hibbitt in the Ninian hot seat in March 1998. But Burrows was immediately a fans' favourite having taken City up before in 1988.

And the man with the flat cap wasted no time in making his mark, clearing out 11 players at the end of the 1997/98 season including legend Dale. He brought in a raft of new faces, including Delaney, Andy Saville, Mark Bonner and Dai Thomas. But even Burrows thought that after such major changes it might take two seasons to get out of football's basement.

But after a poor start to the season, during which City won one in seven, Burrows's men started to improve. Christmas came with the Bluebirds sitting proudly on top of the division and the crowds were now more often in the 7,000 and 8,000 region.

Results were sporadic after the New Year with nine draws from 20 league games – but City had done enough to hang on to an automatic promotion place. They had been in the top two since 1 December and needed just one point against Scunthorpe to clinch a return to the Second Division.

City were certainly not setting the world on fire going into the game. They had managed two goals in a game on just one occasion in their last six. Their strength was in defence though, having conceded just four goals in their last eight. Those stats considered, it was perhaps fitting that City should seal the deal with a 0-0 draw.

The day started on a sour note as a minute's silence for Sir Alf Ramsey, who had died three days earlier, was interrupted by anti-English chanting from pockets of the 12,455 crowd. The *Sunday Mirror* said that the fans had "brought shame on the club".

Scunthorpe also harboured hopes of clinching an automatic promotion spot, so it was perhaps no surprise that there was a nervy, tense opening with neither side wanting to concede first.

Wayne O'Sullivan and Andy Legg, a controversial December signing from Reading due to his Swansea City past, were lively for City and the home side should have been off to a dream start after just five minutes when a Nugent flick put Williams clear but he lobbed harmlessly over the bar.

Four minutes later City leader Ford, who had had an impressive season, was thwarted at the far post after Scunthorpe keeper Tommy Evans got just enough on Legg's corner.

City continued to press and after 13 minutes Nugent's 15-yard drive was charged down after the striker had been picked out by O'Sullivan.

But the best first half openings fell to Scunthorpe, managed by Brian Laws. The Ninian faithful were almost silenced on 33 minutes when Paul Harsley floated a ball in for Gareth Sheldon in space. Seamus Kelly, drafted in for Hallworth who had suffered two broken ribs five games earlier, made a brilliant one-on-one save to stop the striker's effort with his legs. The second chance fell to John Eyre, but he fired over.

And Irishman Kelly did well to stop Eyre's 20-yard effort soon after also. The City defence had done a good job of keeping the league's leading scorer Jamie Forrester quiet.

The decibel levels increased considerably after the break with cries of "Frankie Burrows' barmy army" reverberating around the stands.

The skilful Jason Bowen, a 53rd-minute replacement for fans' favourite Williams, almost raised the roof within seconds of coming on when he latched on to a quick throw-in by Legg. The Welshman eased past Russ Wilcox and set up O'Sullivan, but his effort was straight at Evans.

But as the game went on Scunny, who needed the three points to keep alive their own promotion hopes, threw an extra man up front. The move nearly paid dividends, but Kelly pulled off a stunning save. A corner was whipped over with pace and John Gayle powered a header goalwards. That would have been harmless enough, but Forrester managed to stoop low and get something on it to change the direction of the ball at the last moment. It looked a certain goal, but Kelly flew across his line to tip it on to his bar and City bundled it away. A huge sigh of relief was blown from all four stands.

The tension was clear around Ninian with fans starting to contemplate the possibility of journeying to Mansfield the following weekend still needing to get something from the game to secure promotion. Bizarrely, someone in the PA box decided to play Gary Glitter's "C'mon C'mon" at random breaks of play, much to the disgust of the home fans. Presumably robotic yellow hands would have appeared on a scoreboard with the word 'clap' underneath … that's if the club had a scoreboard at the time.

Bowen held his head in his hands after 73 minutes when he shot into the side netting with only Evans to beat from a tight angle.

City's promotion was all but assured with nine minutes to go when Iron were reduced to ten men. Richard Logan could not resist the temptation of bringing down Bowen when he was clean through on goal and Andy D'Urso had no option but to send him packing.

Gayle tried a 25-yarder but it was no match for Kelly before Bowen spurned the best chance of the game with two minutes to go. The Welsh international collected a Nugent pass and skipped past two men and bore down on goal, with only the keeper to beat. Glory would have been his with just a bit of composure, but instead he fired well over the bar.

The referee found four minutes of injury time from nowhere, but City fans were already getting ready for the customary invasion. Many were halfway over the old fences long before the whistle was finally blown and the celebrations could begin, the club's escape from the doldrums of English football finally in the bag.

Speaking to the *Echo*, Kelly described the terrifying moment one over-excited fan tried to relieve him of his clothing. "They wanted match souvenirs and I was wearing them," he said. "They were trying to pull off my shirt, shorts and boots while I clung on to the match ball. People all around me seemed to be grabbing at me. They weren't being nasty, but it was pretty scary." Bless him.

There were huge cheers from the fans on the pitch as the players emerged in the directors' box guzzling from champagne bottles. But the biggest cheer by far was reserved for Burrows, the man who had transformed City from a team of no-hopers to a workmanlike, hard to beat outfit. He had become the only manager in City's history to win promotion twice.

Speaking to *The Wales on Sunday*, Burrows said, "This time it's an even sweeter moment. I'm older and I left a very good job at West Ham to come back here to Cardiff.

"I'm definitely enjoying it more and I'm going to celebrate tonight. I'm going to get drunk, have a good time. I honestly didn't think it would happen until next season. After the first nine months I thought I would be standing here fending off questions, telling you why I wasn't resigning. For the team to gel together so quickly delights me no end."

Of the game itself, Burrows added, "We were a bit too nervous. I thought the occasion got to the players. But over the course of the season we've done enough to deserve to be in the top three."

Hours after clinching the all-important point, the City players joined supporters at the Coal Exchange for the annual supporters' club presentation night. Ford bellowed out a song karaoke style and off-key, according to the *Echo*. Twenty-one-goal Nugent came away with the player of the year accolades.

City had spent eight of the last 11 seasons playing in the bottom rung of the football pyramid – but there was hope that the club had finally broken the cycle and would never have to stoop so low again. Well-used clichés about the end of 'long trips north' to footballing backwaters were peddled out by the South Wales press. One bloke told the *Echo*, "I've been to Hartlepool seven times – I don't want to go back again!"

Unfortunately it was all misguided. For all the talk of back-to-back promotions and investment, City made an immediate return to the Third Division the following season. Burrows resigned in February 2000 to be replaced by his assistant Billy Ayres – but one suspects it might be a while before he is ousted as the club's only multi-promotion winning gaffer.

33 v Cambridge United 0-0

28 December 1999. Attendance: 4,250
Second Division. Abbey Stadium

CARDIFF CITY:	CAMBRIDGE UNITED:
Jon Hallworth	Shaun Marshall
Winston Faerber	Jason Kavanagh
Ritchie Humphreys	Martin McNeil
Russell Perrett	Clive Wilson
Jeff Eckhardt	Scott Eustace
Jason Fowler (Lee Phillips 46)	Ian Ashbee
Craig Middleton	Alex Russell (Steve Guinan 86)
Mark Bonner	Neil Mustoe
Josh Low	Neil MacKenzie
Richard Carpenter	Trevor Benjamin
Kevin Nugent	Martin Butler
Subs not used: Seamus Kelly, Christian Roberts, Robert Earnshaw, Dai Thomas	Subs not used: Marc Joseph, John Taylor Tom Youngs, James Mercer

Referee: David Elleray (Harrow on the Hill)

O N THE face of it, a 0-0 stalemate on a grey day at the end of the century might not seem like an obvious contender as one of City's all-time great games. But the 502 Bluebirds in a crowd of 4,250 at the Abbey Stadium will remember this as the day Frank Burrows's heroic eight men pulled a point out of the bag against all the odds.

Russell Perrett, Craig Middleton and Lee Phillips were all sent off by Premier League referee David Elleray on a bizarre afternoon between two clubs struggling at the wrong end of the Second Division. Throw in a late penalty save by Jon Hallworth and countless goalmouth scrambles and you've got yourself a classic. Classic, backs-to-the-wall, us-against-the-world, football poetry.

Award-winning football writer Phil Stead's commentary has become almost as famous as the match itself with Cardiff fans. Phil was running the club website at the time and was trialling audio commentaries by recording on a Dictaphone while stood in among the City fans. Ah, those heady pre-Millennium days. His excitable screams towards the end of the match and after the final whistle captured the emotion of an incredible day and put ITV's monotone commentators to shame.

"And it's there, it's all over, and Cardiff City celebrate as they draw 0-0 with eight men – a remarkable performance," he said. "And we celebrate – we celebrate as if we've won the European Champions League. A great day in the history of Cardiff City. This is emotional here in Cambridge. This is what it's all about.

"Cardiff City, the greatest team in the world. They're all heroes. This is one of the greatest days in Cardiff City's history. They're all bouncing up and down. We're surely the greatest team in the history of football. Man United, no. Chelsea, no. Tottenham, no. Barcelona, no. Real Madrid, no. Cardiff City – that's what it's all about."

Maybe Real Madrid was pushing it a tad, but Phil was right – it was exactly what it was all about.

Less than ten years later City would be playing in an FA Cup Final at the start of an incredible period of success in the club's history. Wonderful days. But there were pockets of joy in among the largely woeful 1990s which made the long treks to tin-pot stadiums with roofless toilets all worthwhile.

As City boss Burrows removed his trademark flat cap to perform an Ayatollah and the players were engulfed by the supporters at the final whistle, it was obvious that this was one of those days.

City travelled to Cambridge with renewed optimism in their fight against the drop back into the fourth tier of English football after a 1-0 Boxing Day win against a poor Reading side, Kevin Nugent with the vital goal. That ended a poor run of three consecutive league defeats, and lifted City to the dizzy heights of 17th, ahead of Welsh rivals Wrexham on goal difference. But the preparation for the clash at second-from-bottom Cambridge could hardly have been worse. There must have been some dodgy goings-on at City's Christmas bash as Burrows was without eight players – six of whom would probably have started – due to flu and injuries.

All of the club's 16 available players were named in the squad with the bench severely lacking in first team experience and with an average age of 22-and-a-half. An unused sub on the day was an 18-year-old Robert Earnshaw who was still finding his feet in the Football League. It proved to be little Earnie's last involvement in the City squad before a successful loan move to Scottish First Division side Morton, which in many ways kick-started a glittering career.

It was a disjointed start to the match after skilful midfielder Jason Fowler took a kick to the head from Scott Eustace after just 20 seconds, bringing proceedings to a halt for five minutes. The U's had the better of a cagey opening. Martin Butler shot just past the post after eight minutes then Hallworth was called into making a low save from the same player after a good link-up with a 20-year-old Trevor Benjamin, playing for his first of 18 different clubs.

Despite appearing to be suffering from concussion, it was Fowler who had City's best chance of the half, blazing high over the bar after a decent run. Benjamin then found himself in space for the home side but got caught in two minds between a header and a volley and ended up on his backside.

The first booking of the afternoon soon followed when central defender Perrett went through the back of Butler. On 40 minutes Cambridge's Alex Russell ghosted past three City defenders but his final effort did not match the approach play and was easily gathered.

Three minutes later Middleton, who had made a few errors against his former club, became the second name in Elleray's little black book for a late tackle on Jason Kavanagh and from the resulting free kick Eustace headed over.

So far, just an average error-strewn afternoon of Second Division football – but then the drama began.

As some City fans made a beeline to sample Cambridge's multi-award winning bacon rolls, Middleton was caught napping in his own penalty area. The long-haired midfielder was suddenly under pressure and screwed his clearance to the edge of the area towards Benjamin. Benjamin had his back to goal and was going nowhere but Perrett lunged in late. City fans felt that Benjamin had made the most of the foul and a free kick would have sufficed, but it was no surprise when Perrett received his second yellow and consequently the third dismissal of his career.

That was only City's second red card of the campaign and both times Perrett was the culprit having been sent for an early bath against Gillingham just 32 days previously.

Perrett, a £10,000 summer signing from Portsmouth, had been the Bluebirds' best player up to that point and his departure left an ageing Jeff Eckhardt to cope with United's lively strike-force almost single-handedly.

The half-time whistle blew seconds later, at least giving Burrows the chance to settle his troops. The City fans that had made it back from the bacon bap queue in time were treated to Cambridge's unique take on half-time entertainment as Marvin the Moose paraded around the pitch making gestures with an inflatable sheep.

City's chances of taking anything from the game appeared to take a turn for the worse when Phillips emerged for the second half as a replacement for Fowler, who was taken to hospital still suffering from the effects of that first-minute collision. Welshman Phillips had played just 32 minutes so far that season – and just a handful of games since signing as a trainee in 1996. He went straight into the back four with City looking to sneak something on the break.

But it was City who forced the first save of the second half when the lively Josh Low drove into the box and shot straight at Shaun Marshall. The home side began to make use of their extra man advantage. Benjamin rose for a Clive Wilson cross but flicked his header wide.

Butler then tried a snapshot but there was no venom in the effort before the same player walloped the ball into the car park from a free kick on 50 minutes. Now City's rearguard action was beginning to be tested. Russell chipped over after the City defence had gifted him possession and Neil MacKenzie shot wide.

The Bluebirds enjoyed a rare foray into Cambridge's half just before the hour when Ritchie Humphreys, on loan from Sheffield Wednesday, smashed a vicious shot just inches too high. Humphreys had started his City career in electric fashion having bagged two goals at Colchester on his debut – but he wouldn't find the net again during his three-month stint at Ninian Park.

On 63 minutes City were down to nine men and seemingly staring down the barrel after Middleton picked up his second yellow for going through the back of Butler.

Having witnessed a number of brash U's tackles go unpunished, the City fans were incensed, but Elleray had little option.

Hallworth, an excellent servant to the club, made a fantastic save from the resulting free kick and the City faithful responded by cranking up the volume several decibels.

Cambridge threw striker John Taylor into the mix as they searched for the winner that everyone in the Abbey thought was surely inevitable. But City defended heroically by throwing their bodies in front of every shot and chasing down every ball.

Veteran Eckhardt and Winston Faerber put in a string of heroic tackles while at the other end Humphreys was able to relieve the pressure by holding the ball in the United half for seconds at a time. But just as it looked like City had control of the situation with 15 minutes to go, they astonishingly found themselves down to eight men. A deep cross from the left found Taylor, whose hooked shot was only partially saved by Hallworth. It looked to be heading over the line – it might have even just crossed it – but Phillips dived to produce an expert save, with both hands!

Elleray pointed to the spot and off Phillips trudged as City now contemplated seeing out the final quarter of an hour three players short. On an afternoon which was becoming more bizarre by the minute, it seemed inevitable that Hallworth would save the penalty

– and right on script he gobbled up Butler's tame effort. Butler followed up looking for a loose ball which wasn't there and a mass brawl ensued, bodies and fists flying everywhere.

The siege of the Alamo continued. Butler missed another great chance, Taylor curled inches wide and Benjamin was off target as the City fans taunted "we've only got eight men".

Anywhere would do now as the fans behind the goal celebrated every hoof forward as if it was a goal. City were now playing the unusual 3-3-1 formation with Humphreys cutting a lonely figure up top and captain Nugent filling in as an emergency centre-back.

Cambridge continued with their desperate tactic of lobbing in crosses which were mopped up by the City heroes. And City nearly entered the realms of fantasy when at the other end super-fast Low burst through three defenders and had just one man to beat, but the United defender managed to get a boot in.

Dutchman Faerber was also still venturing forward and he received an ear-bashing from Burrows when instead of holding the ball by the corner flag, he suddenly sent a huge cross to the other side of the pitch which allowed Cambridge a break. City's depleted ranks raced back in time to block Taylor's cross.

With a minute to go all eyes were on referee Elleray once again when Taylor took a dramatic tumble in the penalty area, but the geography-teacher-by-day produced a yellow card for a dive. Elleray found two minutes of added on time – and then another two minutes on top of that – before the final whistle eventually went to signal hysterical scenes of joy from the City fans and mass discontent from the locals.

All of the City players were mobbed as they went towards their adoring fans and boss Burrows danced a merry jig.

After such a gutsy display, no one could have foreseen what was around the corner.

City failed to win any of their next 12 league games, losing five of them. It was a run which cost Burrows his job in February – and replacement Billy Ayre could not save a sinking ship.

Cambridge went on to save themselves while City began the new Millennium by dropping back into the basement division.

34 v York City 3-3

21 April 2001. Attendance: 3,881
Third Division

SUPER LEO Fortune-West headed three goals to ignite a promotion party at York City's Bootham Crescent. The lower league maestro put City one up, then made it 2-1 before equalising late on to seal elevation with three games to spare.

With news that Leyton Orient had lost elsewhere, the 2,000 travelling Bluebirds poured on to the pitch to celebrate the club's tenth promotion since 1910. After embracing each other the supporters gathered in front of the main stand and demanded to see their heroes. The players obliged and threw their shirts into the crowd. Alan Cork, who had taken over as manager in October with City in 14th position, emerged in tears.

It had been a turbulent two years for City after being promoted in 1999, only to plummet straight back down the following year. But things were different now. Sam Hammam had taken control of the club at the end of 2000 and had funded an entirely new team. As we pranced on the Bootham turf there was a firm belief that we would never again return to the depths of the Third Division. As things stand, that belief has turned out to be true. A dismal era of seemingly never-ending disappointment had finally come to an end.

It was fitting that it was Fortune-West's goals that clinched promotion. Few players have won over the fans quite as emphatically as the intelligent, softly-spoken giant. The ungainly striker was ridiculed by City fans after becoming the club's record signing for £300,000 from Rotherham in September. Leo had opted to step down a division to be part of the Hammam revolution and had scored with his stomach on his debut against Halifax. The goals continued to fly in at regular intervals but the supporters never really took to the man with a 50 pence head.

But that was all to change and six foot four Leo finished his Cardiff career with 28 goals in 113 appearances – and with cult hero status. This stellar hat-trick went a long way to securing that standing with supporters. Thank goodness rumours of him winning the lottery and retiring from football a couple of months earlier proved unfounded.

Cork's team went into the game on the back of a thrilling 3-3 draw with Chesterfield thanks to a last-minute Kevin Evans leveller. York, meanwhile, included former Bluebird Nicky Richardson and future Bluebird Lee Bullock and were looking for a point which they believed would guarantee their league status.

City got off to a lively start. Evans's cross from the right was missed by defender Michael Basham but Fortune-West could not direct his header goalwards. Andy Legg used his incredible long throws to create danger in the York defence and from one such effort centre-back Scott Young headed narrowly wide at the far post.

The Minstermen had little answer to the onslaught but City's ploy of playing it out wide for a cross into Fortune-West was a little predictable.

York came close with Basham's looping header sailing inches wide from Graham Potter's free kick. Then after 12 minutes Fortune-West headed down a cross to Paul Brayson but Mark Bower made a vital block. Fortune-West turned provider again but Evans screwed his shot wide from a good position.

The travelling fans grew a little restless as the minutes passed and York's front pair Colin Alcide and Lee Nogan, the brother of out-of-favour City striker Kurt, looked dangerous when they had possession in front of goal. Alcide turned Legg well but was brought down cynically and the free kick came to nothing.

Fortune-West was putting himself about and looking lively. There were those in the away end who took delight in criticising every mistake while others called on him to do the Ayatollah. He was a real Marmite figure.

City's big breakthrough came on 37 minutes in front of their own fans. Legg whipped in an in-swinging corner and Rhys Weston sent a downward header goalwards. York skipper Chris Brass blocked on the line with an upwards header and Leo charged through a crowded area to bundle his header into the bottom corner. The York players asked for a foul on goalkeeper Alan Fettis – television replays showed their appeals were not without substance – but the goal stood and City were on their way back into the Second Division.

Leo celebrated by scowling at his mockers among the away end.

"Going up, going up, going up" chanted the City fans – but they were soon to be silenced by a Brass equaliser just four minutes later. An innocent-looking through ball was chased down by Nogan. Weston put in a solid tackle but referee David Laws saw something that was never there and pointed to the penalty spot. Young and Matt Brazier were booked for their protests. When peace was eventually restored Brass sent Carl Muggleton the wrong way for his first goal for the club.

The shell-shocked City fans fell silent, wondering if the champagne might have to be put back in the fridge. But then Leo gave City a crucial half-time lead with his second goal in injury time. Andy Thompson and man of the match contender Willie Boland combined on the right flank and Boland curled in a superb ball. Leo attacked with purpose, beating two defenders in the air and nodding into the bottom corner on the dive. The double-barrelled striker, who had to wear specs because of short-sightedness, stood statuesque in front of the jubilant Bluebirds fans.

Half-time came with City good value for their slender advantage. Weston, who was beginning to look like the player fans had expected when he signed from Arsenal five months earlier, was still seething about the penalty decision and let the referee know about it as the teams headed off the pitch. Tubby Laws looked poised to take action but City director of football Bobby Gould rescued the full-back by dragging him towards the changing rooms.

Word had spread during the interval that promotion rivals Rochdale were losing and Orient were drawing but were down to ten men. If that stayed the same, City needed just a point to secure promotion.

Soon after the restart Young came close to his 11th goal of the season with a 15-yard volley that was instinctively saved by the legs of Fettis.

Muggleton then got down well to stop Alcide's low drive from 18 yards. Those were rare moments of excitement in a second half that failed to match the first. The atmosphere in the away end had died in the warm spring sun, so much so the home fans politely enquired, "Are you enjoying a jolly nice kip?" Or words to that effect.

It might not have been edge-of-the-seat stuff but City's promotion bid appeared in no danger. Street sellers were already calling suppliers to bulk order souvenir t-shirts. But this City team might have been the best attacking outfit in the division, but it was also defensively shaky. Before this game they had already conceded 49 goals – four more than Darlington in 15th. Strong defenders Danny Gabbidon and David Hughes were both missing through injury.

On 62 minutes the home side had an equaliser out of nothing. Bower played a long ball forward and Alcide beat Young in the air to send a deft flick on between two City players. Nogan found himself completely free and he wrong-footed Muggleton with a 12-yard volley, his sixth goal in ten appearances. The Cardiffian paraded in front of the City fans and pointed to the name on his back of his shirt, presumably in some sort of show of solidarity to his big bro.

And things were to get worse for City when York went ahead for the first time five minutes later. Brazier let the ball drop behind him and Darren Edmondson was in. He sent over a carefully weighted cross which Alcide crashed in with a header from two yards for 3-2.

For a short time it was looking gloomy for City. A couple of heads had dropped. Cork responded by replacing Jason Bowen with the energetic Robert Earnshaw, who had just turned 20 and had scored 23 goals so far that season. He immediately had a couple of chances to run – but it was a header from that man again Fortune-West that made it 3-3 on 71 minutes.

Leo was brought down 30 yards from goal and Leggy curled in a trademark free kick. There was Fortune-West on the edge of the six-yard box to loop his header over Fettis and in off the underside of the bar.

It was Leo's third career hat-trick and the celebrations could resume.

Tough-tackling Scott McCulloch was brought on for Evans to add a bit of steel to the midfield. He was given a warm welcome by City fans who believed he should have been given more game time since Cork's arrival.

The final 15 minutes were tense but news had filtered through that Orient were now two goals behind and a draw was going to be enough. Earnshaw saw a shot bounce just wide after breaking through following a defensive mistake as City looked to finish in style.

There were few dramas in the last few minutes and supporters ran on to mob their idols. Leo was chaired off. As the celebrations unfolded in the directors' box the biggest cheer was reserved for Hammam, the man who appeared to be the saviour fans had been seeking for two decades or more.

Cardiff City's Greatest Games

He said, "When I took over here I said I wanted to bring top flight football and that remains my ambition. It may not happen in my life-time – but I will give it everything I've got.

"But I can only do so much. I don't have a set of magic keys. It has to be down to our supporters to play their part next season by coming along in their thousands and giving us their support. The fans here are just as passionate as those anywhere in the world. Now I want those who have doubted our progress to join them."

Bald Corky, who had been with Sam and Gould as part of the infamous Wimbledon 'Crazy Gang', was also chuffed. Speaking to *The Sunday Mirror*, he beamed, "Promotion is what we wanted this year. We have scraped our way through over the last few games, but have got there. There are a lot of young players in this team having their first season in league football, so this is a great reward for their and everyone else's efforts."

And as if the day could get any better, Swansea's relegation back to the Third Division was confirmed with defeat against Oldham. Footballing perfection.

According to *The Sun*, Cork and Gould brought the team coach to a halt just 150 yards into the journey home and stripped a Spar shop of all its lager. Gould went further with a bottle of Southern Comfort. It must have been some party for the 240 miles back to South Wales.

City eventually finished the season in second position, ten points behind worthy champions Brighton. The Bluebirds had banged in 95 goals, the highest in the whole country and two up on the club record set more than half a century ago. There could certainly be no complaints about the entertainment on offer and there was real excitement around the city that the club was only heading in one direction – upwards.

35 v Leeds United 2-1

6 January 2002. Attendance: 22,009
FA Cup Third Round. Ninian Park

CARDIFF CITY:
Neil Alexander
Danny Gabbidon
Spencer Prior
Scott Young
Andy Legg
Willie Boland
Mark Bonner
Graham Kavanagh
Paul Brayson
Robert Earnshaw
Gavin Gordon (Leo Fortune-West 79)
Subs not used: Leyton Maxwell, Jason
Bowen, Rhys Weston, Josh Low

Referee: Andy D'Urso (Billericay)

LEEDS UNITED:
Nigel Martyn
Danny Mills
Jonathan Woodgate
Rio Ferdinand (Michael Duberry 10)
Ian Harte
Gary Kelly
Lee Bowyer
David Batty
Alan Smith
Mark Viduka
Robbie Fowler
Subs not used: Stephen McPhail, Paul
Robinson, Jason Wilcox,
Frazer Richardson

SUNDAY 6 January 2002 was a landmark day in Cardiff City's recent history – both on and off the field. On the pitch, Alan Cork's team were catapulted into the national limelight with an astonishing FA Cup win over Premier League leaders Leeds United. But one of the club's greatest successes was soured by ugly scenes among supporters both during and after the match. The national press launched a sustained attack on the club and its fans – so much so that it forced actions that changed the club forever.

Leeds had come to Ninian Park, by then in its twilight years, top of the pile in the football pyramid and looking good to win the title for the first time since 1992. Their starting 11 cost more than £48m to assemble and included the likes of Jonathan Woodgate, Rio Ferdinand, Mark Viduka and Robbie Fowler.

The Bluebirds, meanwhile, were tenth in the Second Division and had just been beaten 3-1 at home against rivals Bristol City, causing Cork to question his players' commitment to the cause. They had not won a league game since 8 December. Fifty-four league positions separated the sides.

It appeared to be Mission Impossible as a squad of journeymen assembled for scarcely £2m including Andy Legg, Willie Boland and Gavin Gordon lined up against a club which looked ready to emulate their glory days under Don Revie.

What followed was one of the iconic Cup giant-killings which is still talked about today in the same breath as Hereford v Newcastle 1972. But it was the unique atmosphere, throbbing with aggression, testosterone and excitement, that remains the abiding memory for many and proved to be a great leveller. Peter Ridsdale and Ferdinand, Leeds chairman and skipper at the time, would later liken the occasion to a trip to Galatasaray.

139

Cardiff City's Greatest Games

A capacity 22,009 – the biggest crowd since 1976 – packed into The Old Lady for the Sunday evening game. Looking to cash in on the club's most glamorous fixture in years, City had made a bid to switch the tie to the Millennium Stadium but that was quickly turned down by the FA.

In the week building up to the tie self-absorbed owner Sam Hammam lapped up every moment in the spotlight as the television cameras descended on Cardiff. While playing down his side's chances of winning in a tactical move, he was busy telling anyone who would listen that Cardiff were the bigger club. "This tie is a glimpse of where Cardiff should be," he said, with not a hint of insincerity. "We should be playing the likes of Leeds, Man United and Liverpool every week. Club for club we're bigger than Leeds. If we were in their position we'd be getting 60,000 at every home game. When they come down to Wales they'll be in for a battle because they'll be taking on the whole of the Welsh nation."

Leeds boss David O'Leary, meanwhile, confidently predicted that his team would "start and finish their cup campaign in Cardiff". The final, of course, was being played at the Millennium Stadium at the time.

There was a decent history between the two clubs, despite not crossing paths since 1984. In the 1950s the clubs featured in one of the strangest spells of FA Cup history when for three years running the two clubs were drawn against each other. All three ties were in the third round, all were at Elland Road – and the Bluebirds won the three matches 2-1.

And of course the late, great John Charles, the most complete footballer of his day, had starred for both clubs during the 1950s and 1960s. In a fitting tribute, the Gentle Giant led the teams out. There wasn't really much doubt where his loyalties lay, though. He might have been a proud Welshman, but he was also Leeds through and through.

History, for what it's worth, favoured City. Leeds had been to Ninian Park on 17 occasions – and only won three times.

Ninian was packed a good 20 minutes before kick-off and there was a real air of excitement among City fans as day turned to early evening. Every supporter had been given a copy of the words for Welsh battle song 'Men of Harlech' which was belted out loudly. The tune has been sung by City fans at almost every home match since.

Cork left his players with simple words as they headed out into a cauldron of noise, "If you want to be a hero, today's the day for it."

There was an angry atmosphere around the crumbling stadium and it took less than a minute for the game to be halted when referee Andy D'Urso collected an object from the pitch which had been thrown from the Bob Bank terracing.

Leeds, Champions League semi-finalists in 2001, started the match with purpose, knocking the ball around swiftly and attractively like the classy side they were. City responded with grit and aggression – perhaps a little too much of the latter in the case of Gordon, who went straight through Ferdinand, forcing the £18m defender off the pitch after just ten minutes. The Grandstand waved him farewell, cruelly singing "what a waste of money" as he hobbled towards the tunnel. On came Michael Duberry to link up with Jonathan Woodgate for the first time since the conclusion of the much-publicised 'Leeds-gate' court case.

City had grasped a foothold in the game and were playing with a confident swagger which far exceeded their league standing. Livewire Robert Earnshaw was playing in a wider role than usual which seemed to upset the Leeds superstars.

But then after just 12 minutes, and perhaps slightly against the run of play, the visitors were ahead. Spencer Prior tried a Hollywood pass which was more Haverfordwest and only found Gary Kelly in midfield. He was able to charge forward before passing to Viduka, who lashed past Neil Alexander into the bottom corner from 20 yards.

That could have been the cue for City to capitulate. This was a team without a win in their last four and starting to stutter after a promising opening to the league season.

But City were not fazed and began playing with width and conviction. Boland and Mark Bonner were snapping away in midfield, breaking up Leeds' rhythm, and chances were coming.

First Earnshaw, who had scored 12 goals so far that campaign, reacted first to meet Graham Kavanagh's corner but put his effort over the bar. Then Kav sliced open the Leeds midfield and found Gordon, but his weak shot showed all the confidence of a striker who had only scored eight that term – and five of those were in one game!

But City kept scrapping and a moment of magic from super Kavanagh, the club's first £1m signing, drew the scores level and sent City fans into euphoria. Legg was brought down well outside the area and up stepped Kav to take everybody by surprise by curling a magnificent free kick past England international Nigel Martyn and into the near corner on 21 minutes. The wall should not have been penetrated so easily, but the accuracy was sublime.

Before the match Kavanagh had hit back at Cork's claim that the players didn't care – and he showed there were no hard feelings by engulfing his gaffer. The atmosphere cranked up from red-hot to inferno.

City were turning on the style with some great, free-flowing football and without their rock of Ferdinand Leeds looked vulnerable. Earnie was keen to impress and his direct run was halted by a solid Woodgate tackle. Kavanagh then hit a fierce 20-yard drive which was well blocked. Leeds looked dangerous on the counter-attack, but it was City enjoying the better territory and long throws by Legg were causing panic.

Meanwhile, Paul Brayson, brought in to replace Jason Bowen, gave City extra width while keeping Danny Mills under control. Feisty Mills had earned rave reviews for a stellar performance in Leeds' 3-0 win over West Ham the Tuesday previous but was made to look very ordinary by the little chap from Newcastle.

Fowler, a recent £11m signing from Liverpool, had to wait until the 37th minute before he threatened for Leeds, but Alexander comfortably gathered his shot. Fowler tried again four minutes later, but this time he curled his effort above the woodwork.

Cork's men were handed a major boost shortly before half-time when a young Alan Smith was sent off for an elbow on Legg after a tangle. It was a harsh decision – Leggy himself later said a yellow card would have sufficed – but Smith's reputation went before him. At just 21, it was the sixth red card of his career. He was afforded no sympathy from the City fans as he headed off the Ninian turf.

The second half saw more nervous, edge-of-the-seat action for City fans but chances were at a premium. Leeds regrouped and stifled City's attacking play more efficiently with ten men than they had managed with their full complement. One suspects they would have been more than happy to leave the bear-pit with a draw and a replay.

Boland had a chance to put City ahead after 55 minutes when Woodgate scuffed a clearance, but the Irish midfielder was anything but prolific during his time at City and fired straight at Martyn. Gordon then drove a shot into the keeper's arms and Bonner went inches wide soon after.

City looked the more likely to nick a goal, but blue hearts were in mouths as a clearly offside Viduka latched on to a long ball forward and went one-on-one with

Alexander on 75 minutes. Somehow Scott Young found enough in his tank to catch up with the Australian and snatch the ball from his feet with a hooked tackle just as he was about to pull the trigger. Moments later super Young flew in again to win another crucial tackle.

Then with ten minutes to go Cork shuffled his pack. Gordon had been a spent force for a good quarter of an hour and was finally hauled off for the uncompromising figure of six foot four Leo Fortune-West.

There was another stoppage on 81 minutes as D'Urso received treatment after being hit on the head by a coin.

As the game moved into its latter stages, the belief grew among the home supporters that something special was just around the corner. With three minutes remaining, there it was. As Hammam controversially lingered behind the Leeds goal with his bodyguard, along came three consecutive City corners, taking their tally to seven for the game.

Cries of "Leo, Leo Leo" echoed off the Grange End tin roof as the giant striker Fortune-West bounced around like a child on Christmas morning. In came the Kavanagh corner, down went the header from Fortune-West, which hit David Batty on the line. It came back out for Young and time stood still before the defender – Pontypridd-born and Cardiff's longest-serving player – volleyed in from close-range.

Ninian had seen some big moments, but as Young ducked and dived around his team-mates in front of a euphoric Bob Bank, it was hard to imagine that many had been as sweet.

"Even in my wildest dreams I could never have believed that this would happen," Young told *The Mirror* afterwards. "I've been involved in two promotions in my ten years at the club but I can never remember a day like this. The roar from the crowd almost deafened me. They deserve it more than anyone."

Hammam's Ayatollah-frenzy lap of honour continued as City hung on tight before a final whistle which was greeted by wild celebrations. Cardiff had dumped the great Leeds United out of the FA Cup – and nobody could deny that it was utterly deserved.

Fans poured on to the pitch and Leeds midfielder Lee Bowyer was attacked as he tried to make the tunnel.

Hammam was lifted on to supporters' shoulders with a Welsh flag grasped in his hand. His ridiculous black eyebrow dye ran down his smirking face to create a snapshot that would become synonymous with his topsy-turvy, controversial and eventually ill-fated six years with the club.

But while some City fans were on the pitch to innocently celebrate a great result, others headed straight over to the 2,000 Leeds fans caged in the Grange End. Riot police with dogs and batons had to force them away. All in front of the TV cameras.

Hammam saw O'Leary, football's biggest whinger, later that day and quipped that he was spot on with his prediction that their cup campaign would start and finish in the city. O'Leary reportedly responded by grabbing the City chief by the lapels. "Thank God my chairman Peter Ridsdale and three directors were with me," said O'Leary. "I was pulled away. Otherwise, it would have gone into a heated exchange."

Days of media frenzy followed. *The Daily Mail* called it "a new phase of hooliganism". David Lacey of *The Guardian* wrote, "Ninian Park is a land that time forgot, a place where raptors still rule."

The BBC radio commentator gasped at what he was witnessing. The club undeniably had its problems for a few years after the Millennium, but the reporting was sensationalist and over the top and even led to parliamentarians calling for the closure of football grounds where trouble was occurring.

Unfortunately City's cause was not helped when undercover filming by the BBC revealed Hammam making light of the violence with a trusted group of supporters he had summoned to the ground. The club was eventually fined £20,000 by the FAW and Hammam was banned from taking his stroll around the pitch during games.

The crowd trouble threatened to overshadow what was a remarkable victory by the Bluebirds but in the end it proved to be a turning point for the club. Steps were taken which finally saw the Ninian fences removed in 2006 and the club was even named Family Club of the Year in 2011 and 2013.

In typical fashion, the following Saturday City slumped to a dismal 2-0 home defeat against Peterborough United on an afternoon with a peculiar atmosphere. They were knocked out of the Cup in the fourth round at Tranmere and eventually finished the season in fourth position, though they lost out in the play-offs against Stoke City.

As for Leeds, the match was also a bit of a milestone for them. They didn't win a single game in their next nine, finished the season in fifth position and missed out on a place in the Champions League. That had serious financial implications and two seasons later they were relegated.

36 v Oldham Athletic 7-1

16 March 2002. Attendance: 6,786
Second Division. Boundary Park

CARDIFF CITY:

Neil Alexander
Rhys Weston
Scott Young
Spencer Prior
Andy Legg
Danny Gabbidon (Michael Simpkins 76)
Willie Boland
Graham Kavanagh (James Collins 66)
Andy Campbell (Gethin Jones 75)
Leo Fortune-West
Peter Thorne
Subs not used: Mark Walton,
David Hughes

OLDHAM ATHLETIC:

Andy Goram
Michael Clegg
Stuart Balmer
Julian Baudet
Chris Armstrong
Matty Appleby
Cristian Colusso (Tony Carss 34)
Paul Murray
David Eyres (Darren Sheridan 83)
Carlo Corazzin
Allan Smart (Lee Duxbury 45)
Subs not used: Dean Holden, David Miskelly

Referee: Colin Webster (Shotley Bridge, County Durham)

"THERE'S ONLY one Andy Goram" mocked the travelling City fans as the overweight goalkeeper, a shadow of his former self, wobbled to his goal-line at the start of the second half. The 37-year-old had answered an SOS call to return to the club where he launched his distinguished career 21 years earlier. Now 45 minutes into his second debut as an Oldham player, former Rangers and Scotland man Goram had conceded five.

Sublime City had smashed five first-half goals without reply for the first time since walloping Liverpool 6-1 at Ninian Park in 1957. Lennie Lawrence's Bluebirds went on to tonk useless Oldham 7-1, an astonishing result against play-off rivals. The 2,400 vocal City fans wildly celebrated one of the most sensational afternoons in the recent history of the club.

Goram, who just a year earlier had been called in to ease a goalkeeping crisis at Manchester United, was slow and cumbersome. He was at least partly at fault for three of City's goals – but that is to take nothing away from this devastating performance by Lennie's Lions.

While the career of one Andy appeared to be on a sharp decline, the future of another looked like it was just about to take flight. That man was ginger Bluebirds striker Andy Campbell. The 22-year-old had joined City on loan from home-town club Middlesbrough at the end of February and had scored three goals in as many games before hitting a fantastic hat-trick in this match. Campbell, who had made four Premier League appearances that season, appeared to have the electric pace and natural finishing ability to reach the very top.

Campbell's stellar performance earned rave reviews from the Sunday nationals – but this was far from the achievement of one man. The Bluebirds were brilliant from front to back, from Spencer Prior's solid defending, to Willie Boland's tenacity. The *South Wales*

Echo's Terry Phillips, in fact, hailed it one of the most remarkable performances he had witnessed in 33 years as a journalist.

Much of the credit had to go to Lawrence, who was beginning to look like football's equivalent to Einstein. This was the experienced leader's sixth league game in charge after taking over from Alan Cork – and he'd now managed four wins and two draws.

The match at Boundary Park looked set to be Lennie's toughest test to date. Before kick-off Oldham and City were locked on 61 points in seventh and eighth, four points behind Bristol City in the last play-off place in the Second Division. But Lawrence's plans had been disrupted by a monster injury list. Fourteen players were doubts and just one of those – Rhys Weston – made it into the threadbare 17-man squad which included every fit senior player on the books.

A huge re-shuffle was needed with Danny Gabbidon moved to left-back and Andy Legg pushed up into midfield. But Lawrence's genius was to name three up front with Peter Thorne just behind Campbell and Leo Fortune-West. The move bamboozled Oldham, who had injuries of their own and just could not live with City's firepower.

City, wearing red, looked nervous in the opening exchanges as they adapted to their unfamiliar set-up. First David Eyres's long corner found Stuart Balmer at the back post but the Latics defender stubbed his shot into the ground and it bobbled through to City keeper Neil Alexander.

A minute later Matty Appleby fed Cristian Colusso out wide on the left. Colusso slid the ball forward for Paul Murray but the midfielder's shot was hit wildly over the bar.

But then after just six minutes came the goal which set City on the way to Seventh Heaven. Legg, who once held the record for the longest throw-in, hurled a trademark howitzer to the back post. Goram and his defence stood motionless as centre-back Scott Young headed down and inside the post with ease.

But City were still not firing on all cylinders as Oldham – a Premier League club just eight seasons before – poured forward looking for an immediate response. Alexander had faced the brunt of the City fans in recent weeks but silenced his critics with two smart saves.

First Colusso tried his luck from 20 yards but the Scot made easy work of the block before from a corner midfielder Murray saw his snapshot brilliantly stopped at point-blank range. Sandwiched between those saves Carlo Corazzin found the ball at his feet after some pinball football in the City area but hopelessly scooped his shot over the bar from just five yards.

There were a few jitters in the away end as it looked as though an equaliser might be imminent but City always looked a threat on the break with some devastating runs from Campbell and Thorne. On 22 minutes it was 2-0 as an excellent in-swinging corner by Legg, Cardiff's first of the match, was glanced in at the near post by the unmarked Fortune-West. Goram continued his one man game of musical statues. It was super Leo's seventh goal of the season, but his first in 15 appearances.

A minute later and there was mayhem among the travelling fans as Thorne made it 3-0. It was another in-swinging corner by Legg which did the damage, to the far post this time for the classy striker to charge in and power his header home. Three goals from three set-pieces – and another drought over, too, with Thorne's first in nine.

Oldham were in disarray and City smelt blood. The Latics chased the ball aimlessly as City sprayed it around midfield with ease. Gabbidon came close with another header from a corner before with 30 minutes played, it was 4-0 and game over.

A sloppy pass by Balmer was picked up by Thorne and he carved the Oldham defence wide open with a through ball for Campbell. For once Goram did respond and charged out but it ricocheted back off the striker and into the empty net. You know it's going to be your day when you get those sorts of breaks.

The home fans were, understandably, growing frustrated, and Campbell didn't help matters by standing directly in front of them with his arms stretched high in the air. He was pelted by anything the Oldham fans had to hand – including a pork pie. Police waded in and took several fans into custody and Campbell was booked for his part.

The Latics badly needed to steady the sinking ship but instead they found themselves down to ten men straight from the kick-off as 29-year-old Appleby was sent off for an appalling high lunge on Gabbidon. It was his second yellow card but it could easily have earned him a red card on its own. Manager Mick Wadsworth said afterwards, "Matt is not a baby, he is a senior player who should have a lot more sense."

Wadsworth took immediate action as former Bluebirds player Tony Carss came on for Argentine midfielder Colusso. Carss, who played 50 games for City in 1997 and 1998, was a late inclusion in the Oldham squad after David Beharall pulled a muscle during the warm-up.

Graham Kavanagh hit a speculative 30-yard dipper which Goram managed to tip over before Oldham enjoyed a rare attack. Allan Smart cannoned a header against the bar and Corazzin headed the rebound woefully into Alexander's arms. The ball was cleared up the pitch and seconds later City made it a fantastic first-half fistful of five.

This time it was lively Kav who dinked in the perfect cross from the edge of the area and Leo was there to head high into the net.

Thorne could have made it six in injury time as Goram got down well to push his effort wide and from the corner Chris Armstrong lashed clear.

The Oldham supporters – the ones who hadn't already darted for the nearest exit – booed their team off the pitch. That was no surprise, but I'm not sure I've ever before witnessed fans boo their players as they came back out for the second half as well!

Goram can't have been looking forward to the second half, not least because he had to endure 45 minutes of being within earshot of the City fans. After "there's only one Andy Goram" came "there's only two Andy Gorams", a reference to the keeper's battle with a mild form of schizophrenia, and chants of "Scotland's number ten". Goram didn't rise to the bait and stood with his hands on his hips.

Oldham brought on midfielder Lee Duxbury for striker Smart as they turned to damage limitation.

Prior cleared an Oldham corner off the line before Legg burst through and should have made it six. He latched on to Prior's thump downfield, bundled through three challenges but blasted over the bar with Leo much better placed to his side.

On 57 minutes Fortune-West sent a header over before three minutes later Campbell shot forward with the ball at his feet but this time Goram was out fast to claim the loose ball.

A sixth goal was around the corner, though, on 64 minutes after some more schoolboy defending. Armstrong's back-pass was pathetically under-hit and Campbell was able to race on to it, take it past Goram and slide into an empty net. It was the finish of a man bursting with confidence.

Number seven of an incredible afternoon – and Campbell's hat-trick – was only nine minutes in the making. Again the loan man's pace was just too much for the Oldham defence as he came tearing through from Gabbidon's pass. Julian Baudet managed to deflect his initial shot on to the bar but it fell nicely for Campbell to bury his third of the game.

It was the second time that rampant City had scored seven in the 2001/02 season having embarrassed Rushden & Diamonds 7-1 in the LDV Vans Trophy in October.

A minute later the few home fans left did have something to cheer when Balmer steered in a soft consolation goal from a free kick. Celebratory music blasted out from the PA system, causing a chuckle or two from the City faithful.

City played keep-ball for the final 15 minutes, though James Collins almost added an eighth goal from a cross by fellow substitute Michael Simpkins.

The afternoon got better for City when news filtered through that Bristol City had lost at Notts County. There was now just one point between the teams and dreams of the play-offs were back on. When Lennie took the job that gap was eight points. One of the game's wisest craftsmen was working his magic.

The result goes down as City's best away win since joining the Football League in 1920. There were 7-0 and 7-1 wins at Torquay and Watford in the 1945/46 season, but as there was no relegation and promotion in that immediate post-war campaign the victories do not form part of City's official record.

Wadsworth, reflecting on Oldham's first home defeat in the league since taking over as coach in November, pulled no punches. "I have never had a day like this as a manager or coach," he said. "We made a cow's backside of it in every sense."

Delighted Lawrence, meanwhile, said, "This shows we mean business, and sends a message out to our rivals. Now we have to carry it through. Every time we went forward we looked like we would score."

Stunning City went on to win six and draw one of their final seven league games, which saw them finish nicely nestled in fourth position, eventually ten points ahead of seventh-placed Bristol City and just one behind second-placed Reading.

v Stoke City 2-1

37

28 April 2002. Attendance: 21,245
Second Division Play-Off Semi-Final, First Leg.
Britannia Stadium

CARDIFF CITY:

Neil Alexander
Rhys Weston
Spencer Prior
Scott Young
Gary Croft
Graham Kavanagh
Willie Boland
Peter Thorne (James Collins 90)
Mark Bonner
Leo Fortune-West
Robert Earnshaw (Andy Campbell 77)
Subs not used: Jason Bowen, Leyton
Maxwell, Stephen Bywater

STOKE CITY:

Neil Cutler
Wayne Thomas
Peter Handyside
Sergei Shtaniuk
Clive Clarke
Bjarni Gudjonsson (Jurgen Vandeurzen 81)
Tony Dinning
James O'Connor
Marc Goodfellow (Deon Burton 77)
Chris Iwelumo (Rikhardur Dadason 84)
Andy Cooke
Subs not used: Jani Viander,
Ian Brightwell

Referee: Tony Leake (Darwen)

ERRATIC CENTRE-BACK Spencer Prior scrambled off the line in the dying moments to ensure Cardiff clinched this superb result in the Second Division play-off semi-finals.

The Bluebirds had survived a deluge of pressure from Stoke, thanks in no small part to the inspirational form of goalkeeper Neil Alexander. Breakaway goals by little and large combination Robert Earnshaw and Leo Fortune-West had given City a shock 2-0 lead.

But the Potters turned the screw and when Deon Burton hammered in with six minutes remaining, City's advantage looked fragile. Only last-gasp heroics by the giant Prior made sure the Bluebirds went into the return match with their beaks in front.

One foot in the Millennium Stadium final – or so fans thought. City's second leg implosion has soured the victory at the Britannia Stadium. But time is a healer and now supporters can look back and doff their hats to what was a joyous day in Staffordshire.

City had enjoyed a stunning end-of-season charge to book their place in the play-offs as they went in search of back-to-back promotions. With Sam Hammam's cash blurring all sense of perspective, supporters had been promised a promotion challenge.

In had come a clutch of expensive players including Prior, £650,000 from Manchester City, and Stoke pair Graham Kavanagh and Peter Thorne for £1m and £1.7m. Des 'Disco' Hamilton, Leyton Maxwell and Michael Simpkins looked like good free signings while Andy Campbell was also bought in March after an electrifying loan spell.

But City had slumped to 11th position, five points shy of the play-offs, before Alan Cork was sacked as manager following a dismal 4-0 defeat at Wigan in February. In came the experienced and thoughtful Lennie Lawrence – and the turnaround was immediate.

The Bluebirds embarked on a 13-game unbeaten run which included ten wins to finish in fourth position, just one point behind second-placed Reading. Thirty-three points from a possible 39 – not a bad way to start your managerial reign.

But despite City's sensational form, there was plenty of confidence in the red corner as well.

Stoke had won seven of their last 11 and boasted the best defensive record in the league, having conceded just 40 goals. Gudjon Thordarson, their Icelandic manager, certainly wasn't short of belief. "No one can stop us if we play to the best of our ability," he had boldly written in the match programme.

It was City's first involvement in the play-offs since 1997 when they were beaten by Northampton Town in the Third Division. It was a different story for Stoke, though, who were under pressure having failed in the end of the season knock-outs the previous two seasons.

There was plenty of buzz about the fixture. Cardiff and Stoke had developed a bizarre and bitter rivalry despite almost 150 miles separating the two cities. It had started in 2000 when an otherwise routine Second Division fixture was tarnished by some of the worst crowd violence at a football match in recent years. The pot was stirred when Kavanagh and Thorne made the switch from the Potteries to South Wales within the space of a couple of months.

The history between the club's supporters and the importance of the game meant a huge police operation for this semi-final. Just 2,500 Cardiff supporters were allowed to travel – and only on coaches under armed escort like hostages travelling through a war zone. The convoy set off at 9am from Ninian Park, a full five hours before kick-off. When the coaches did arrive at the Britannia supporters were greeted by 200 police officers – many wearing balaclavas – helicopters and horses. It was an intimidating atmosphere and added an extra edge to an already tense mood.

Stoke cranked up the volume inside the ground by parading former club favourites including Gordon Banks to the crowd. There was also a rousing rendition of club anthem 'Delilah' with the City fans joining in and acting as conductors.

City could have been forgiven for starting cautiously in the Britannia bear pit, but Lawrence's three-pronged strike-force of Thorne, Fortune-West and Earnshaw immediately took the game to the Potters. Fortune-West had a good chance inside the first minute after a trademark head down from Thorne but the big striker miscued his effort. A minute later Thorne fired a warning shot straight at Neil Cutler.

The home side looked to be finding their feet in the swirling wind and rain and won a corner which came to nothing. At the other end, Rhys Weston of all people caused a panic when he embarked on a sterling run from deep inside his own half.

City favourites Thorne and Kavanagh were, predictably, given a torrid time from the home fans. But Thorne found the perfect reply by creating the opening goal on 12 minutes.

The move was started by Kavanagh on the halfway line, who played a short pass to Earnshaw in some space behind the Stoke midfield. Earnie knocked inside to Thorne, who found the Welshman's darting run with an instinctive first time ball through the heart of the defence. Earnie was under pressure from three players in stripes but neatly tucked his shot into the bottom corner. It was Earnie's 15th goal of a decent season – and his first following his return to action after a hamstring injury disrupted his campaign.

From then on it was Stoke who made all the running. Five minutes later Marc Goodfellow pounced on a loose ball but his low shot from the edge of the area was dealt with comfortably enough by Alexander.

Chris Iwelumo then headed wide from a central position from 18 yards before City were given a huge let-off on 20 minutes. The ball broke loose after a Prior challenge and the lively Goodfellow crossed for Bjarni Gudjonsson but the manager's son got his feet in a tangle and shot well wide from just 12 yards with the goal begging. Daddy's boy must have had his pocket money docked after a torrid game from start to finish.

Iwelumo sent a shot from the edge of the six-yard box wide before City came desperately close to squeezing into a 2-0 lead against the run of play. Kavanagh's free kick from outside the box was only half cleared and headed back goalwards by Mark Bonner. Leo, with his back to goal, flicked it on but saw his smart effort come back off the post.

The game became frantic as Stoke tried desperately to pinch an equaliser before half-time. Gudjonsson and Clive Clarke were booked in quick succession. Alexander kept out efforts from Wayne Thomas and James O'Connor before Iwelumo glanced a header just inches wide from Gudjonsson's free kick.

There was a torrential downpour during the half-time break. As a section of Stoke fans darted for cover, the City fans mocked, "You're afraid of water!"

Stoke came at City from the start of the second half and Alexander saved a firm Thomas drive from 20 yards after five minutes. Alexander then capped a superb personal display with an excellent one-handed save at full stretch from O'Connor after a mazy run by the midfielder.

Nine times out of ten that effort would have been good enough to make it 1-1 – but just before the hour City stunned the Potters with a priceless second goal. Earnshaw went down under a Thomas challenge and Kav curled in the free kick from the edge of the area. Prior got a good head on it from six yards out but Cutler was able to push it on to his post. Leo was in the right place though to smash into the roof of the net from two yards – right in front of the delirious City fans.

Unfortunately that was the cue for Stoke's Neanderthals to turn nasty and the match was stopped for five minutes as riot police waded in with batons and shields. For once it wasn't the City fans causing the bulk of the disturbance. In scenes resembling London riots, police surrounded the pitch to keep the thugs at bay as missiles rained. Thankfully, it will be difficult for fans who have only started to travel away with Cardiff in the last few seasons to associate with this type of madness. For a few seasons it was all too common.

The break did City no favours and when play resumed it was the Potters pushing forward again and Goodfellow brought another sharp save out of Alexander in the 73rd minute.

Now 2-0 down and with an away leg to come, Stoke knew they had to go for it, but by doing so they would inevitably open themselves up to the counter-attack. With Earnshaw in the team, City possessed the perfect dynamite weapon to exploit any gaps. Minutes later Thorne put Earnshaw through but for once he was a little slow out of the blocks and Cutler was off his line fast enough to smother the shot. If Earnie had been as clinical as he had been early on then City would surely have been celebrating a place in the play-off final.

Earnshaw was replaced by £1m man Campbell on 77 minutes while Stoke brought on Burton, who was on loan from Derby. He had spent a month on loan at Ninian Park as a fresh-faced 20-year-old at the end of 1996, scoring twice on his debut before heading back to Portsmouth. Belgian Jurgen Vandeurzen also came on for Gudjonsson.

Stoke threw everything they had at City in the closing stages – and eventually the pressure paid off as the subs combined six minutes from time. Vandeurzen's swirling cross was misjudged by Prior, who had been otherwise excellent, and the ball landed at Burton's feet for the Jamaican international to gleefully half-volley into the roof of the net.

Suddenly City's lead looked anything but impenetrable as Stoke laid siege on Alexander's goal. Five minutes of injury time were announced, largely due to the trouble in the stands. There were some terrifying moments. Prior cemented the man of the match award when he raced back to spectacularly hook off the line after Burton had Alexander beaten again with a header.

Thorne was replaced by defender James Collins as City switched to an unorthodox 9-1-0 formation.

There were wild celebrations from the City fans at the final whistle. Cardiff ruled Britannia and a place in the Millennium Stadium final appeared almost a formality. The Potters had pushed hard and shown plenty of passion, but City still looked like the better of the two sides. *The Daily Mirror* said, "There was just a feeling of superior quality about Lennie Lawrence's in-form team. Their investments in the past few years are paying off with annual dividends."

With the benefit of many failed play-off attempts since, that confidence was always misplaced. A single goal lead going into the second leg of a play-off is far from insurmountable. Wise Lawrence knew better. "It's not all over yet," he said. "We shall go flat out to get the first goal again in the second leg as is our method with our three-forward system. Stoke threw the kitchen sink at us at the end and could even have equalised. They deserved a goal but we deserved to win, and we have had a good start to the tie."

Thordarson said the first goal in the second leg would be vital, "Some people might think that the job is done. But there's still 90 minutes to go."

The second leg was nothing short of a disaster for City. The Bluebirds appeared to have done enough to book their final ticket. "Would supporters please stay off the pitch so Sam and the lads can do a lap of honour," said tannoy man Ali Yassine moments before O'Connor levelled the tie in the last minute of normal time. Souleymane Oulare bagged the winner with five minutes of injury time left to leave Cardiff in tears.

The two extremes of football emotion separated by just three days. That's life as a Cardiff fan for you.

v Bristol City 0-0

38

(Cardiff won 1-0 on aggregate)

13 May 2003. Attendance: 16,307
Second Division Play-Off Semi-Final, Second Leg.
Ashton Gate

CARDIFF CITY:

Neil Alexander
Rhys Weston (Gary Croft 37)
Spencer Prior
Danny Gabbidon
Andy Legg (Mark Bonner 76)
Willie Boland
Graham Kavanagh
Gareth Whalley
Chris Barker
Robert Earnshaw (Andy Campbell 86)
Peter Thorne
Subs not used: Martyn Margetson, Jason Bowen

Referee: Jeff Winter

BRISTOL CITY:

Steve Phillips
Louis Carey
Tony Butler
Daniel Coles
Matt Hill (Peter Beadle 78)
Scott Murray
Tom Doherty
Joe Burnell (Kevin Amankwaah 71)
Brian Tinnion
Christian Roberts (Leroy Lita 60)
Lee Peacock
Subs not used: Mickey Bell, Mike Stowell

FOR TENSION, nerves and ultimately magnificent joy, this goalless play-off draw at City's closset English rivals is well worth its place in the history books. About 1,700 City fans made the short journey over the Severn Bridge with a bit of hope but not a lot of expectation. Peter Thorne's fine header in the first leg at Ninian Park had given the Bluebirds the most slender of advantages on the road to the Millennium Stadium Second Division play-off final.

But fans feared that a 1-0 head start at Ashton Gate was not going to be enough. The memories of play-off heartache against Stoke City just 12 months earlier were still raw. City had taken a lead into the second leg of that tie, too, but imploded spectacularly.

This time the challenge looked even tougher. Lennie Lawrence's City had finished the season poorly, taking just two points from their final five league games and scoring just once. They hadn't won since mid-April. Pundits often say that play-off success is all about momentum. City had crawled over the line with little conviction.

Bristol City, meanwhile, were a decent side. They had finished third in the league, just three points behind second-placed Crewe. No team had won more league games (15) or scored as many goals (43) in front of their own supporters. They had twice beaten City 2-0 in the league, had lifted the LDV Vans Trophy at the Millennium Stadium just five weeks earlier and had won their last eight home games.

And City could draw no comfort from history, either. The Bluebirds had not won at Ashton Gate since 1969.

But despite all the omens pointing to failure, this heroic City team somehow kept its nerve to produce a defensive display of sheer brilliance. The home side had the vast bulk of possession – at times it was a tide of red – yet somehow Lennie's lads limited their rivals to just two serious attempts. Three hours of football and the teams were separated by just one solitary goal. City had booked their ticket to a dream play-off final in their home city.

"We'll never see you again," taunted the delirious City supporters as the frustrated home fans filed out, their season brought to an unexpected halt. Many of the Bristol City players slumped to the ground in despair while the City heroes at the other end of the spectrum of emotions embraced and danced.

Ten minutes of celebration passed in a flash before the City players returned to the pitch with "We're Going to Cardiff" banners.

There was sheer delight – and a bit of shock – on the face of every City player. But four Bluebirds, all club legends in their own right, really stood out: Andy Legg, Thorne, Robert Earnshaw and Graham Kavanagh. Earnie somersaulted and sambaed, Leggy was passion personified and for Kav and Thorne there was relief. The best mates had both suffered play-off misery in the last three consecutive seasons.

But the biggest cheer, as ever was the case, was reserved for Sam Hammam. The crackerjack chairman allowed the players their moment before emerging from the tunnel with his trusty Welsh flag. A couple of hours later, when the City fans had finally made it back to Cardiff and into the Lansdowne pub to continue the party, there was Sam again making sure he didn't miss a single pat on the back. Crazy days indeed.

With hundreds of fans watching on the big screen back at Ninian Park, the evening had started with plenty of tension in the air but also plenty of noise. City wore blue after a bizarre poll on the official website gave fans the choice between their traditional colours or their away colours, yellow. More than 90 per cent went for blue.

The game kicked off at a blistering pace. Bristol City's Scott Murray, who had scored 27 goals that season, was hacked down by Leggy inside the opening minute. Murray was not a favourite with City fans after he celebrated a goal in 2001 at Ninian by running the full length of the pitch performing the Ayatollah.

City had been woefully slow starters for almost the entire season – but for once they had begun with a buzz about their play. Thorne headed a Rhys Weston cross comfortably wide in the game's first noteworthy chance.

The Bluebirds were trying to frustrate the Robins by playing keep-ball but it nearly went all wrong after 14 minutes. Kavanagh was robbed in midfield by Brian Tinnion who then fed Christian Roberts. The former Bluebird skipped past the desperate challenges of Weston and Kavanagh before testing Neil Alexander with a fierce drive. The City keeper, playing his 100th game for the club, got across well to save.

Bristol continued to enjoy much of the possession but their cutting edge had deserted them at the worst possible time. Too often the final ball was not good enough. It was City who were looking most threatening on the counter-attack, even if *The Independent* did report that the Bluebirds "flapped around with little direction".

Gareth Whalley fired a shot against the side netting from a tight angle on 26 minutes after a blunder by Daniel Coles. Minutes later 36-goal Earnshaw met a lofted ball over the top by Thorne with a first-time volley that dipped just over the bar.

Earnie had been sparked into life. Three minutes later he had the audacity to try a snap overhead kick from a Chris Barker cross and a Thorne knock-down. The connection was true enough but he was slightly off target. Earnie, after an electric start to the season, had scored just once in nine games but that had done nothing to dent his confidence.

City suffered a blow on 37 minutes when Weston was forced off after a collision. Left-footed Gary Croft, who is now working as an actor, filled in at right-back.

Legg almost found the net direct from a corner before a great move between Thorne, Earnshaw and Kavanagh almost broke the deadlock with eight minutes of the half remaining. Thorne charged upfield, found Earnshaw, who flicked the ball to Kav and Steve Phillips did well to tip his instinctive shot over.

Such was the dominance of City centre-backs Spencer Prior and Danny Gabbidon that the Robins had to wait until the 42nd minute for their first genuine chance. Joe Burnell whipped in a decent cross but Tom Doherty didn't get enough on his glancing header and the ball fizzed past the upright. It was Doherty's mistake that led to City's goal in the first leg – how he would have loved to have made amends.

A minute before half-time Matt Hill had to recover well to scramble clear after his poor headed back-pass looked for a second to have gifted Earnie an opening.

Bristol-based Tony Robinson, most famous as Baldrick from *Blackadder*, entertained supporters at half-time and he would have been hoping that Robins boss Danny Wilson had a cunning plan up his sleeve.

With the tension increasing on and off the pitch, the second half began aggressively. Roberts escaped a booking for chopping down Croft, but Croft himself was not shown the same leniency when he went into Jeff Winter's book for a high challenge on Doherty.

City continued to throw players in front of everything. Irish pair Willie Boland and Kav had an iron grip on the centre of midfield. They were simply outstanding. Thorne and Earnshaw gave Bristol's defence no time on the ball by persistently chasing and harrying.

With half an hour left, Wilson moved to change his attack. Off came Roberts, who had looked dangerous early on but was now losing his cool, and on came 18-year-old starlet Leroy Lita.

City were now being pinned back and it took a wonder save by Alexander on 68 minutes to keep the scores at 0-0. Veteran midfielder Tinnion threw himself at a Louis Carey cross from the right and the Scottish keeper was at full stretch to palm the point-blank diving header out for a corner. "Scotland's number one" bellowed the City faithful.

Lawrence was on his feet urging his troops forward to kill the tie and Earnie almost created something out of nothing when he tried a half-volley from 25 yards which Phillips just managed to grasp under the bar.

The game was now entering the period when managers earn their crust. Lightning quick winger Kevin Amankwaah was brought on for Bristol with 20 minutes remaining. Murray switched to the left in a desperate attempt to create an opening. Five minutes later a jittery Lawrence made a move of his own, Mark Bonner replacing Legg in a bid to tighten up the midfield. Just three minutes later Wilson went for broke by switching defender Hill with striker Peter Beadle.

The Robins were playing a 3-3-4 formation and the crosses were flying into the area almost relentlessly. A frustrated Murray was trying shots from anywhere. Alexander, though he had been criticised by some City fans throughout the season, was the calmest man in the house and his handling was faultless.

The final ten minutes were excruciating for Cardiff fans – but Bristol City could not break down the rock solid blue wall. Andy Campbell came on for Earnie with four minutes remaining to add a bit of new energy up front.

Three minutes of added-on time were announced. Thorne had a chance to put the icing on the cake when he broke clear but screwed his shot wide. That would have just been greedy, anyway.

When Campbell won a corner towards the end of injury time the cheer from the City fans was so loud that Kav thought the final whistle had been blown and fell to his knees in delight. He must have felt a bit daft having to get to his feet to continue.

But just moments later the final whistle did come and City celebrated a famous triumph. There have been some wonderful occasions of players celebrating with the City fans over the years – the FA Cup semi-final in 2008 springs to mind – but this was special. There was togetherness between supporter and star which is too often sorely missing in today's game.

Lennie hailed his Lionhearts. "It was our best defensive performance since I've been at the club," he told the *Western Mail*. "All credit to Bristol. They threw everything at us but we were absolutely determined and they met an unmovable force. I expected the pressure to last for 15 to 20 minutes at the start of the second half but it lasted for about 35 to 40. Normally we would have conceded but we held on superbly.'"

Amid the rejoicing there were uncharacteristic words of comfort from Hammam. "My heart goes out to Bristol City," he told the *Daily Telegraph*. "They finished third and they are the ones who should be promoted. This devalues the competition, we all have to feel sorry for them."

But Hammam did find time to wheel out some of his usual patter. "This is the game for the whole of Cardiff and the whole of Wales," he said. "What we can achieve is something great for the whole of Welsh football."

The thought of a showpiece final at the still gleaming Millennium Stadium, the 74,000 capacity arena supporters had watched grow from the ashes of the Arms Park, exhilarated the capital's population.

City had achieved a feat that many thought was impossible. And the rest, as they say, is history.

v QPR 1-0

25 May 2003. Attendance: 66,096
Second Division Play-Off Final. Millennium Stadium,
Cardiff

CARDIFF CITY:
Neil Alexander
Rhys Weston (Gary Croft 70)
Danny Gabbidon
Spencer Prior
Chris Barker
Willie Boland
Graham Kavanagh
Gareth Whalley
Andy Legg (Mark Bonner 116)
Robert Earnshaw (Andy Campbell 79)
Peter Thorne
Subs not used: Martyn Margetson, Jason Bowen

Referee: Howard Webb (South Yorkshire)

QUEENS PARK RANGERS:
Chris Day
Stephen Kelly
Danny Shittu
Clarke Carlisle
Gino Padula (Tom Williams 79)
Kevin Gallen
Marc Bircham
Steve Palmer
Kevin McLeod
Richard Pacquette (Andy Thomson 60)
Paul Furlong
Subs not used: Nick Culkin, Brett Angell, Terrell Forbes

LOVE THEM or hate them, the play-offs have a never-ceasing ability to create drama, tension and heroes by the bucketload. Paul Dickov was the last-minute hero for Manchester City in 1999, Dean Windass fired Hull City to the Premier League in 2008 and on 25 May 2003 it was the unlikely figure of Andy Campbell who earned legend status for Cardiff City.

Campbell had signed for City for almost £1m from Middlesbrough the previous season after impressing on loan, scoring six goals in five explosive games. But Campbell was forced to play second fiddle to star striker Robert Earnshaw during the 2002/03 campaign and had managed just six goals in 40 appearances (25 as a substitute, to be fair) before the play-off final.

There were grumbles around the Millennium Stadium from the City fans when 35-goal Earnshaw was taken off on 79 minutes by boss Lennie Lawrence. Earnie, who had scored a winner for Wales against Germany at the stadium almost a year ago to the day, shook his head in disbelief as he trudged off.

QPR had been the better side in a hard-fought if unspectacular play-off showpiece. The 35,000 City fans watching their team in their home city were preparing for another addition in the book of hard luck tales.

But this was to be Campbell's career highlight – and one of the all-time City success stories. With just six minutes of extra time remaining and the scores locked at 0-0, leaving penalties looming, the carrot-haired striker ran on to Gareth Whalley's ball over the top. One bounce, two bounces, then an inch-perfect lob over the QPR goalkeeper from the edge of the area. It was a goal of sheer quality which earned City promotion into the second tier of English football for the first time in 18 years.

Sam Hammam had splashed the cash and delivered on his promises. Goodbye Mansfield Town, Stockport County and Cheltenham Town. Hello Nottingham Forest,

Derby County and Sheffield United. Sam's darlings had won two promotions in three seasons and were back in the big time. "ONE-DERS" screamed the front page of the *Welsh Daily Mirror* with a photo of an ecstatic Campbell with the cup the following day.

That was probably the peak of Hammam's six years at City. As he paraded around the Millennium turf before his adoring public, it seemed only a matter of time until the Bluebirds would take their place in the Premier League alongside Manchester United, Liverpool and Arsenal. But even that wasn't enough for Hammam. "The nation of Wales deserves a top-notch Premiership club but reaching the Premier League is only a step," he said. "We have the fan-base to take on any club in Europe, so our aim is not to be in the Premier League but to be in the top echelon of the Premier League and consequently in the Champions League. That is the only place which Welsh people will accept."

Madcap Hammam had done everything he could to steal the headlines in the build-up to City's biggest game in many years. It was widely reported that the Lebanese businessman had hoped to lead a march of thousands of City fans from Ninian Park to the Millennium Stadium before the match on the back of an elephant. In the end supporters had to make do with the Cwmaman Institute Silver Band leading the procession over the river and into battle in scenes reminiscent of *Braveheart*.

Vince Alm, chairman of the Cardiff City Supporters' Club at the time, told *The Wales on Sunday*, "We'd love to see Sam on the back of an elephant!" Earnshaw said, "He's (Hammam) a god in Wales now. He's turned everything right round for this club and if we go up it's down to him because it's his dream."

Just a few years later there would be plenty of supporters who would have been happier to see Hammam underneath an elephant than on top of one.

City went into the game having scraped past Bristol City 1-0 on aggregate in the semis. But their form prior to that two-legged tie was far from electric. The Bluebirds had lost three and drawn two in their previous five, including a dismal 3-0 home defeat against mid-table Colchester. Serious questions were being asked of boss Lawrence and his often unusual tactics.

Ian Holloway's Rangers, meanwhile, were the form team in the Second Division having lost just one of their last 14 games. They had finished a couple of points ahead of City. The omens didn't look good for City, who had won the toss to play in blue but were then allocated the 'unlucky' south end changing room at the stadium, though it was not as unlucky as it once was.

The Millennium started hosting major finals in 2001 while Wembley was being rebuilt – and the first 12 winners of major cup finals had all used the north changing rooms. The hoodoo was finally broken by Stoke in the Second Division final a year earlier.

The demand for tickets was huge. Systems crashed and fans queued for up to six hours to ensure they were there to witness City's big day. Rangers, too, managed to shift an impressive 31,000 tickets to make for a huge crowd of 66,096 and a raucous, tense atmosphere.

Much of the pre-match hype had focused on whether the National Anthems of England and Wales would be sung prior to kick-off. In the end, the Football League decided to scrap both. But such was the atmosphere inside the stadium – and indeed around the streets of Cardiff – that the row had paled into insignificance by the time Graham Kavanagh introduced 'dignitary' Tory minister Brian Mawhinney to the City squad. The tension must have robbed the sense from some fans as there were four marriage proposals, all shown on the big screen.

Despite City's poor form, Lawrence stuck with the same starting 11 which had battled valiantly over two legs against Bristol City. In central defence there was the experienced if a little one-paced Spencer Prior alongside Welsh international Danny Gabbidon. They had built up a steady partnership since Gabbidon had returned from a four-month absence following a back problem. Willie Boland was a consistent performer in the centre of midfield, Whalley offered a little creativity and Earnie was a goal machine, despite a drought of one goal in ten leading up to the final.

But it was Kavanagh and then-record signing Peter Thorne who were the lynchpins of this team. Both had signed from Stoke in 2001 and are remembered fondly by City fans. But the close friends were battling their own demons having suffered the heartbreak of losing in the play-offs for the previous three seasons, twice with Stoke and once with City. After finally breaking the run, man of the match Kav told *The Daily Mirror*, "It got to the stage where I hated the very words play-offs. But now – it's still an unbelievable feeling to have got through."

In fact Thorne nearly missed the game. The hard-knock striker, who scored 16 goals that season, including the crucial one in the semi-final win over Bristol, woke up on the morning of the match with a crick in his neck. Just as Lawrence was considering changing his team Thorne was given a painkilling injection which, thankfully, worked.

Significantly, QPR were without Richard Langley after the star midfielder was sent off in his team's play-off semi against Oldham. He was considered one of the best outfield players in the division and had scored the decisive goal in a 2-1 win against City at Ninian in April. Langley signed for Cardiff during the summer before later returning to Loftus Road in 2005.

City had the better of the early exchanges. Earnie snatched at a shot after a trademark Andy Legg long throw.

Yet it was QPR who forced the first meaningful save after just seven minutes. The Bluebirds defence was expecting Kevin Gallen, QPR's player of the year, to whip in a cross from a tight angle towards the corner flag but instead he lashed a shot goalwards and Neil Alexander did well to tip it over the crossbar.

Then on 25 minutes a long goal kick by Hoops number one Chris Day was flicked on and the usually dependable Gabbidon slipped, allowing 34-year-old forward Paul Furlong a decent sight on goal. He should have taken it closer to Alexander's goal but instead attempted a cheeky lob and was left red-faced as it sailed harmlessly over.

Despite some neat probing build-up play, City were struggling to get a foothold in the match. Too many long balls were being pumped up to the little and large combination of Thorne and Earnshaw and were being gobbled up by the excellent Rangers centre-backs Clarke Carlisle and Danny Shittu. Both were six feet-plus and were starting to earn the rave reviews which would later see them playing Premier League football.

But a couple of decent opportunities did fall City's way just before half-time. Legg, playing what turned out to be his last game for the club at the age of 36, side-stepped Stephen Kelly before delivering a dangerous cross from the left that Kavanagh headed over. Midfielder Whalley then saw his angled drive deflected out for a corner by Shittu.

Holloway's team started the second half well. Marc Bircham chipped in to Furlong, who showed neat control inside a congested penalty area. Gallen took over but in the end could not get it from under his feet and Alexander made light work of a tame shot towards the bottom corner. A minute later Furlong's close-range effort was blasted high and wide. City were surviving by the skin of their teeth as the Hoops fans cranked up the volume.

On 61 minutes Britain's brainiest footballer Clarke Carlisle played a deep free kick to the edge of the area and Furlong flicked it on. Kavanagh completely missed his kick when trying to hoof to safety and it fell to Gallen, who took one neat touch to the side before volleying just inches over.

Kav did, however, make amends moments later with a key challenge on Kevin McLeod as the midfielder prepared to let rip.

Without question, Rangers were on top. The fingernails of City supporters took a battering as the team in white pushed on for the winner their dominance probably deserved. They were tougher in the challenges and playing all the football.

City fans were baying for Lawrence to make a change but they were not expecting to see Campbell replace Earnshaw. It was a gamble by the experienced City boss – and he was about to cash in big time. For QPR, Tommy Williams replaced Padula.

Campbell almost made an immediate impact on 86 minutes when a punt forward was won in the air by Prior and Campbell looked to have a yard to spare on the six-yard line. He was eventually crowded out yet still managed to force a cross of sorts for Thorne. The forward won it but could not get enough on his header with Shittu and Furlong in close proximity. There was a healthy shout for handball, particularly from Prior, but Howard Webb was having none of it.

Then came QPR's big chance to clinch promotion in the last minute of injury time. Prior, who was not averse to the odd calamity during his time with City, tried to calmly head back to Alexander but was way, way short. Substitute Andy Thompson, aware that he had three blue shirts closing in on him, tried to loop a header over Alexander who had come off his line but the effort bounced agonisingly past the post. It is hard to see how Prior could have played for the club again if that had dropped in. Prior gave a wry smile, only too aware of the fact.

Campbell looked bright and set up Whalley, who failed to connect properly while at the other end another Prior slip let in Thompson but his pass to Furlong hit Gabbidon. Furlong had annoyed Gabbidon before the game by intimating that he knew nothing about the rising star. "He knows who I am now," Gabbidon said afterwards.

Carlisle then came close, heading Gallen's perfect cross wide. And there was still time for the save of the match. A wicked Kavanagh free kick was met by the busy Prior, whose downward header from point-blank range was superbly saved by Day at the near post. Day had enjoyed a relatively quiet afternoon but his reactions were razor sharp when required.

The match looked for all the world to be heading for penalties. Alexander had never once saved a penalty for City and only once dived the right way. It did not bode well – and the strain on the faces of the City fans showed it.

Four minutes after the turnaround, Williams blew a golden opportunity for Rangers. The defender embarked on a dazzling, if slightly fortuitous, run from inside his own half and held off Gary Croft near the byline. He had to pull it back for either Furlong or Andy Thomson, who were waiting unmarked. Instead he lost his composure, went for glory and hit the side netting.

Then, after almost two hours of tense football, Whalley picked the perfect pass and Campbell struck his incredible winner. The ball seemed to hang in the air for an eternity before mayhem among the City supporters.

There were still six minutes for QPR to salvage their season and bring an abrupt end to the wild celebrations, but they looked like a beaten team. Then the final whistle came and 18 years of stagnation were over. "We're going to the show, baby," screamed little Earnie, but it was Campbell that everyone wanted a piece of.

Campbell scored just three more goals for City in 43 appearances as his career nose-dived. Fortunes can change so quickly in football.

A podium was erected on the pitch and the fireworks crackled as Kav lifted the cup. Prior looked like his head was about to explode, understandably so when you consider he bagged a reported £250,000 promotion bonus.

"It wasn't a classic match," Lawrence said, "but no one connected with Cardiff will ever forget it." Ain't that the truth.

The following day much of the paper talk was about how long it would take City to make the final step and earn promotion to the Premier League. There seemed no stopping the juggernaut CCFC. A new stadium was surely now inevitable and we were about to put Wales firmly on the map, or so we thought anyway.

Two days later City were splashed all over the back pages again as it was revealed that a rogue fire alarm may have played its part in City's triumph. Neil MacNamara, an ex-minder of Hammam, had been spotted on CCTV triggering the alarm at the hotel where QPR were staying the night before the game, causing the players to get up at 3am. MacNamara was later given a five-year ban from attending football matches. It could only happen at City.

Sunday 25 May 2003 is a day City fans will never forget. Winning promotion is special. Doing it by the play-offs is even better. To do it in your own city … well that's fairytale stuff. Hammam had brought an end to a generation of yo-yoing between the bottom two divisions – but in years to come it would prove that it came at a huge financial cost.

40 v **Middlesbrough** 2-0

9 March 2008. Attendance: 32,896
FA Cup Quarter-Final. Riverside Stadium

CARDIFF CITY:

Peter Enckelman
Kevin McNaughton (Darcy Blake 87)
Roger Johnson
Glenn Loovens
Peter Whittingham
Tony Capaldi
Gavin Rae
Aaron Ramsey
Stephen McPhail
Paul Parry (Trevor Sinclair 82)
Jimmy Floyd Hasselbaink (Steve Thompson 76)
Subs not used: Michael Oakes, Darren Purse

MIDDLESBROUGH:

Mark Schwarzer
Luke Young
David Wheater
Emanuel Pogatetz
Robert Huth
Gary O'Neil (Adam Johnson 59)
Stewart Downing
Julio Arca
Fabio Rochemback
Afonso Alves (Mido 46)
Tuncay
Subs not used: Ross Turnbull, Jonathan Grounds, George Boateng

Referee: Mike Dean (Wirral)

THIS WAS the day when City fans dared to dream the unthinkable. More than 3,000 supporters got up at the crack of dawn to make the 300 mile journey to the North East for City's first FA Cup quarter-final since 1927. Many had brought inflatables and giant tinfoil cut-outs of the famous trophy.

Optimism was high. The FA Cup had already thrown up some stunning shocks that season. Just the day before Barnsley had inexplicably dumped holders Chelsea out of the competition to book their place in the semi-finals. All the other big guns had also fallen by the wayside. Surely City couldn't repeat the feat at Premier League Middlesbrough, could they? You bet they could – and with consummate ease. Early goals by the outstanding Peter Whittingham and Roger Johnson set the Riverside Stadium bouncing and City fans into dreamland.

Out of nowhere, City, not previously famed for their cup exploits other than an historic triumph 81 years previous, had secured a place in the last four at Wembley. And with just one Premier League team, Portsmouth, remaining in the semi-finals for the first time in 100 years, it really was anybody's game.

"I am going to Wembley and cannot believe it," beamed veteran striker Jimmy Floyd Hasselbaink after the win.

City had beaten Chasetown, Hereford and Wolves to reach the last eight of the competition – hardly the toughest draw imaginable, but a decent run all the same.

But their form was poor heading to Middlesbrough with just one win in seven and four games without a goal. The effects of a paper thin squad and a long season were taking their toll and even chairman Peter Ridsdale conceded that reaching the play-offs was unlikely.

Off the pitch, the club faced a High Court trial over a £24m loan to creditors Langston, represented by former chairman Sam Hammam. The very survival of the club was being questioned – not for the first time. Perfect timing, then, for an uplifting cup run to galvanise the club.

On a personal note, the day would prove to be an unusual one. I had made my way back to Cardiff from Eastbourne, where I was studying at the time, to travel up on one of the Valley Rams coaches as I didn't trust my car to do a 660-mile round trip. Two hours into the journey and on to my third can of Carling, I received a call from Cardiff City media manager Barrie McAuliffe asking if I would do a match report for the official website from the Riverside press box. I had been doing a bit of work for the club from time to time in exchange for the occasional free ticket and Barrie had to do some video work. I had a match ticket in my pocket and wanted to be in among the fans for such a special match. And I was hardly dressed for the occasion either wearing my blue Joma shirt and jeans, but I reluctantly agreed.

After a stop-off in a village pub outside Middlesbrough, we finally made it to the Riverside and I picked up a laptop off Barrie before taking my place in the press box next to the great and good of football writers from all the big titles – still in my Cardiff top and undoubtedly stinking of booze and cigarettes. I don't suppose I did much to change the rugged image of the club that day.

The match had all the ingredients of an upset. City's recent form was poor, but Boro were struggling in the league, above the drop zone only by virtue of the poor standard of the other teams.

Boss Gareth Southgate was under pressure from the fans and a rare Riverside 33,000 full house did little to settle the home team's nerves. Dave Jones made three changes to the side which had drawn at Crystal Palace during the week. Seventeen-year-old Aaron Ramsey came in for old boy Trevor Sinclair, Gavin Rae replaced Ricardo Scimeca and Hasselbaink was chosen ahead of Steve Thompson.

City had Boro under control from as early as the fifth minute and Ramsey made some encouraging surges forward before Whittingham's magnificent goal after nine minutes set the tone for the rest of the afternoon.

Poor defending by Mark Schwarzer and Robert Huth gave full-back Tony Capaldi the chance to launch a long throw into the area. Julio Arca made the initial header but it only went as far as Stephen McPhail, who won the ball with his forearm, but that went unnoticed by referee Mike Dean. It fell to Whittingham, who showed phenomenal close control to create space with a little drag-back before twisting and turning past Luke Young, Fabio Rochemback and Arca and curling a deft shot into the top corner off the post. Of all the goals the genius Whittingham scored in a City shirt, it has to be up there as one of the best.

I let out a yelp of joy from my elevated position surrounded by suits – but how I longed to be in the away end where unrestrained scenes of jubilation were unfolding.

From that moment, you just knew that it was going to be City's day. Jones's men started to play with a swagger. It is a cliché, but if you had watched the game not knowing which team was from the Premier League, you would have definitely gone for City.

McPhail bossed the centre of the park and Glenn Loovens was a colossus in defence.

Hasselbaink, who spent two years at Boro between 2004 and 2006, nearly made it two just a couple of minutes later when he met Capaldi's cross with a stooping header just seven yards out, but the 36-year-old's effort fell just the wrong side of the post. On 20 minutes good work by Ramsey saw him feed Paul Parry, whose shot went just wide.

With Boro heads already down, it came as no surprise when City doubled their advantage three minutes later through super Johnson. The centre-back got the wrong side of Emanuel Pogatetz and dived to head Whittingham's free kick back across Schwarzer and in at the far post. Booming renditions of 'Que Sera Sera' echoed around the Riverside as the natives grew increasingly restless.

There was, at last, some sort of a reaction from the woeful home side, though little to seriously concern Peter Enckelman in the City goal. The Finnish keeper had just one meaningful save to make after a speculative shot from £12m man Afonso Alves.

England winger Stewart Downing was off target with a free kick and appeals for a penalty when Alves hit the deck under a Kevin McNaughton challenge were waved away before the half-time whistle, which was greeted by boos. Southgate replaced Alves with Mido at half-time, though the Egyptian forward did not fare much better.

The home side came out with fists pumping the air as if to signal that a rousing fight-back could be on the cards, but their enthusiasm soon waned. They needed to score early to rattle Cardiff, but Southgate's men rarely looked capable of doing that.

The second half lacked the excitement of the first, but that was fine as far as the City fans were concerned, who continued to enjoy a party of a lifetime. Instead it was City who continued to look the greater threat in attack.

On 53 minutes Whittingham skipped past his man and dragged it back for McPhail on the edge of the area. The City skipper curled a low shot which appeared to strike the hand of Rochemback yet nothing was given.

Boro came close on the hour just as their play was becoming more desperate. Hasselbaink's handball gifted the locals a free kick just a yard outside the area and Rochemback missed the upright by a whisker.

As each minute passed chants of "We're the famous Cardiff City and we're off to Wembley" became ever more believable.

Many Middlesbrough fans were already heading for the exits as Southgate stood helplessly rubbing his chin. City grew slightly more cagey as the game went on but Boro could not create a meaningful opening, their afternoon epitomised by substitute Adam Johnson's effort from the edge of the area which was neither shot nor cross and floated harmlessly wide.

Substitute Thompson could have embarrassed the top flight club still further with eight minutes to go but his header from a Whittingham cross went straight into the keeper's arms.

An awful thump over the bar by Boro defender David Wheater was the cue for droves of home supporters to stream out of the stadium and some even joined in with cries of "Premiership, you're having a laugh" on their way.

After the final whistle and I had filed my report, I took a call from Barrie, who asked if I could take some reaction from Southgate and Jones from the press conference. There were some difficult questions for shell-shocked Southgate as he faced the local journalists. This was supposed to be the day that he won over the doubters and took Boro a step closer to a return to European football, yet it had ended disastrously for him.

"In a strange way the Cup has been a release for us and we haven't spoken about winning it because it has been a case of let's see how we get on," said Southgate. "Then with everybody going out yesterday it suddenly dawned on us that we had a fantastic opportunity. Whether we froze or the occasion was too much I don't know. Cardiff played good football with the freedom we wanted. We just couldn't get a grip. We have to hold our hands up. Cardiff were better throughout." Then it was Jones's turn to take the stand.

This was a day of almost unrivalled joy for the club, but he said, "Someone asked for champagne but for what? We have not done anything yet. We have not reached the final or won it so the champagne will be for the staff." And the players' reaction to that? "I ducked," he said.

As for rewriting history, Jones added, "You've got to dream it could be our year, I've had 1927 rammed down my throat every day. I've always maintained it is the history of the club and should be put where it belongs."

Afterwards I decided to stay in Middlesbrough with my brother-in-law Tom. It turned into a good night of celebratory drinking and I was even treated to a Teesside delicacy, a Parmo, chicken beaten until it's flat, covered in breadcrumbs, fried and then smothered in butter and melted cheese. It was no match for curry off the bone from Caroline Street, but when in Rome.

A message board post by Cardiff vice chairman and lifelong Bluebird Steve Borley summed up the excitement around the city perfectly. He wrote, "What an amazing day and amazing result. The chaps at the FA will raise a few eyebrows with us coming to town. Great scenes, grown men crying, fans cheering and great performance from the team. The fans played a great part today and should be applauded for silencing a big Boro crowd. We're the famous Cardiff City and we're going to Wemberlee, Wemberlee."

The following day City fans were glued to the TV and radio for the semi-final draw.

Number four, Barnsley, will play number one, Cardiff City. Get in there. I nearly cried with joy. All of a sudden a repeat of 1927 looked a real possibility. Unbelievable.

Two days later City won their High Court case with the judge ruling that Langston did not need to be repaid until 2016. All was well with the world and City fans could savour four weeks of excitement and build-up before the semi showdown.

Cardiff City had achieved something its long-suffering supporters never dreamed could be possible – a date at Wembley.

v Barnsley 1-0

6 April 2008. Attendance: 82,752
FA Cup Semi-Final. Wembley Stadium

CARDIFF CITY:

Peter Enckelman
Kevin McNaughton (Aaron Ramsey 47)
Roger Johnson
Glenn Loovens
Tony Capaldi
Joe Ledley
Gavin Rae
Stephen McPhail
Trevor Sinclair (Steve Thompson 61)
Peter Whittingham
Jimmy Floyd Hasselbaink (Riccy Scimeca 88)
Subs not used: Michael Oakes, Darren Purse

Referee: Alan Wiley (Staffordshire)

BARNSLEY:

Luke Steele
Marciano van Homoet
Stephen Foster
Dennis Souza
Rob Kozluk (Jacob Butterfield 86)
Jamal Campbell-Ryce
Bobby Hassell
Brian Howard
Martin Devaney (Diego Leon 68)
Kayode Odejayi
Istvan Ferenczi (Michael Coulson 65)
Subs not used: Kyle Letheren, Sam Togwell

A S 33,000 delirious Welshmen made the new Wembley Stadium shake with a rendition of 'Men of Harlech', I turned to my dad on my left. "Dad," I said, my eyes welling up, "we're going to see City in an FA Cup Final." If there was one sentence I never thought would leave my lips, there it was. My old man, a City veteran of some 40-odd years, smiled back numbly.

This heroic City team – a mixture of journeymen, promising youngsters and just one or two mercenaries – had done the unthinkable. We had shocked the football world to its core by booking a place in the final of the FA Cup by beating Barnsley. We had gone a long way towards bringing the romance back to a competition which was starting to look more Nessa and Smithy than Romeo and Juliet.

And to complete the glorious fairy tale, it was local lad Joe Ledley who had scored the decisive goal with a strike of sheer brilliance.

The celebrations continued long after the final whistle. As the players ran towards the fans hand-in-hand, there were beautiful scenes among the supporters. Pensioners more accustomed to relegation battles than Cup semis danced side by side with nine-year-olds with their idol's name printed on their backs.

Who needs John Terry and Cristiano Ronaldo when we've got Roger Johnson and Trevor Sinclair? We had finally made it. The sleeping giant was alive and kicking.

Hundreds of column inches had been given to the game in the weeks and days before, many focusing on loud-mouthed Swansea City fan Leighton James. West Wales's most famous lollipop man, who made 88 appearances for the Swans between 1980 and 1983, earned himself a suspension from his job as a pundit on the BBC's *Wales on Saturday* programme for foolishly announcing he would be supporting Barnsley.

He also had to cry off from an appearance on the Real Radio phone-in. Bitter rivals Swansea were top of League 1 under Roberto Martinez yet the eyes of the football world were on the capital – and James hated it.

165

There were some classic outbursts from the former Wales international as City fans took the mick. On one phone-in in the build-up to the big game he told one Bluebird, "Don't sit there and pontificate to me and be super-serious and say that you weren't laughing when the Swans got beat by Havant & Waterlooville." The Jacks' Cup dreams had ended in January with a defeat against the non-league team. And you're right, Leighton, we were pissing ourselves.

As fate would have it, Barnsley boss Simon Davey was also Swansea-born and desperate to earn the freedom of his home city by ending Cardiff's dreams. "Being a Swansea lad it'll always be nice to put Cardiff out," said Davey, who made 50 league appearances for Swansea between 1989 and 1992.

In the blue camp, there was even an air of excitement from boss Dave Jones. He said, "If the players need to be told that they are in the semi-finals of the FA Cup then they are not on the same planet, to be fair. I think they realise what the game is all about. It's the biggest game in the history of the club for many, many years – and we want to do ourselves proud and the supporters proud."

The days dragged as City fans waited for 6 April. There were 28 days between City's heroic quarter-final win at Middlesbrough and the Barnsley semi, during which time there were five Championship games. Quite remarkably, City won three of those and drew the other two to cling on to faint hopes of reaching the play-offs – but the league campaign felt like something of a sideshow.

One of those games, a 1-0 win against Hull City at Ninian Park, attracted 17,555 spectators, more than 4,000 up on the previous home attendance, after the club announced that those with stubs would have priority for buying semi-final tickets.

Eventually the talking was over and one of the biggest days in the club's history dawned. And it was as momentous as expected from start to finish. City fans had been waiting for a trip to Wembley for 81 years – and they were going to make the most of every second. But there was a shock when supporters opened their curtains to find a winter wonderland staring back at them. Inches of the white stuff had fallen overnight causing a brief moment of panic that weeks of pre-match build-up would have to be repeated because of suspension. But the match was never in serious doubt and the long wait to see City take their place on the big stage was over.

The M4 was a sea of blue and white as thousands upon thousands of fans made their way to London. Most had arrived at the £757m arena hours ahead of the 4pm kick-off to soak up every moment. Walking along Wembley Way with sporadic chants of 'Little Pick and Shovel' swirling around the cold London air was absolutely a dream come true. Little did we know that over the next four years Wembley would become something of a second home.

The game itself was certainly no classic, more a tense and ferocious clash between two decent, if unspectacular, Championship sides. City started as slight favourites. Jones's men were nine places and ten points better off than the Tykes, who had slipped down the league since their Cup exploits.

Barnsley had followed their 2-1 win at Liverpool with a defeat and three draws before beating Chelsea 1-0 in the quarters. They spanked Ipswich 4-1 the Tuesday after, but then embarked on a run of three back-to-back defeats before the game at Wembley.

City made two changes to their starting line-up, Trevor Sinclair in for Paul Parry, who suffered a muscle strain, and veteran Jimmy Floyd Hasselbaink preferred to Steve Thompson up front after completing a three-match suspension.

Hasselbaink, 36, had been through a mixed season. City fans had expected big things from the Dutch master. He had shown glimpses of brilliance – his goal on the turn in the 2-0 Cup win against Wolves will live long in the memory. He had managed only eight goals before the Barnsley match but was popular with supporters. In comparison to fellow ageing striker Robbie Fowler, who was at City at the same time, he was a living legend. There was no place in the squad for Fowler, who was recovering from a hip injury.

The first five minutes of the tie were as expected: frantic and nervy as both teams got to grips with the huge occasion. Midfielder Brian Howard cannoned a shot against the City defence before Johnson came close to connecting with a Peter Whittingham free kick after sneaking in at the back post.

The match appeared to be settling into a cagey pattern but after just nine minutes came the moment of genius from Ledley which would be immortalised for eternity.

A long throw by Tony Capaldi was headed clear by Barnsley defender Rob Kozluk and the opportunity looked over. But it fell to man of the match Ledley towards the back of the area, who hooked his left leg around the ball and volleyed over his shoulder and into the corner.

For City fans watching from the opposite end of Wembley, it took an age to hit the back of the net. But when it did, the noise was incredible.

If any City fans were thinking they were in for a stress-free afternoon, those thoughts were quickly dispelled as the Tykes hit back strongly. They should have been level within two minutes after City were caught out by Kozluk's pass. Kayode Odejayi beat Peter Enckelman to the ball and his header was goalbound but Johnson was on the line to clear. Defender Stephen Foster was next to go close to forcing an equaliser when he rose to meet Howard's corner on 13 minutes. Enckelman floundered but was relieved to see the ball drift wide of the post.

The game had a feisty edge to it with snap tackles right across the pitch. As was a regular feature of Jones's reign at the club, City dropped back after taking the lead and invited the opposition forward.

On 16 minutes Jamal Campbell-Ryce clipped the ball into the area for Istvan Ferenczi and Odejayi to attack but the City defence somehow managed to scramble the ball to safety.

Martin Devaney was next to get in behind an increasingly static Bluebirds defence as he raced on to Howard's pass, but Odejayi's finish from the resulting cross was weak.

For City, it was Hasselbaink and Sinclair, with a combined age of 71, who looked most impressive.

Hasselbaink set off on a solid run, only to be cut down by a lunging tackle by Kozluk.

Then from Whittingham's free kick Ledley again went close when he brought a save from Luke Steele.

City chances were at a premium. The best came after 21 minutes when Whittingham and solid midfielder Gavin Rae combined to set up Hasselbaink. Steele spilled Jimmy's initial shot but managed to recover to smother as Sinclair eyed one more moment of glory in a wonderful career.

Barnsley really piled on the pressure for the rest of the half and City went into the dressing room at 1-0 by the skin of their teeth.

Marciano van Homoet fired over a great cross that Ferenczi headed wide with the goal gaping before the same player saw a fierce drive hacked off the line heroically by Sinclair.

Odejayi thought he was through on goal on the half hour as he raced on to Campbell-Ryce's header, but the striker's second touch was far too heavy and it went out of play. Barnsley had a great chance in the dying seconds of the half but a comical mix-up from the free kick between three Barnsley players meant it went begging.

City fans breathed a collective sigh of relief when the half-time whistle finally blew.

Jones was forced to make a change just two minutes into the second half, injured full-back Kevin McNaughton replaced by 17-year-old midfield wonder kid Aaron Ramsey. The Welshman was already attracting interest from Sir Alex Ferguson despite making just 14 appearances for the Bluebirds. He had scored his first goal for City in their 3-1 win at Chasetown at the first juncture on the road to Wembley.

It was the creativity of Ledley, by far the best player on the pitch, which nearly gave City some breathing space. The 21-year-old broke down the left, beating two red shirts before firing the perfect ball over for Rae. But Rae, who scored just eight goals in 153 appearances for City, put his header straight into Steele's arms.

Dennis Souza made a brave block from a Hasselbaink pile driver before Enckelman did well to claw away Devaney's near post cross.

It is written in the laws of sport – right next to England always losing penalty shoot-outs – that on big occasions for every hero there has to be a villain. Step forward Odejayi, who celebrated a career high little over a month earlier by bagging the winner against Chelsea. On 66 minutes he too easily beat the offside trap and ran through on goal, with just Enckelman to beat. Barnsley fans behind the goal already had their arms stretched high, but Odejayi passed the ball into the side netting with the whole goal at his mercy. It is a moment he has undoubtedly replayed in his mind time and time again since.

Had Barnsley scored, they likely would have gone on to win the game, but as it was City were able to push on. Hasselbaink had a good effort deflected wide and then Whittingham's 71st-minute shot left Steele rooted to the spot but brushed the roof of the net.

Rae again found himself free in the area soon after, but his first touch was poor, allowing the keeper to block with his chest. City shut up shop in the last 15 minutes, Johnson and Stephen McPhail heroically throwing themselves in front of everything.

The four minutes of injury time were fraught and nerve-racking – but finally the celebrations and the tears could begin.

City players ran in every direction while Odejayi stood with his head bowed. Football can be such a cruel game. Celebratory songs blared from the Wembley PA system and soon only the blue shirts remained in the giant stadium. The supporters could not believe what they were witnessing – and neither could the players. "I have been with Chelsea to a Cup Final but this is unbelievable," Hasselbaink told Sky Sports.

It was the stuff of dreams. We had all seen minnows defy the odds in the FA Cup, but this was on a different scale – and Cardiff were the talk of the football world. Every City fan that night went to bed dreaming of McPhail lifting the Cup. Jones's team had already given us so much to be proud of, but eternal glory now looked within touching distance.

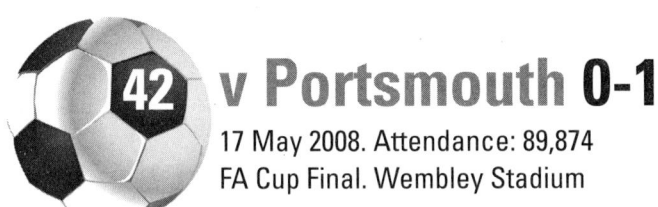

v Portsmouth 0-1

17 May 2008. Attendance: 89,874
FA Cup Final. Wembley Stadium

CARDIFF CITY:

Peter Enckelman
Kevin McNaughton
Roger Johnson
Glenn Loovens
Tony Capaldi
Joe Ledley
Gavin Rae (Trevor Sinclair 86)
Stephen McPhail
Peter Whittingham (Aaron Ramsey 61)
Paul Parry
Jimmy Floyd Hasselbaink (Steve Thompson 70)
Subs not used: Michael Oakes
Darren Purse

Referee: Mike Dean (Wirral)

PORTSMOUTH:

David James
Glen Johnson
Sol Campbell
Sylvain Distin
Hermann Hreidarsson
John Utaka (David Nugent 69)
Pedro Mendes (Pape Bouba Diop 78)
Lassana Diarra
Sulley Ali Muntari
Niko Kranjcar
Nwankwo Kanu (Milan Baros 87)
Subs not used: Jamie Ashdown, Noe Pamarot

CARDIFF CITY Football Club had waited for 29,611 days to be back on the biggest stage of them all in the final of the FA Cup. For those City fans old enough to remember 1927 and that famous win over Arsenal – including my 92-year-old granddad, John – it had not only felt like a lifetime, it had been a lifetime.

Now the class of 2008 – Loovens, Capaldi and Ledley – had their chance to become immortals alongside Watson, Ferguson and Keenor.

The six weeks between City's semi-final triumph over Barnsley and the Portsmouth final had been incredible. The atmosphere in the city gradually increased until it reached its crescendo in the final days before the clash. Flags were erected all around Cardiff as everyone went Cup crazy. People with no previous interest in football were discussing whether Dave Jones should start with Aaron Ramsey or whether Jimmy Floyd Hasselbaink could provide one more moment of magic. Pubs which had been rugby strongholds for decades all of a sudden had bunting strewn across their beer gardens. A giant flag proclaiming "Cardiff City FC, Pride of Wales" had been hung on the NCP car park in Dumfries Place in the heart of the city centre. Welsh boxer Joe Calzaghe appeared at a weigh-in in Vegas wearing a City shirt.

And there were Cup Final songs aplenty. The official offering came from James Fox with 'Bluebirds Flying High', which was catchy if a little cringeworthy:

"With Parry, Rae and Ledley
The outcome seems so likely
Little Rambo's like a tank
Scoring goals there's Hasselbaink."

A comedy version of La Macarena recorded by 50 City fans, called 'Do the Ayatollah', attracted a lot of attention but the pick of the bunch, by a country mile, was written and performed by striker Steve Thompson.

It started:

"And on that bonny pitch in Chasetown, when we went one nil down.

Written off at the Riverside, but we took it all in our stride.

When your thoughts are far away, are you dreaming about Wembley?

And on the 17th of May, you can go down in history."

The 'official video' with the players lurking around Thommo straight-faced and hands in pockets looked a little awkward, but there was a rather more animated performance at the Vale of Glamorgan Hotel on 4 May when a couple of hundred supporters forked out to attend the celebration dinner.

After a rendition of Bob Marley's 'Redemption Song', a well-oiled Thommo announced "here we go, Cardiff City, let's stick it up every bum in the country" before shouting his way through his Cup Final song while playing acoustic guitar.

Darren Purse, Riccy Scimeca and Trevor Sinclair sang along loudest as the camera bulbs flashed.

It is ridiculous, but watching the video still makes the hairs stand on end. Whatever we achieve in the future, that group will always be heroes in my eyes. Stuff the Premier League, we were living the dream.

The City team left Cardiff Central Station by train the day before the match to a hero's send-off. The excitement was almost unbearable – and this from a club which just seven seasons earlier was attracting crowds of just four or five thousand in the Third Division. Proper *Roy of the Rovers* stuff.

City had, of course, been to Wembley for the Barnsley semi-final, but familiarity made the journey along the M4 no less special. The demand for corporate seats for the final meant there were less of us this time – 25,000 instead of 33,000 – but the Welsh invasion looked just as impressive. Scarves fluttered from cars and flags adorned with the names of every South Wales valley covered bus windows.

The atmosphere inside Wembley prior to kick-off was fantastic. All City fans had been given a black and yellow flag to wave while at the other end Portsmouth fans were equally as colourful. It was an incredible sight. Meanwhile, giant banners of Joe Ledley and Thommo were rolled on to the hallowed turf while at the other end there were David James and Nwankwo Kanu.

The English FA caved into pressure and ruled that the Welsh National Anthem would be sung along with 'God Save the Queen' before kick-off. 'Hen Wlad Fy Nhadau' has rarely be sung with such gusto and pride – and also booed so ferociously. The Welsh anthem was sung before the 1927 final, but only in English and just the first two verses. It was an emotional couple of minutes, and I would wager that the FA will never let it happen again.

As well as bending the rules on anthems, after much deliberation the FA also announced that City would qualify for the UEFA Cup should they lift the trophy. If winning the Cup, £1m prize money and eternal fame wasn't enough, there was the cherry on top of re-living those great European nights of yesteryear.

Despite much speculation, disaster signing Robbie Fowler did not make the 16-man squad after five months out with a hip injury. Instead Paul Parry took his place along Hasselbaink up front.

In midfield, Jones opted for experience over flair by naming emerging star Ramsey on the bench, Peter Whittingham, captain Stephen McPhail, workhorse Gavin Rae and Ledley making up the four in the middle. In defence there were no surprises with Tony

Capaldi, Roger Johnson, Glenn Loovens and Kevin McNaughton offering the protection for goalkeeper Peter Enckelman.

Harry Redknapp's Portsmouth, meanwhile, had just finished an incredible season in the Premier League, eventually finishing eighth after flirting with a Champions League spot for a spell. The team, which consisted of players from nine different countries, was littered with expensive and experienced talent. There were Glen Johnson, Sylvain Distin, Lassana Diarra, John Utaka and Kanu to name but five. Though public support was marginally in City's favour, Pompey were the clear favourites to lift the Cup for the first time since 1939.

But City were encouraged by Pompey's awful run of form in the lead up to the final. They had forgotten how to win. Redknapp's team had lost their last four Premier League games, scoring just once in the process. They had only picked up four points since beating West Brom by a single goal in the semis. City, meanwhile, had just ended a run of two defeats and a draw with a convincing 3-0 win over Barnsley in a re-run of their own semi-final fixture.

With Jermain Defoe, a January signing from Tottenham, cup-tied, Redknapp went for Kanu ahead of Milan Baros and David Nugent with Pompey sticking to their 4-1-4-1 formation.

The game got off to a frantic start in front of a global television audience of an estimated half a billion. Diarra won an early free kick after surging through midfield and Sulley Ali Muntari tried his luck from all of 40 yards, but Enckelman was equal to it.

City, wearing their 'lucky' black shirts which had served them well against Middlesbrough and Barnsley, settled well and had their first opening moments later when Parry raced through on goal. The makeshift striker was thwarted by 'Calamity' James, who did well not to concede a penalty. Parry was a handful throughout but how City could have done with the natural finishing of Michael Chopra, who had been sold to Sunderland the previous summer.

It was City who looked the more urgent of the two teams in the early exchanges as they looked to become the first team from outside the top flight to win the Cup since West Ham United beat Arsenal in 1980. Loovens made a rare sortie forward and was only inches away from getting on the end of a Ledley pass.

Hasselbaink then tried to chase down a pass which might have put him clean through. And then on 13 minutes came the big chance that City's pressure had merited. Ledley played a perfect ball inside Sol Campbell for livewire Parry and James had to be quick off his line to save with his feet.

A deflected Whittingham shot then had James wrong-footed and the effort fell just wide of the post. The City fans that had made the journey more in hope than expectation were now starting to believe.

There was a nervous moment at the other end as Enckelman flapped unconvincingly at a Muntari cross when it looked like it was going wide. Distin headed back across goal but Kanu was unable to control and City fans could breathe again.

The first gilt-edged chance fell to Kanu on 22 minutes. The Nigerian put Loovens on his backside with a nonchalant touch inside the area, went round Enckelman with a shimmy of the hips before contriving to jab against the outside of the post from just three yards and with the goal at his mercy. It was the type of miss that would have been replayed a thousand times over had the talented striker not redeemed himself later in the game.

City hit back immediately with a succession of set-pieces, the closest of which had James rooted to the spot as Johnson's header from a Whittingham cross sailed just inches over the bar.

But the Premier League side went ahead undeservedly eight minutes before the break. Utaka, who had been kept relatively quiet on the right, made enough room to bend a cross past Capaldi, who should have been closer. Enckelman spilled it like a bar of soap and Kanu – officially 32 but believed to be in his 40s – was able to bundle home from a yard under pressure from Johnson.

How ironic that City's fate should be sealed by a goalkeeping howler after the legendary tale of hapless Arsenal keeper Dan Lewis allowing a shot to slither under his body 81 years earlier.

Even then there were chances for Jones's men to claw their way back into the match before half-time. McNaughton was almost an unlikely hero when he prodded an effort just wide from a Parry cross after sprinting the entire length of the pitch to offer his support.

And then in injury time Loovens had the ball in the net with an inch-perfect lob following a James flap – but he had controlled the ball with his elbow beforehand.

But City were not the same side after the interval as Pompey worked on keeping possession and City legs grew tired. Some City fans thought the superb Johnson had made it 1-1 after 53 minutes but the defender's header from a Whittingham cross tickled the side-netting.

Kanu then saw a shot deflected over before Muntari pinged an effort just too high. With Pompey starting to take control of the game, it was Jones who blinked first by bringing on Ramsey for Whittingham after 61 minutes. Twelve months earlier the 17-year-old was sitting his GCSEs – now the hopes of a nation lay on his shoulders as he became the second youngest player to play in an FA Cup Final behind Millwall's Curtis Weston.

The Welshman, arguably the most naturally talented player to ever pull on a City shirt, made an impact with his ability to keep possession, and he also threw himself into some crunching tackles.

The decibels dropped inside Wembley as City ran out of ideas and Pompey were happy with their goal advantage. Nugent came on for Utaka after 70 minutes and Jones responded a minute later by bringing on Thompson for Hasselbaink. The big Dutchman had enjoyed a decent season for City and was popular with supporters, but he had struggled to make an impact on the biggest stage of them all. It would prove to be his last game for the club. A dull spell followed before Enckelman did well to turn Nugent's fierce shot round the post from a narrow angle. With ten minutes to go Loovens powered a diving header so firmly against the turf that it bounced agonisingly over the bar.

But Pompey's success that season had been built around a strong defence. They had conceded just 40 goals in the Premier League and a tiring City team were struggling to get behind their back-line.

Jones threw on Sinclair for the final four minutes for Rae as City desperately searched for an equaliser. Ramsey looked ready to pounce in the area but the ball just wouldn't fall for him and then Johnson had a half-chance but his effort was blocked and scrambled to safety.

Referee Mike Dean brought an end to the game and an end to City's dreams. It had not been the vintage match neutral viewers were hoping for, but it had been a hard-fought tie with sporadic moments of excitement. The heartbroken and shattered Cardiff players slumped to the floor while Pompey revelled in their success. There were tears aplenty among the City fans.

The City stars embarked on the long walk up the famous Wembley steps to collect their runners-up medals and received warm applause from all sides of the ground. There was a word in the ear for McPhail from Bobby Robson, but the captain barely acknowledged it.

After the game there were generous comments about City's achievement in reaching the final, but it was difficult to force a smile. *The Telegraph* quipped that Jones was so low he made Steve Coppell sound like Brian Blessed. "You've got to let us wallow in our self-pity," the City boss said. "I've just lost a cup final. Being a Championship club doesn't soften the blow. I wanted to win."

There was immense pride about that Cup run – it was simply fantastic. But at the same time, when I find myself drifting off into the land of fantasy, changing the outcome of games through willpower alone, it is this one I nearly always come back to. What if Jones had played Ramsey from the start? What if Enckelman had kept a firm grasp on that goal? What if the footballing gods had been smiling on us just one last time?

The following day a welcome party had been arranged at Roald Dahl Plass in Cardiff Bay. Thousands turned up to welcome the team, who arrived in style by boat. All the City players were wearing suits – apart from Ramsey, who was in a tracksuit! He might have had a Cup Final medal in his pocket, but he wasn't quite a man yet.

Thommo took centre stage once again. With his tie around his head like a naughty schoolboy, he sang his song and we all sang with him. The players smiled bravely, but it was emotional. The past month had been like nothing we had ever seen before, but now the fairy tale was over. There was immense pride at what had been achieved, but it was impossible not to think about the party that could have been.

43 v Bristol City 6-0

26 January 2010. Attendance: 13,825
Championship. Ashton Gate

S O MUCH for Ashton Gate being a bogey ground. Harold Wilson was Prime Minister and old money was still in circulation the last time City had won at rivals Bristol City more than 40 years earlier. But the Bluebirds made a mockery of that statistic by tearing the Robins to shreds. This was Dave Jones's promotion-chasing team at its scintillating best and the 693 City fans who made the 53-mile journey over the bridge under police escort loved every second.

The team of 2009/10 boasted some of the classiest players to ever pull on the blue shirt, including Peter Whittingham, Joe Ledley, Michael Chopra and Jay Bothroyd. There were times when the combination just didn't work and City were often embarrassed by lesser teams – but this was a night when everything went right with some stunning football and ruthless finishing.

Remarkably, this was the third Severnside derby in just a fortnight. A last-minute Bristol equaliser had forced a replay in the FA Cup on 12 January but a solitary own goal was enough to send City through in the replay at the Cardiff City Stadium seven days later. City had been impressive in their 4-2 win over Leicester City on the following Saturday, a result which set up a tasty fifth round tie against Chelsea, but there was no hint of what was to come on an historic winter night.

Jones and his Bristol counterpart Gary Johnson had described the match as a six-pointer. Though still fifth, City's promotion challenge had faltered having drawn their last four Championship games. Bristol City, too, were stumbling but were just four points behind in tenth position. A draw would probably have been considered a decent result but this was a night where everything City touched seemed to end up in the back of the net.

It was City's biggest away win since the 7-1 trouncing of Oldham eight years earlier – and their biggest ever success over their fiercest English rivals, eclipsing the previous best of 5-1 on the last day of 1966.

Bristol City made a bright enough start. After about five minutes Gabor Gyepes beat Patrick Agyemang in the air after a dangerous cross and City eventually scrambled clear with Nicky Maynard poised to pounce. A minute later Cole Skuse tried a shot from distance after a good link-up with the powerful Agyemang but his effort was powder-puff and easily gathered by David Marshall.

It was the home side who looked the more urgent and from a 12th-minute corner debutant Jamal Campbell-Ryce hooked the ball back into the area and Marshall did well to punch it to safety from the head of Agyemang, who was also making his first Robins appearance. Chopra, playing furthest forward, had barely had a sniff though Ross McCormack looked eager.

Whittingham had a pot shot for the Bluebirds with the outside of his boot after some neat play between McCormack, Bothroyd and Ledley but was well over. Minutes later at the other end future Bluebird Maynard had Marshall worried with a 25-yard drive which flew just inches wide.

But the tide was about to change dramatically after 19 minutes. From a Marshall goal kick, Bothroyd flicked his header on to Chopra, who played a short pass to McCormack and set off on a run. McCormack spotted his colleague's move and played it over the top. Confusion reigned in the Bristol defence between goalkeeper Dean Gerken and Liam Fontaine. The defender eventually headed the ball at his goalkeeper from a yard, the keeper could only parry and super Whittingham was on hand to sweep the ball into the empty net.

The *Bristol Evening Post* described the mistake as "a moment of pure farce". It was Whittingham's 18th goal of the season, and his 15th in his last 20 games.

Lively Campbell-Ryce had a chance to hit back immediately but he sent his shot bobbling harmlessly past the post from inside the area.

And then, with just 23 minutes on the clock, more calamitous defending by Bristol City gifted Dave Jones's men an almost unassailable two goal advantage. Again it started from the boot of Marshall.

Again Bothroyd won the header, Chopra played out wide for Whittingham, who lobbed a first time volley over the top of the back-line for Gavin Rae. There was no way Rae would score but somehow his mis-hit cross (or was it a shot?) squirmed its way between Bradley Orr and Gerken and there was McCormack at the back stick to poke home from all of two yards.

Suddenly City had one of the softest two-goal leads you will ever see. "Easy, easy, easy" chanted the Cardiff fans gathered at the other end of Ashton Gate.

Incredibly, less than 60 seconds from the restart, it was three. McCormack picked the ball up well within his own half, controlled with his chest and instinctively sliced open the Bristol defence again with a long, inch-perfect volleyed pass to Chopra. He had Bothroyd joining in support but didn't need him, firing a fantastic, controlled drive across Gerken and into the bottom corner from the edge of the area. Chops cupped his ears in front of the furious home supporters as the City fans went wild. Three goals in five explosive minutes.

City were purring against Bristol's chaotic defence, yet at the back of everyone's minds was the embarrassment at London Road less than a month earlier when rampant City stormed into a four-goal lead against Peterborough, only to draw 4-4.

Jones had put together one of the greatest attacking teams in the club's history and when it all clicked, it was electrifying to watch. Before this game City had already smashed six past Derby and scored four against Scunthorpe, Watford, Sheffield United, Peterborough and Leicester. Even before this game City were the second highest scorers in the league with 44 goals from 25 league games – but the defence was a problem at times.

After 32 minutes Maynard found some space in the box after more good work by Campbell-Ryce on the left up against Adam Matthews but completely missed his kick. A couple of minutes later Whittingham wasn't too far away with a shot from 30 yards.

City, wearing all yellow, were starting to knock the ball around confidently in midfield, frustrating the home supporters with every completed pass.

Embarrassment turned to humiliation for Bristol City on 43 minutes as Cardiff made it 4-0. And from the home team's perspective, it was the worst of the lot. Whittingham passed to Chopra out wide and he fired a hopeful ball into the danger area. Bothroyd was in the general vicinity but there was no explanation for Fontaine slicing into his own net. The City players walked casually back to the centre circle, too embarrassed to muster a celebration.

Half-time was greeted, unsurprisingly, by loud boos from the locals – those who hadn't already gone home.

Whatever Gary Johnson said to his players at half-time clearly had little impact as after just 52 seconds City had the ball in the net again through Chopra. A lovely little flick took Bothroyd past Fontaine and he bundled it through for Chops, who finished one-on-one with the keeper with aplomb into the bottom corner. Chops aeroplaned away in front of the City fans, who could now relax knowing that a Peterborough re-run was not on the cards. That was 5-0 with 44 minutes remaining. Statisticians were checking for details of the biggest ever league win.

Skuse screwed a shot wide from the edge of a crowded area for Bristol and then after 49 minutes at the other end Whittingham pinged the ball over the bar after Bothroyd's pull-back.

It was nearly six on 56 minutes when Whitts picked up a ball from Matthews, skipped past Campbell-Ryce and substitute Lewin Nyatanga, and dodged his way through the desperate tackles of Marvin Elliott and Fontaine before firing a left-footed shot from the edge of the area that Gerken did well to save. The first corner was headed clear but from the second attempt, McCormack played a one-two with Whittingham and from an acute angle fired through a crowd of players and into the bottom corner. McCormack had his second, City their sixth and it was a riot. Fortunately Ashton Gate has a scoreboard.

Confident Chopra tried his luck from 30 yards after 65 minutes but it was too close to Gerken. City fans were running through the full repertoire of the big win hymn book, including "we want seven", "we're going to score in a minute" and "all we are singing is give us a goal".

Campbell-Ryce nearly pulled one back for Bristol from a tight angle but Marshall, a spectator for most of the game, saved with his legs. A few minutes later Ledley got his back in the way to block a goalbound Elliott shot. But City's counter-attacking was sublime and impressive play between McCormack and Chopra almost created an opening for a seventh goal.

Skuse hit the side netting for Bristol before Maynard's header was easily caught by Marshall from Nyatanga's cross.

As so often is the case after a team scores their sixth goal, the game reduced to almost walking pace for long periods. City might have bagged another in the 85th minute, though, when Whittingham played a short corner to McCormack and he played along the floor to Ledley in the box. Ledley laid it back for Chopra for his hat-trick but his first time shot was cleared off the line.

In the closing minutes Marshall had to be at full stretch to push a magnificent Maynard free kick on to the post to preserve the clean sheet for City's defence and make it a perfect evening for the Bluebirds. Hundreds of programmes, handed out to supporters for free at the turnstiles as part of a trial initiative, rained on to the pitch from disgruntled home supporters.

One angry Robins fans posting on the This is Bristol website simply said, "It was the most inept match I have seen played in this ground for many, many years."

The resounding result lifted City into fourth position in the Championship above Swansea City, and though there was still a long way to go, the scoreline was just the boost that supporters needed. The Bluebirds had only had eight shots on target in comparison to Bristol's five but the finishing was clinical.

Jones tried his best to keep a level head after the match. "I thought it was an emphatic performance from us and I think it was well deserved. We totally dominated," he said in the *Western Mail*. "Everything we seemed to hit seemed to go in, but there was a bit more to it than that. That five-minute spell in the first half gave us a grip on the game and we just continued from there. It was just one of those days where everything comes off for you. It's still too early to read anything into the table, but we are hanging in there."

There was no hiding for Jones's mate Johnson, who had to deal with a group of disgruntled Bristol City fans who had stayed behind to complain outside the dressing room. He was fast losing the support of the fans. "It's the sort of night when it is best not to say much," he said. "Whatever reason I try to offer for that performance will be picked apart. We have a lot of soul-searching to do over the next few days before our next game at Middlesbrough. It wasn't that we forgot how to defend, we just couldn't defend on the night. Full credit to Cardiff. I had my say at half-time but now we have to collect our thoughts and come up with the right response."

The result should have spurred City on to to greater things but Jones's teams often struggled with consistency. They won just three of their next nine Championship games and only a decent spell in March salvaged a play-off finish. The season ultimately ended in disappointment at Wembley – but the Ashton Gate massacre will never be forgotten.

44 v Swansea City 2-1

3 April 2010. Attendance: 25,130
Championship. Cardiff City Stadium

CARDIFF CITY:

David Marshall
Anthony Gerrard
Darcy Blake
Adam Matthews
Gavin Rae (Joe Ledley 63)
Peter Whittingham
Stephen McPhail (Aaron Wildig 89)
Tony Capaldi
Michael Chopra
Jay Bothroyd
Ross McCormack (Kelvin Etuhu 70)
Subs not used: Peter Enckelman, Aaron
Morris, Soloman Taiwo, Warren Feeney

Referee: Phil Dowd (Staffordshire)

SWANSEA CITY:

Dorus de Vries
Ashley Williams
Alan Tate
Angel Rangel
David Edgar
Leon Britton
Darren Pratley
Andrea Orlandi
Cedric van der Gun (Mark Gower 84)
Nathan Dyer (David Cotterill 69)
Gorka Pintado (Shefki Kuqi 76)
Subs not used: David Cornell, Garry Monk,
Joe Allen, Lee Trundle

E VERY GOAL against your bitter rivals is sweet, but few match up to Michael Chopra's injury time winner against Swansea in 2010 for sheer unbridled jubilation. The loveable Geordie, who had earlier levelled for the Bluebirds, etched his name into Cardiff City folklore with a 92nd-minute winner in the first South Wales derby at the new stadium.

The crucial Championship match in front of 25,130 passionate fans appeared to be heading for a draw as the fourth official announced three minutes of added-on time.

In truth, City would probably have taken that. Swansea had looked the more comfortable on the ball for long periods and City goalkeeper David Marshall had heroically just produced a wonderful reaction save from Swans striker Shefki Kuqi.

But Chopra almost always shone on the big stage – and the £4m man gave Sky TV a grandstand finale once again. Marshall launched a hasty ball upfield, a last throw of the dice. Welsh defender Ashley Williams could only head into touch, giving Adam Matthews the chance to wind up one final long throw.

An audible sense of anticipation whipped around the stadium bowl. A Swans head cleared, but only as far as the edge of the area. It was forced on by the head of Aaron Wildig – his first touch since coming on as a substitute seconds earlier – and fell for Chops, who smashed into the bottom corner past Dorus de Vries.

Swans hands shot up into the area, convinced that a man with so much space in the area must surely have been offside. But the flag correctly stayed down and Chopra darted towards the Canton Stand, veins bulging from his neck, before completing a rather unorthodox roly poly near the corner flag. The City fans burst with excitement – and, at last, the Cardiff City Stadium felt like our own.

It was City's first league win against the Jacks since 1997, but those 13 years of hurt had been wiped away in one unforgettable moment. And boy, did the home supporters rub it in to the 1,900 West Walians who had made the journey along the M4 under over-the-top police escort.

Thousands of fans remained in the stadium ten minutes after the final whistle – many by now bare-chested – as The Automatic's 'Monster' blared out, prompting rousing renditions of "what's that coming over the hill, it's Michael Chopra".

Swansea boss Paulo Sousa admitted after the game that his side, the Championship's lowest scorers in 2009/10 with a woeful final tally of just 40, desperately needed a Chopra among their ranks. Such was the ecstasy that many City fans only remembered the importance of the fixture in terms of league standings as they reached Sloper Road.

This was billed as the most important South Wales derby in living memory – and for once the headlines were entirely justified. City went into the game in fourth position, just three points ahead of the Jacks in fifth. And their form was devastating. With the likes of Peter Whittingham and Jay Bothroyd really starting to purr, City had managed 13 points from their last five games to leapfrog their rivals.

Swansea, meanwhile, for all the plaudits they were starting to receive for playing their easy-on-the-eye passing game, had not won in their previous five and were dropping like a stone. There was a growing belief among City fans that top flight football was a real possibility.

This win stretched that gap from City to the Swans to six points – and meant City retained their eight-point cushion over Blackpool in seventh in the chase for the play-offs. With just five games to go, that was a lead too big to throw away, even by City's standards.

City boss Dave Jones had been criticised by Cardiff fans for down-playing the derby in the years before he finally broke his duck. His record against the Swans before this fixture stood at two defeats and two draws. In fact, in the 24 derbies he had been involved with as either a player or a manager prior to this springtime clash, Jones had tasted success on just three occasions.

True to form, there was little excitement from the surly Scouser after the game.

He told *The Wales on Sunday*, "It's an important three points but I haven't changed anything or done anything differently. People say I play it (the derby) down, but it was nice to get the three points more than anything. If they think I don't care I'm not in the mood to change that attitude."

The South Wales police agreed to a 5.20pm kick-off at the command of the TV bosses, which gave City fans valuable extra drinking time before the big game.

That played its part in creating a fantastic but tense atmosphere as the 52nd meeting between the clubs got under way.

Excitement nearly turned to euphoria inside two minutes when City striker Ross McCormack was played in by Whittingham on the edge of the area, but the Scot curled his shot wide of the post.

The pitch was showing the tell-tale signs of a relentless season of coping with both rugby and football. And it was a not untypical bobble which led to Swansea's first chance of note, but Andrea Orlandi fired high and wide.

Marshall nearly notched an unlikely assist with the pass of the game shortly after, but his good work was undone as McCormack did well to progress to the edge of the Swansea box from halfway, only to screw wide once more with Whittingham screaming for the easy ball to his left.

But 'Swansealona' – a cocky name created by their own fans – started to find their feet and to pass ball around in the stylish manner they were becoming known for.

And, somewhat fortuitously, the visitors had the lead on 29 minutes.

Marshall thought he had done enough to stop the ball going out of play after Angel Rangel's cross had taken a nick, but the linesman thought differently. Corner ball.

Orlandi curled in the cross and Marshall, under pressure from Williams and having strayed too far off his line, punched the ball into his own net.

There were a few half-hearted appeals for a foul on the keeper, but there wasn't much in it. "I thought it was a foul," said Marshall afterwards. "But I think people like to see keepers getting a bashing these days."

The Swans fans went wild as they anticipated the prospect of doing the double in the South Wales derby for the first time, having won the reverse fixture 3-2 in November.

The goal settled Swansea, but half chances continued to come the Bluebirds' way.

Shortly after a long ball forward by Marshall was nodded on by Bothroyd and McCormack tried to fashion an overhead kick but was off target.

City's attempted route to goal was a direct one, in contrast to Swansea who nearly always started a move among their back four, but with Bothroyd working tremendously hard and winning almost everything up front, it did not look like a bad option.

Swansea could have had a second five minutes before the break when Darren Pratley's through ball caught Anthony Gerrard flat-footed and Cedric van der Gun bore down on goal, but the Dutch midfielder's shot lacked the power to beat Marshall low down.

And that miss proved absolutely crucial.

Stephen McPhail, who had been sent off twice in the South Wales derby in the previous season, showed some neat footwork to play in Bothroyd, who hit the ground with characteristic ease in the Jacks' half. McPhail played the free kick out to Matthews, who launched a long ball towards Bothroyd's head. The big man beat pantomime villain Alan Tate to the ball and his header found Chopra, who got in front of Williams to poke into the roof of the net.

Chops had been suffering one of his all-too-regular droughts and had not found the target for eight games, but that was his 18th of the campaign nonetheless.

And three minutes before the interval, it could hardly have come at a better time.

When Chopra broke his scoring duck, another goal, or two, or three, was so often around the corner. And he almost gave City an unlikely half-time lead when McCormack played a wonderfully weighted chip into his path, but Chopra couldn't quite find the lob over de Vries's head.

Swansea started the second half on the offensive and David Edgar came close to bagging his first goal for the Jacks with a tame effort that eventually bobbled the wrong side of the post.

City had a golden opportunity to force their noses in front on 52 minutes following one of the best moves of the match. Matthews ghosted past Edgar, jinked past three more and found Whittingham on the edge of the area. Whittingham showed fantastic vision to find Chopra on the wing, he went past van der Gun with ease and drilled across the six-yard box, but no one was there to apply the finishing touch.

Local lad Joe Ledley came on for Gavin Rae after 63 minutes, making a surprise comeback after a double hip operation. But his arrival could not provide the creative spark required in a game which was intriguing and tense, but now lacking clear cut opportunities.

As was often the case under the management of Jones, City dropped further into their shell and City fans feared a late Swansea winner. Marshall was called upon to deal with a shot from Cardiff-born David Cotterill's drive as substitute Kuqi started to cause problems.

The Finnish striker – famed for his belly flop celebration – was so nearly the Jacks' hero on 90 minutes when he found himself unmarked from a Cotterill free kick and his flicked header was expertly saved by the legs of Marshall.

A winner looked beyond City, whose fans were now in a state of nervous panic and baying for the final whistle.

But one last hoof upfield, one last long throw, a gritty challenge by Wildig and a poacher's finish by Chopra lifted the roof at the CCS.

For those with long enough memories there were shades of 1980 and John Buchanan's last-gasp equaliser – but this time it was all three points for City. It was a special moment for Chopra, who had been slammed by the national press for missing a sitter in the Tyne and Wear derby for Sunderland against his former club Newcastle.

The joy on his cheeky face was clear for all to see.

"I can't describe my emotions," he beamed. "I have played in a lot of derbies and this one caps it all off – and to score the winning goal means a lot to me."

Jones paid tribute to his marksman. "They were two great finishes from Chops," he said. "He's a pest, if there's something going on he's in it, but his work rate is phenomenal."

While Chopra stole the headlines – as was so often the case – there were heroes aplenty. Gerrard had one of his more solid displays in defence and Darcy Blake showed some fantastic, composed touches. "We are your capital" boasted the City fans as Bluebirds soaked up every priceless, beautiful second of a long, long overdue derby day success.

City did indeed make the play-offs that season while the Swans missed out, but the Bluebirds were left bitterly disappointed after losing out to Blackpool in the Wembley final.

v Leicester City 2-3

(3-3 on aggregate. City win 4-3 on penalties)

12 May 2010. Attendance: 26,033
Championship Play-Off Semi-Final Second Leg.
Cardiff City Stadium

CARDIFF CITY:

David Marshall
Kevin McNaughton (Paul Quinn 97)
Mark Hudson
Darcy Blake
Mark Kennedy
Chris Burke (Kelvin Etuhu 60)
Stephen McPhail
Joe Ledley
Peter Whittingham (Ross McCormack 91)
Jay Bothroyd
Michael Chopra
Subs not used: Peter Enckelman, Gabor
Gyepes, Tony Capaldi, Aaron Wildig

LEICESTER CITY:

Chris Weale
Nolberto Solano
Jack Hobbs
Alex Bruce
Bruno Berner
Paul Gallagher (Jay Spearing 72)
Ritchie Wellens
Andy King
Lloyd Dyer (Martyn Waghorn 72)
Matty Fryatt (Yann Kermorgant 97)
Steve Howard
Subs not used: Conrad Logan, Michael
Morrison, Dany N'Guessan,
James Vaughan

Referee: Howard Webb

BREATHLESS. THAT is the only way to describe this epic Championship play-off semi-final against Leicester City which put the Bluebirds within 90 minutes of reaching the top flight for the first time since 1962.

Peter Whittingham had given City a 1-0 first leg advantage with a magnificent free kick at the Walkers Stadium. But one goal is rarely enough in the play-offs – and so it proved on a night of high drama and incredible tension in South Wales.

Eventually goalkeeper David Marshall proved to be the hero with the decisive saves in the penalty shoot-out, but this was a night when every player from back to front showed immense character and resolve.

Michael Chopra had fired City into a 2-0 aggregate lead but then some shoddy defending allowed Leicester to move 3-1 ahead on the night and the dream looked to be evaporating. But there was no self pity from a very strong City side. A penalty by Whittingham took the tie to extra time and eventually spot-kicks before a celebration to match any other in the stands of the Cardiff City Stadium.

Boss Jones heaped praise on his players, who had gone a long way towards shaking off their 'bottlers' tag. He told the BBC, "One minute you are out then you're back in it. I've nothing but admiration for my players. It is a fantastic achievement for everyone at the football club. We played scintillating football. We missed two or three glorious chances. We showed great character."

Sparky City should have been ahead inside four minutes when Chopra picked the ball up in his own half, and came forward ten yards before playing an incredible weighted ball beyond Solano and into the path of Whittingham. The midfielder had already cracked 24 goals that season, including that free kick in the first leg, but this time with Chris Weale rushing off his line he slid his shot inches wide of the post.

Minutes later Chris Burke was hacked down by Alex Bruce on the edge of the area, well within Whittingham range. This time he was on target but Weale got over well and got two gloves on his save.

And City came close again when Darcy Blake won a defensive header and it was flicked on again by Joe Ledley. One more first time touch sent Chopra racing through and the CCS held its breath. Chopra, with Bruce on his tail, went for the audacious chip but got it all wrong and his effort bounced harmlessly wide.

Soon after a huge hoof forward by Mark Hudson was nabbed off clumsy Bruce by hard-working Jay Bothroyd. He played a one-two with Chopra and then fizzed his shot just wide. There were some City fans who were quick to question Bothroyd's drive and determination but this was a chance fashioned entirely by his honest endeavour.

Supporters had feared an early Leicester onslaught as the underdogs tried to scrap their way back into the game, but City were buzzing and slicing the Foxes' defence open with ease.

Chopra had another half-chance after good build-up play between Burke and Bothroyd. The ball eventually found Whittingham on the edge of the area and his mis-hit shot almost landed at the feet of Chopra just eight yards out but the Geordie wasn't expecting it and his first touch deceived him.

At the other end a Nolberto Solano ball was nearly forced in by Matty Fryatt but then on 21 minutes City's brave attacking play was rewarded when Chopra scored the goal which City fans believed would take them through to Wembley. Stephen McPhail found Bothroyd in space and his header penetrated the Leicester back-line. Chopra raced on and kept his nerve to slide the ball through Weale's legs for one of the most important goals he will ever score. It felt like a gigantic step towards the Premier League.

But play-off semi-finals are rarely that straightforward – unless it's City v West Ham. The celebrations had barely died down when suddenly the game was back on a knife-edge four minutes later. Fryatt played a high ball to Steve Howard, so often a thorn in City's side, and continued his run. Howard beat Ledley in the air too easily and Fryatt was able to squeeze inside Blake and somehow force his shot between Marshall's legs and over the line … just.

Whittingham didn't get any power behind a 30-yard effort after Chopra had dragged half the Leicester team out of position and then shortly after Bothroyd powered his way into the area and felt he might have had a penalty after he was bundled off the ball by a combination of Bruce and Solano. City continued to create the better chances. Burke's shot took a hefty deflection and whizzed just over.

But then, after 36 minutes, almost out the blue, the game was dumped on its head. Bruce's long free kick was helped on by Howard and then pinged off Hudson's head, wrong-footed Marshall and nestled in the top corner. Nigel Pearson's Leicester were now level at 2-2 on aggregate and their players and supporters celebrated an unlikely comeback. There was an uneasy feeling around the CCS with shades of the Stoke play-off in 2002.

The Foxes' tails were up. Bruno Berner chipped a ball to the back stick which was again won by Howard but this time Hudson was able to get it clear. City had a great chance to go into half-time all square on the night when a poor Leicester clearance came to Chopra in a crowded area but he blazed over the bar.

The first opening of the second period fell to City's flying winger Burke. It was the familiar routine that created it: a long Marshall goal kick on to the head of Bothroyd. It was only partly cleared as far as Burke, who managed to get his foot above the ball to keep it low, but it was comfortably gathered by Weale.

It had been a positive start by Jones's men but just four minutes into the second half sloppy marking allowed Leicester to go 3-1 ahead on the night – and in front in the tie for the first time. Weak defending by Bothroyd and Chopra gave Paul Gallagher the chance to cross and Andy King rose under a half-hearted Ledley challenge to head past Marshall.

It was the first time that Cardiff had conceded three at their new ground. It could hardly come at a worse time. City's confidence was shot – both the players' and the fans'. Leicester had turned a two-goal aggregate deficit into a one-goal advantage and City's chances of progressing looked in grave danger.

A clever corner routine created a City chance minutes later. Burke played a short one to Whittingham and he found Mark Kennedy in the area with a low pass. His first touch took him past Gallagher but Jack Hobbs flew in to block and deny the full-back a rare moment of glory.

Ledley then glanced a header wide from a Burke cross before Lloyd Dyer nodded straight into Marshall's arms from an accurate Solano cross. The Cardiff City Stadium was growing more tense as each minute ticked by, City's promotion dreams hanging by a thread.

Leicester could have put the tie to bed on 64 minutes when Gallagher's in-swinging corner was won by Hobbs. Fryatt went for the overhead kick and missed the ball, but King did manage to get something on it and City were fortunate to have Whittingham on the line to hook clear.

But just as the game looked to be slipping away from City, the home side were handed a huge lifeline by World Cup referee Howard Webb. Hudson's teasing ball looked like it had sent Chopra through but he had his ankle tapped by Bruce and down he went. Penalty. A moment's hesitation between Bruce and his goalkeeper had cost Leicester severely.

With so much at stake, even ice-cold Whittingham looked fazed but the midfielder fired smack into the middle of the net to give this most dramatic of semi-finals another intriguing twist.

Minutes later excellent Bothroyd almost raised the roof when he smashed the crossbar from a tight angle after drifting past tiring Solano. And soon after a perfect ball over the Foxes' defence was brought down by Chopra who hooked a shot past Weale but Hobbs had made it back in time to just nudge it the other side of the post.

A wonderful chance to win the game inside the 90 fell to Whittingham on 82 minutes after Solano had brought down Chopra right on the edge of the area. Whitts thundered his free kick over the wall and against the crossbar.

City were attacking with real drive and purpose yet it was not one-way traffic. With just two minutes remaining Howard, who scored in the Championship fixture in March, came buttock-clenchingly close to bagging a dramatic winner with a half volley which Marshall had to be at full strength to palm out for a corner.

It had been a stressful 90 minutes and in the end both sides were grateful to have taken the match to extra time, despite both having chances to score more.

Ross McCormack came on for the injured Whittingham at the start of extra time and the lively Scot fired a bobbling shot goalbound almost immediately. McPhail then picked his pass to find Chopra in the area but the striker's weary legs could only manage a tame effort.

After the break Kelvin Etuhu, who had come on for Burke on the hour, had a decent crack at goal from an acute angle but he might have been better looking for the unmarked McCormack at the back post. City were now looking the more dangerous but Leicester still had plenty to offer on the counter-attack.

Neither side could force a winner, however, and a place in the Championship play-off final, often described as the wealthiest game in football, had to be decided on penalties.

Jones told his players to pick a spot and stick to it. Now it was all about which team could handle the enormous pressure best. With so much hinging on the outcome, the atmosphere inside the stadium was almost unbearable, yet incredible at the same time.

Berner finished confidently for the Foxes in front of the Grange End but Chopra looked just as assured to make it 1-1. Howard smashed into the top corner to edge Leicester ahead and McCormack responded emphatically.

Solano was next up and his experience told with a great penalty, 3-2 Leicester. Weale went the right way but could not stop Ledley's low shot.

And then came the decisive moments. Moments that City fans will cherish forever. Yann Kermorgant, a 97th-minute substitute for Fryatt, tried a ridiculous little dink down the middle and Marshall was able to slap clear from a seated position. It was a stupid decision of epic proportions by the Frenchman – and it turned out to be his last competitive involvement for the club.

The calamity inspired a smash-hit YouTube song to the tune of Bonnie Tyler's 'Turn Around', including the line, "Confidence is something but you took it too far. Did someone tell you you were Eric Cantona?"

There was no mistake by Kennedy to give City match point. Martyn Waghorn came forward for the Foxes and Marshall saved with an outstretched right arm to spark some of the greatest celebrations City fans will ever enjoy.

The players mobbed their hero goalkeeper and supporters were soon pouring on to the pitch to join in. There was nothing a piece of string held hopefully by stewards could do to stop the inevitable invasion, an outpouring of joy and relief.

Once the string had done its job in coaxing the fans back into the stands, Dato Chan Tien Ghee, the Malaysian businessman and prospective club chairman, did a lap of honour with the players. Long before talk of re-branding, the Malaysians appeared to have delivered where so many others had failed.

'Hey Jude' belted out on the sound system as fans contemplated a third trip to Wembley in two years. It truly was an unforgettable 15 minutes of celebration.

Twelve months earlier Jones's job had been called into question after City missed out on a place in the play-offs by a single goal with defeat at Sheffield Wednesday. Now just little old Blackpool stood between Cardiff and a dream promotion to the Premier League. Surely there was no stopping us this time.

46 v Blackpool 2-3

22 May 2010. Attendance: 82,244
Championship Play-Off Final. Wembley Stadium

CARDIFF CITY:
David Marshall
Kevin McNaughton (Anthony Gerrard 74)
Mark Hudson
Darcy Blake
Mark Kennedy
Chris Burke (Ross McCormack 58)
Stephen McPhail
Joe Ledley
Peter Whittingham
Jay Bothroyd (Kelvin Etuhu 15)
Michael Chopra
Subs not used: Peter Enckelman, Paul Quinn,
Tony Capaldi, Aaron Wildig

Referee: Andre Marriner

BLACKPOOL:
Matthews Gilks
Seamus Coleman
Alex Baptiste
Ian Evatt
Stephen Crainey
Keith Southern
Gary Taylor-Fletcher (Ben Burgess 53)
Charlie Adam
David Vaughan (Barry Bannan 90)
Brett Ormerod (Stephen Dobbie 60)
D.J. Campbell
Subs not used: Paul Rachubka, Rob Edwards,
Billy Clarke, Jason Euell

CITY FANS shuffled out of Wembley Stadium towards the trains and buses in almost complete silence. There was shock and despair as each of the 37,000 Bluebirds processed what they had just witnessed.

Twice City had led in the so-called "richest game of football", but the dream of becoming the first Welsh team to play in the Premier League had been mercilessly extinguished by the Tangerine Army. Blackpool, the paupers of the division, had denied Cardiff their finest moment. And it hurt.

Some might be surprised that an afternoon which ended in such disappointment has squirmed its way into a book about greatness. But this is Cardiff City and a £90m Wembley final watched across the globe still has to go down as one of the club's proudest days.

The following paragraphs contain content that some City fans might find disturbing. Those not ready to re-live the match are advised to carry on to the next chapter.

City went into the game in splendid form and favourites to be playing top flight football for the first time in 48 years. Play-off semi-finals aside, Dave Jones's talented side had won seven of their final 11 games in the league, losing only at Derby on the last day of the campaign with a weakened team. Automatic promotion hopes had long since evaporated as Newcastle and West Brom romped over the line, but City finished a very creditable fourth behind Nottingham Forest in third.

There was a lot of excitement in the build-up – James Fox had even tweaked and re-released his FA Cup Final song from two years previous – but there was an equal measure of nervousness. The pressure was undoubtedly piled on City while Blackpool, suddenly the nation's darlings, had little to lose. The Tangerines were among the favourites for relegation before the season started but had shocked even themselves by pipping Swansea to sixth place.

Their players still took their kit home to wash, but their team togetherness could not be questioned. They had developed an exciting, if slightly risky, style of play and had won six of their final eight regular Championship games. In the play-off semis they had put in a stunning display to beat Forest 4-3 on aggregate.

Both managers made no bones about the importance of the game. Jones, not normally one for hyperbole, said, "If we achieve what we want, we are not just taking a football club up into the Premier League, we are taking a whole nation up; it's life-changing for everyone."

Of course, there was one part of Wales where the locals weren't dreaming of Cardiff City at Old Trafford. Two Swansea City fans went as far as having their garage doors painted tangerine orange in support of the Seasiders.

Holloway, a good friend of Jones, was more accustomed to providing sound bites. "This is it," he said. "It's crunch time. We could do something absolutely marvellous, something that no-one expected – this is our time to step forward and show what we're made of."

Jones was able to name the same starting line-up that had squeezed past Leicester City in the semis. Jay Bothroyd was passed fit despite a troublesome calf and Darcy Blake was preferred over Anthony Gerrard in central defence alongside Mark Hudson. Holloway also went for the same 11 that had played the last six games for Blackpool.

It was a lively start to the game on an absolutely scorching afternoon. A thermometer on the pitch side showed temperatures topped 42°C at times.

Some sunburnt fans hadn't even found their seats when Michael Chopra thumped the crossbar after just three minutes. Peter Whittingham played a one-two with Bothroyd and fizzed an inch-perfect first time low ball in for Chopra, who got himself in front of Ian Evatt and poked his shot against the woodwork from six yards. Matthew Gilks was beaten but the ace marksman just could not keep it down.

But just six minutes later Chopra was absolutely clinical from outside the area to give the Bluebirds a priceless advantage. Whittingham jinked past two Blackpool players ten yards inside their half and slid a pass through to Chopra, who managed to steal some space on Alex Baptiste by drifting back from an offside position. He needed just one touch to drill his shot from the edge of the area across Gilks and accurately into the bottom corner.

The City fans could not believe what they were seeing. Sure, City had expected to win, but fans certainly hadn't anticipated a lead after just nine minutes. Thoughts turned to Stamford Bridge, Anfield, The Emirates …

But the more experienced City supporters knew better. Things were seldom dull where this Blackpool team was involved. They had scored 74 goals in the league and conceded 58. On 13 minutes they were back on level terms at 1-1.

A free kick was given against Stephen McPhail ten yards outside the area for blocking a cross with raised arms. Charlie Adam stepped up nonchalantly, ignored the howls from the City fans behind the goal, and curled a magnificent shot over the wall and into the top corner. It was Adam's 19th goal of the season and his second against City. Not bad for £500,000.

That silenced the City fans, but worse was to come. Bothroyd had been limping since the seventh minute and now he was heading off. So much of City's play revolved around Bothroyd that season. He oozed class and could hold the ball up excellently to bring midfielders into the game. Now Kelvin Etuhu, a loan signing from Manchester City who hadn't scored a single goal, was being asked to play 75 minutes of the biggest game in Cardiff's history. You could hear the groans from the supporters. It was a massive blow.

Blake had to be at full stretch on 17 minutes to clear a Keith Southern cross with Gary Taylor-Fletcher ready to pounce before David Marshall was fast off his line to nab it away from Brett Ormerod as Blackpool enjoyed a period of possession.

On 19 minutes D.J. Campbell hit an air shot in a dangerous position on the edge of the area and soon after Welshman David Vaughan wasn't too far away with an effort from distance after bursting past Joe Ledley.

Jones looked on concerned as the orange tide continued to surge forward, though a 29th-minute cross by Whittingham gave City a decent opening. Chopra watched it float across his body but mis-hit his volley and it bobbled harmlessly out for a goal kick.

Then against the run of play City, incredibly, were back in front on 37 minutes – and it was the genius Whittingham at the heart of it again. Ledley knocked a first-time pass to Whitts in the centre of the field and instinctively set off on a run through the Blackpool centre-backs. The weight of Whittingham's pass was just beautiful and Ledley defied the circumstances by showing remarkable composure to slip his shot past the oncoming Gilks from an ever-narrowing angle. It was Ledley's second goal at the new Wembley, the Welshman having scored the winner in the FA Cup semi-final against Barnsley two years earlier. Party back on.

There had been just three goals in the previous three Championship play-off finals – the attacking styles and defensive frailties of Blackpool and Cardiff had already matched that.

There was never any realistic chance of the score staying that way. Just two minutes later Taylor-Fletcher, until recently a lower league journeyman, thumped the foot of the post with a curling half volley. But the midfielder did have the ball in the net from the resulting corner.

Vaughan curled it in, Marshall flapped at it under pressure from Adam and Evatt fired a volley goalwards. Mark Kennedy was well placed to block off the line but Taylor-Fletcher showed good bravery to stick his head in and beat both Ledley and Chris Burke to the ball to scramble home. City fans stood in silence and complete shock at what was unfolding.

And Blackpool weren't finished. Fifteen seconds into injury time Campbell, on loan from play-off semi-finalists Leicester, slipped while trying a shot and fortuitously it ran to Ormerod. Hudson, Kevin McNaughton and Kennedy had already dived in to block the anticipated Campbell shot, leaving Ormerod free to smash into the near corner through Marshall's legs from ten yards.

Blackpool were in front for the first time and City fans had that familiar sinking feeling.

City thought they had bagged an immediate equaliser on the stroke of half-time when Blake volleyed in from a Whittingham free kick but the makeshift centre-back was clearly offside.

Jones stood on the touchline roasting in the May sun, still with his hands on his hips but looking ready to unleash a barrage of abuse on his defenders.

What a half.

There were encouraging signs for City early in the second half. Etuhu flashed a cross over which didn't miss Chopra's head by too much while Blake bravely blocked a Campbell shot.

Then on 57 minutes City were two inches away from levelling the match and taking an almighty step towards the Promised Land when Chopra smashed the crossbar again.

Burke, who had been unusually quiet, scrapped the ball through to Chops and he leathered it from the edge of the area against the frame of the goal.

Burke was immediately replaced by Ross McCormack, who had played second fiddle to Chopra and Bothroyd all season and had only scored five. Maybe the sun was all a bit too much for tricky Scot Burke.

Just before the hour Ledley got in front of Gilks and flashed a header just wide from an in-swinging Whittingham corner before Southern, nicknamed 'Gnashers' because of his plentiful teeth, went straight up the other end and fired a shot over the bar.

McNaughton came off injured after 74 minutes with Gerrard his replacement.

The chances kept coming, albeit at a slower rate. On 75 minutes a poor Kennedy cross should have been easily gathered by Gilks but he spilled it under hopeful pressure by Chopra and was relieved to see it bounce just the wrong side of the post.

Suddenly Blackpool looked a little ragged for the first time and City were enjoying almost all of the possession. City had scored 15 goals in the last ten minutes of matches. Another now would be invaluable.

Blake set off on a jinking run into the area but his low shot was comfortably gathered before Gerrard was thrown up front for the final five minutes.

Four minutes of injury time were shown – but it was no good. Ledley's tame header from 18 yards was the best the Bluebirds could muster and Blackpool were in the big time for the first time in 39 years.

There were tears on the pitch and tears in the stands as men and women in orange celebrated an incredible achievement. From relegation candidates to play-off winners in ten months. The players had plenty of reason to smile – they had just scooped a share of a £5m bonus.

The general consensus was that Jones deserved another crack at promotion – and that's exactly what he got.

Speaking after the game, the City gaffer said, "Emotions are raw. It's a huge disappointment for everybody, players, fans, all of us. But I will be sitting down with the club's new owners on Monday when we'll go over a few things. I can't stop all the speculation about my future and the future of my players. But my heart and my mind are with the club. I hope I'm still manager next season."

Holloway, meanwhile, left the one-liners to one side for once. "I am so proud," he said. "It was magnificent and not just for the team, but for our whole area. My players showed great spirit."

I had never watched the game back, not until I came to write this chapter. It was therapeutic. Yes, City lost. Some will always say Jones and his well-paid players bottled it. But this was an exceptionally talented City side who came up against a Blackpool team riding the crest of the wave and in the end, perhaps the Bluebirds were just a tad unlucky.

And of course, now that our time in the top league has finally come, it makes it just a little bit easier to accept.

47 v Leeds United 4-0

25 October 2010. Attendance: 20,747
Championship. Elland Road

CARDIFF CITY:	LEEDS UNITED:
Tom Heaton	Kasper Schmeichel
Kevin McNaughton	Paul Connolly
Mark Hudson	Alex Bruce
Gabor Gyepes	Neill Collins
Lee Naylor	George McCartney
Chris Burke	Robert Snodgrass
Peter Whittingham	Jonathan Howson
Seyi Olofinjana	Amdy Faye (Adam Clayton 81)
Craig Bellamy	Bradley Johnson (Max Gradel 64)
Michael Chopra (Andy Keogh 73)	Davide Somma (Ramon Nunez 57)
Jay Bothroyd	Luciano Becchio
Subs not used: David Marshall, Gavin Rae, Stephen McPhail, Jason Koumas, Darcy Blake, Aaron Wildig	Subs not used: Jason Brown, Neil Kilkenny, Andy Hughes, Leigh Bromby

Referee: Michael Oliver (Northumberland)

THERE HAVE been some terrific tussles between Cardiff and Leeds United in recent years. It started in 2002 in the FA Cup, the first meeting between the two working-class clubs in over 17 years. On that day Second Division City famously toppled the leaders of the Premier League.

In 2005 Jason Koumas curled in a free kick to give City victory at Elland Road and then in 2007 the Bluebirds held on to win by the same scoreline with nine men at Ninian Park.

Going into this Monday night game in 2010, City had won the last four against the once-mighty Whites and were unbeaten in nine, a record stretching back to 1984.

But this magic night in West Yorkshire, in which ruthless City secured their biggest ever victory over their old foe, was one of the most enjoyable.

Ten years and a day earlier Leeds had drawn at home against Barcelona in the Champions League. They had then famously plummeted all the way down to the third tier of English football but appeared to be on their way back up having achieved promotion the previous season. There had been optimistic talk of back-to-back promotions after a respectable start to the season – but this night only served to underline the gulf in class between the sides.

This was a formidable City squad desperate to bounce back after defeat in the play-off final in their last season. The majority of the big-hitters had remained at the club to give promotion another go, including Chris Burke, Peter Whittingham, Michael Chopra and Jay Bothroyd.

And there was one key addition to complete the fabulous front five, a signing which hit the headlines right across the world. That man was Craig Bellamy, who had agreed to drop down a division to join his home-city club on loan from Manchester City. Cardiff had been berated for taking on a player and only paying a small percentage of his astronomical wages, but it was nothing but jealously. Great players joining the Championship from the Premier League was not unheard of, but this was a player still in his pomp, still Champions League standard. His delicate knees might have been a concern, but his arrival had lifted the gloom of that terrible day at Wembley.

Bellamy hit the ground running and with Bothroyd also in top form, City went into this game knowing a win would put them level on points with leaders Queens Park Rangers. The Bluebirds had won their last three on the bounce against Barnsley, Bristol City and Coventry and appeared destined to end their 48-year exile from the top flight.

And Jones's men made a composed start to the match with Bothroyd and Bellamy clearly in the mood to entertain. It was, however, Leeds who had the first chance of note when Alex Bruce sent a header wide from Robert Snodgrass's corner. Jonathan Howson also flashed a shot wide from 25 yards after Amdy Faye had bundled his way through a Seyi Olofinjana tackle.

But the Bluebirds, wearing their black strip, soon took control. Whittingham struck a free kick straight into the wall and the home defence charged out to block the rebound.

Minutes later City demonstrated their attacking pedigree by breaking the full length of the pitch. Bothroyd played a neat touch inside for Chopra, who lofted a ball down the wing for his strike partner. Bothroyd, one month before winning his solitary England cap, dragged two players out of position and rolled it back for Bellamy. The City skipper slipped the ball to Olofinjana, who darted past Howson – but the big man's final shot from a central position lacked power and was easily gathered by Kasper Schmeichel.

The away end at Elland Road was only ten per cent full at kick-off as West Yorkshire Police made more than 600 frustrated supporters wait at a service station on the outskirts of Leeds for more than an hour. But most City fans had made it inside to see their team go ahead on 22 minutes in comical fashion.

Goalkeeper Tom Heaton pumped a huge ball downfield which bounced on the edge of the Leeds area. Both Bruce and Schmeichel went for it and in the confusion the United keeper spilled the ball hopelessly into the path of Bothroyd to poke simply into the empty net from 18 yards.

Peter Schmeichel and Steve Bruce had enjoyed an almost telepathic understanding as goalkeeper and centre-back while at Manchester United – but that had clearly not been passed down to their offspring. Bruce senior was in the stands and shook his head despairingly as Schmeichel junior berated his son's latest gaffe.

Leeds had conceded 11 goals in their last four games, including half a dozen at home to Preston in an astonishing 6-4 home defeat. That had prompted boss Simon Grayson to recall both Bruce and Schmeichel back to the starting line-up. He was surely now questioning whether it was too soon.

"The first port of call is for Alex to head it and not let it bounce, and it's just gone under Kasper," Grayson told the *Daily Mail*. "An individual mistake has cost us a goal and when you do that against teams like Cardiff they've got players who can punish you."

Leeds responded brightly for a team whose early season promise was evaporating fast. Six-goal Luciano Becchio shot tamely at Heaton from a tight angle when there were team-mates better placed.

Leeds stuck at their task manfully but City always looked the classier side and were a constant threat on the counter-attack with some fast and fluid passing. The confidence oozed from Jones's star-studded side and there were step-overs, back-heels and feints aplenty.

It might have been a more level playing field if Bothroyd had been dismissed shortly after for a late, dangerous, studs-up tackle on Becchio. Little was made of the challenge at first and Becchio bounced straight back to his feet but, as the game was live on Sky, it received the slow-mo-from-every-angle treatment. A week later Grayson was still bleating about it – but the FAW made it clear that retrospective punishment could only be considered if the officials didn't see the incident.

Bellamy's influence on the game grew as it went on. The Welsh international saw his thumping volley saved by his former Manchester City team-mate on 32 minutes before Bothroyd fired wide from an angle with Chopra screaming for the ball in the centre.

Heaton was called into action again before half-time to make a solid save from Snodgrass and just before the whistle a Bradley Johnson effort fizzed across the City goal.

If the first half had been easy on the eye for City fans, the second was a fairytale as Bellamy, Bothroyd and Co. tore the once-great Whites to shreds. George McCartney had to head off the line from Gabor Gyepes three minutes in – but that merely delayed the rout that was to follow.

The three points were never in doubt after the 52nd minute when Mark Hudson won a tackle against Faye well within his own half and his punt luckily sent Chopra through. Chops might have been an inch offside but the flag stayed down and the striker took two touches to take it to the edge of the area before firing across Schmeichel into the bottom corner. It was a trademark Chopra goal, and his third of the season.

Five minutes later it was 3-0 – and it was another stunning City move. Brilliant Bellamy drove from deep inside his own territory to the halfway line and found Bothroyd, who dribbled to the edge of the area and played in Burke on the overlap. The Scottish midfielder's pull-back was perfect and untracked Bothroyd was left with the simple task of sliding in his 11th goal of the season from close-range. A move which was beautiful in its simplicity.

The Bluebirds were flying to the top of the table faster than Lee Trundle charging towards a burger van. On the hour left-back Lee Naylor made it four, drilling into the bottom corner with his weaker right foot from 25 yards after finding himself with all the time in the world from Bellamy's pass. Schmeichel did not flinch. Three goals in nine second half minutes – lovely jubbly.

Shell-shocked Elland Road descended into silence. Substitute Ramon Nunez drilled a shot over the bar from the home side and then Becchio thought he had pulled one back on 73 minutes when he headed in but he was correctly ruled offside.

Boos rang around a once-proud stadium at the final whistle while the small but vocal band of City fans celebrated a fantastic result. At last this magnificently talented City team was playing to its potential and appeared destined for the Premier League.

The result made it 16 points from a possible 18 and moved City six points clear of third-placed Swansea after 13 games. After the same number of games in 2006/07 City were top, in 2008/09 they were fourth and in 2009/10 they were third. But a history of falling away after strong starts had done nothing to dampen the enthusiasm of the pundits, both local and national.

South Wales Echo reporter Terry Phillips was the most confident as he prepared to swap the crowded press box of Glanford Park for the luxuries of Old Trafford.

In his report he said, "The Bluebirds team boss is itching to work in the Premier League again and he must know now that he's on his way back to the Promised Land."

That was swiftly followed by, "There is a long, long way to go, but I simply cannot see how a team with this amount of talent and character can fail to go up this season."

Not that the *Echo*'s long-serving writer was alone in his gushing praise for this City team. Even the BBC said, "The Bluebirds are looking like real contenders for automatic promotion" while Grayson hailed City as favourites to win the league.

Bellamy said the victory was a serious statement of intent and the bookies also slashed City's odds for winning the title to 2-1 second favourites, in from 10-1 just two months before.

Just about the only one keeping his cool was Jones. "It's early days, we're 13 games in and we've a long, long way to go," said the City boss. "I think we earned the right to play. It was a tough first 45 minutes and very evenly contested. I felt if we stayed solid and built from the back, with the players we have we are likely to score goals."

But unfortunately for City, November was just around the corner – and under Jones that inevitably meant a severe dip in form. Jones won just six out of 30 games in November during his time at the club. City followed the win against Leeds with a 3-1 home victory against Norwich City the day before Halloween but then lost three, drew one and won just one during the nightmare month.

City eventually finished in fourth and crumbled in the play-offs, losing 3-0 at home to Reading in the semi-finals after drawing 0-0 at the Madejski Stadium. It was the final straw for Jones, who was sacked after six years at the club.

He might have ultimately failed to deliver promotion – but there were certainly some stunning performances under his reign. This was one of the best.

48 v Liverpool 2-2

(AET, Liverpool won 3-2 on penalties)
26 February 2012. Attendance: 89,044
League Cup Final. Wembley Stadium

CARDIFF CITY:	LIVERPOOL:
Tom Heaton	Pepe Reina
Kevin McNaughton (Darcy Blake 106)	Glen Johnson
Mark Hudson (Anthony Gerrard 99)	Martin Skrtel
Ben Turner	Daniel Agger (Jamie Carragher 86)
Andrew Taylor	Jose Enrique
Don Cowie	Jordan Henderson (Craig Bellamy 58)
Peter Whittingham	Steven Gerrard
Aron Gunnarsson	Charlie Adam
Joe Mason (Filip Kiss 91)	Stewart Downing
Kenny Miller	Luis Suarez
Rudy Gestede	Andy Carroll (Dirk Kuyt 103)
Subs not used: David Marshall, Robert Earnshaw, Craig Conway, Lee Naylor.	Subs not used: Doni, Maxi Rodríguez, Jay Spearing, Martin Kelly
Referee: Mark Clattenburg (County Durham)	

THE 2011/2012 season was supposed to be one of rebuilding. Dave Jones had departed after six largely successful years following City's latest play-off failure. Big-name players including Jay Bothroyd, Craig Bellamy and Michael Chopra had all left. Malky Mackay had been brought in after showing some promising signs as Watford boss and had signed a raft of young, relatively inexperienced replacements. A season of consolidation was anticipated – and perhaps even a scrap against relegation. A League Cup Final and a fourth trip to Wembley in as many years was certainly not in the script.

Malky had brought a refreshing new attitude to the club. His mantra was all about team spirit and togetherness. The players had now taken up yoga and were living their day-to-day lives on the advice of sport scientists and food nutritionists. Pasted on the walls of the training facilities there were inspirational comments from the likes of Michael Jordan. Things had changed quite dramatically in a short space of time and there was plenty of optimism among supporters about the long-term future.

City had scrambled their way through to their first League Cup Final with wins over Oxford United (3-1 AET), Huddersfield Town (5-3 AET), Leicester City (2-2 AET, 7-6 on penalties), Burnley (1-0), Blackburn Rovers (2-0) and Crystal Palace (1-1 on aggregate AET, 3-1 on penalties). City had needed extra time on four occasions and penalties twice, including in a thrilling two-legged semi-final against Palace. In total, City had played 750 minutes of football before facing Kenny Dalglish's Liverpool.

Liverpool, meanwhile, had played just 540 minutes in the competition but had seen off Premier League opposition in Stoke City, Chelsea and Manchester City.

For me, the build-up to the game was strange. Unlike the FA Cup Final in 2008 and the play-off final in 2010, it was subdued. That was partly because it was City's fourth appearance at the home of English football and partly because there was a stark shortage of belief.

Speaking to a Liverpool fan on the tube before the game, I predicted a 5-0 hammering for City – and I meant it. City weren't playing well. They had lost three of their last four, including a dismal 3-0 thrashing at the hands a very average Ipswich side the weekend before. Liverpool, in contrast, had trounced Brighton 6-1 in the FA Cup seven days earlier, who were just four points behind City in the Championship.

One fan on Wembley Way, speaking to the BBC, said: "If we can keep them below six we'll be alright." It was sixth in the Championship versus seventh in the Premier League. City's squad cost £4m to assemble, Liverpool's £135m. Punters could get 15/2 on City to win the match in 90 minutes. In the TV build-up pundit Alan Shearer, who was almost named City boss less than 12 months earlier, said bluntly, "I can't see Cardiff doing it today."

Liverpool's last visit to Wembley was in 1996 in the FA Cup. That match has become as famous for the squad's decision to wear white suits as it has for Eric Cantona's late winner. Their last piece of silverware was the FA Cup in 2006, ironically won in Cardiff at the Millennium Stadium while Wembley was being rebuilt. If anything, it meant more to Liverpool than it did Cardiff. We wanted it but Liverpool – and King Kenny, in his first (and last) full season of his second coming – needed it.

There was some good banter between supporters on Wembley Way as City fans taunted their counterparts with chants of "shall we show you where to go?" and "we're Cardiff City, we'll be your tour guides".

There was a surprise in the City line-up as Rudy Gestede was named up front playing in a more advanced position ahead of Kenny Miller. Young forward Joe Mason also played in a midfield role. Malky had been a staunch supporter of 4-5-1 throughout the season but had named a very attacking line-up for his biggest challenge so far.

Tom Heaton, who was second choice in the league but had been given a run in the cup, started ahead of number one David Marshall in goal. Mark Hudson was passed fit after recovering from a calf strain to replace Anthony Gerrard for his first game in a month and took the captain's armband.

In the Liverpool line-up there was no place for Bellamy, who had achieved hero status while on loan with the Bluebirds during the previous season. Instead it was Stewart Downing and Jordan Henderson either side of the talismanic Steven Gerrard.

Unlike the FA Cup Final in 2008, there were no national anthems this time but 'You'll Never Walk Alone' echoed around the giant Wembley arena before the game. Large red and white and blue and white sheets were rolled out on to each half of the pitch as millions of people in an estimated 151 countries worldwide watched on.

The game kicked off to a cauldron of noise inside the famous arena – and Liverpool could have been ahead inside two minutes.

Gerrard picked the ball up deep inside his own half and powered forward before passing out wide to Downing. He played a first time ball inside for Glen Johnson on the edge of the area, who took one touch and curled a magnificent effort goalwards. Heaton was helpless as it hit the underside of the crossbar, with just one minute and 46 seconds on the clock. Gerrard wellied the follow-up over. If City fans were pessimistic before kick-off, they were positively terrified now.

Liverpool were making all the early running. Andy Carroll was putting himself about and Hudson did well to block a low Downing cross.

Those opening minutes could have shook the City players, but it is to their credit that they continued to look forward when they had the ball. The first chance came on ten minutes after good build-up play. Andrew Taylor passed low to Don Cowie, whose neat flick found Miller a yard inside the area. The Scot had to hit the target but leant back and slashed over.

On 15 minutes Carroll rose well above Hudson to win a Charlie Adam cross, but his header was comfortably off target and then the same player won another ball in by Luis Suarez, but this time his effort lacked the power to beat Heaton.

Then on 19 minutes came one of the greatest moments in City's modern history. Kevin McNaughton played into Miller's feet, he showed great awareness to knock past Daniel Agger and Jose Enrique into the path of Mason, who needed just one touch to finish through the legs of Pepe Reina.

The 32,500 Bluebirds erupted as the 20-year-old, a £250,000 bargain buy from Plymouth, wheeled away in delight. It was a supremely cool finish by a player of boundless natural talent. You could have bought 140 Masons for Carroll's £35m price tag – but there was no doubt which player you would rather have in your team at that moment.

The Liverpool fans, many of whom had turned up expecting an easy ride, were silenced. It was against the run of play, no question. City had had just 35 per cent of the possession up until that point. Did the City fans care? Not a jot.

McNaughton was dealing well with Liverpool striker Suarez, who had re-discovered his scoring touch after returning from an eight-match ban given for racially abusing Manchester United's Patrice Evra.

Liverpool felt they should have had a penalty on 31 minutes when Henderson's cross brushed the arm of Taylor on its way in, then moments later Adam, who had broken Cardiff hearts for Blackpool in the play-off final two years earlier, was just off target with a low drive from outside the area. Eight minutes before the break Carroll tried a one-two with Suarez and looked to have got around Hudson, but City's excellent captain did well to hook his leg around the ball and poke clear.

A minute later Liverpool should have had their equaliser when Downing got the better of McNaughton and whipped a cross in. Henderson completely missed the volley but it ran through to Gerrard, who side-footed over the bar. City were under the cosh but some heroic defending gave Malky's men a dream lead going into half-time.

City started the second half brightly and had a decent opening on 48 minutes. Peter Whittingham found Cowie in the area, who in turn back-heeled for Miller, who pulled his low drive wide. Miller, playing deeper than he was used to with Gestede providing the nuisance factor ahead of him, was putting himself about but had not scored in six appearances and there were signs of a lack of confidence.

Bellamy entered the fray for the useless Henderson on 57 minutes and the Welshman received warm applause from both sets of fans.

Two minutes later City hearts were crushed as Liverpool finally forced the equaliser. Downing took the corner, Liverpool's eighth of the game to City's zero. Carroll nodded on and Suarez helped it against the post from just six yards. City looked like they would escape but Martin Skrtel finished through Heaton's legs from close-range.

The millions watching around the world would have anticipated a City cave-in. But Mason then had a decent strike at goal which Reina was alive to while at the other end Taylor just managed to get his toe to a Suarez cross to divert the danger.

Liverpool continued to enjoy nearly all of the possession but centre-backs Hudson and Ben Turner were putting in a monumental shift. Heaton did well to stop Skrtel bagging a second of the game with a low volley from yet another corner then on 77 minutes the City shot-stopper had to scramble across his line to block Downing's low drive.

For all their dominance and corners, Liverpool were largely being restricted to pot shots outside the area. And City, too, looked dangerous when they did venture forward. With seven minutes remaining, a quick throw caught Dalglish's men out and Cowie's in-swinger was painfully close to being nodded in at the back stick by man mountain Turner.

But City's big chance – the one which will haunt Miller forever more – was still to come. With 87 minutes on the clock, Whittingham played a short free kick to Cowie, who knocked a neat pass in for Miller with the outside of his boot. The first touch to spin around was sublime but with his second he looped the volley inches over. An in-form Miller would have scored nine times out of ten. That would have sparked celebrations on an unimaginable scale. If only.

Speaking after the game, Miller, who has scored match-winners in finals at Hampden Park and the Millennium Stadium, did not shy away from blame. He told the *Western Mail*, "I just had to hit the target and it was a goal, as simple as that. I was in disbelief when it went over. It was a fantastic chance and if it had gone in your name's on the cup."

City hung on for the four minutes of added time and a League Cup tie involving Cardiff went to extra time for the fifth time that campaign.

Slovakian Filip Kiss came on for Mason at the start of the additional 30. Heaton was called up to palm a Suarez shot round the post early doors and then from the resulting corner Turner was in the right place on the post to clear the Uruguayan's header off the line. Warrior Hudson, who had been limping for at least 15 minutes, was finally forced off on 99 minutes. Anthony Gerrard, cousin of Liverpool's Steven, came on and the script writers sharpened their pencils. "There's only one Gerrard," sang the City faithful, but there were one or two worried faces.

On 102 minutes Carroll rose well to meet yet another corner but was unlucky to miss the target. That was his last involvement as Dirk Kuyt came on. Soon after Bellamy cut inside McNaughton before curling a firm effort over.

Seconds into the second period an injured McNaughton was replaced by Darcy Blake.

Out of nothing, Kuyt looked to have won the cup for his team on 108 minutes when he made full use of his fresh legs to power past Cowie. His first shot was poor but Gerrard inexplicably gave it straight back to him and the Dutchman fired first time into the bottom corner from just inside the area. That, surely, was that.

Not a bit of it. Aron Gunnarsson was riddled with cramp but on 117 minutes he summoned the energy to hurl a long throw towards Gestede and Skrtel headed out for a corner, only City's second of the match. Whittingham whipped it in and Kuyt unbelievably headed off the line and out for a corner from Kiss's shot. City fans could not believe what they were seeing.

But then, with two minutes left, came the moment that City fans will take with them to their graves. Whittingham whipped it in, it was nodded across by Gunnarsson and this time there was nothing Kuyt could do on the line as Turner bundled the ball past Reina and into the net from a yard. Turner ripped his shirt off, as did Taylor. Amazed City fans went absolutely bonkers. It must surely be the loudest single Bluebirds cheer ever, and one of the loudest at the new Wembley.

After such drama, there appeared to be just one winner as the epic game went to penalties. City had been absolutely magnificent for 120 minutes. It seemed destined that it would be blue and white ribbons hung on the cup's ears.

Heaton, the penalty hero against Palace, pulled off an incredible one-handed save to deny Gerrard from the first kick, but Miller compounded a poor afternoon by hitting the post. When Adam blazed yards over the bar for Liverpool and Cowie made it 1-0, it looked like City's day.

But then Kuyt made it 1-1 and a tired Gestede thumped the foot of the post. Downing made no mistake and Liverpool were ahead for the first time until cool-as-ice Whittingham made it 2-2.

Johnson scored to the top left and it fell to centre-back Gerrard to keep City in it. He looked confident enough – until he screwed it wide and fell to his knees in despair. It just had to be Gerrard.

Stevie G tried to put a consoling arm around his cousin but was pushed away despairingly. That night Anthony tweeted, "Sorry to everyone. I can't close my eyes without seeing that penalty. It's going to haunt me for the rest of my days. My head is mashed!"

As the other Gerrard lifted the cup for Liverpool and the tinsel fell, there were tears, of course. To lose a cup final on penalties is cruel, I can certainly vouch for that. But what a bloody effort. The players could barely climb the Wembley steps to collect their losers' medals they were so exhausted.

Mackay was typically dignified at the final whistle. "We wanted to come here and win today but the players have done the club proud," he told the BBC. "I think today we were playing against a top team and I think we have got a lot to be proud of. You have seen two teams who have put everything into that game."

The praise was lavished on City at the final whistle from all quarters. "I've got lots of respect for Cardiff, their manager and supporters," said Kuyt. "Cardiff played sensationally for 90 minutes plus extra time," said Alan Hansen. "CCFC lost a penalty shoot-out but won many friends," tweeted the *Daily Telegraph*'s Henry Winter.

City had gone into the game looking to complete a remarkable Welsh weekend hat-trick after Wales had won the Six Nations Triple Crown against England and boxer Nathan Cleverly had successfully defended his WBO light-heavyweight title. In the end City recorded a different kind of hat-trick – beaten finalists in the FA Cup, the play-offs and now the League Cup.

But there was a different feeling among City fans as they streamed out of Wembley this time. Not disappointment or despair, but pride.

49 v Charlton Athletic 0-0

16 April 2013. Attendance: 26,338
Championship. Cardiff City Stadium

CARDIFF CITY:
David Marshall
Kevin McNaughton
Andrew Taylor
Ben Turner
Leon Barnett
Kim Bo-Kyung
Craig Noone (Tommy Smith 71)
Aron Gunnarsson
Jordon Mutch
Rudy Gestede
Craig Bellamy
Subs not used: Joe Lewis, Ben Nugent, Peter Whittingham, Don Cowie, Craig Conway, Joe Mason

Referee: Scott Mathieson

CHARLTON ATHLETIC:
Ben Hamer
Michael Morrison
Rhoys Wiggins
Chris Solly
Dorian Dervite
Andy Hughes (Mark Gower 81)
Johnnie Jackson
Bradley Pritchard (Danny Green 88)
Callum Harriott
Yann Kermorgant
Ricardo Fuller (Jonathan Obika 81)
Subs not used: David Button, Matt Taylor, Lawrie Wilson, Salim Kerkar

CARDIFF CITY in the Premier League. That doesn't sound bad, eh? Some 51 years since their last appearance in the top division of English football, the Bluebirds finally made their triumphant return by storming the Championship in 2012/13.

It came after years of bitter disappointments and near-misses. In 2008/09 City spectacularly missed out on the play-offs by a single goal scored – despite having an eight-point and a goal difference cushion of 18 over Preston, the team who eventually finished sixth, with just four games to go. A year later and it was despair at Wembley against Blackpool, followed by back-to-back semi-final losses against Reading and West Ham.

City fans were beginning to wonder whether it would ever happen. Then on a special April evening at the Cardiff City Stadium, keeper David Marshall delivered one final punt up the pitch, referee Scott Mathieson put his whistle to his lips and fans surged on to the pitch from every direction. A 0-0 draw against Charlton had secured City's place among the elite with three games to spare. The tag of perennial chokers had been binned.

The outpouring of joy and sheer relief was palpable. Within seconds every blade of grass was covered with supporters. Two smoke bombs were let off. Super Kevin McNaughton, his eyes bulging from his head, was lifted on to some bloke's shoulders. Kev knew what this meant; he had felt every heart-wrenching blow with us over the last seven years. Now, finally, he was a hero. They all were.

The younger element among City's fan base jumped and screamed their delight, and who can blame them. But more poignantly, almost everywhere you looked, were men and women in their 40s, 50s and 60s with tears in their eyes. Some undoubtedly spared a thought for those Bluebirds who had passed on, the ones for which this promised day did not come soon enough.

Eventually the hordes were somehow ushered back into the stands and the players were allowed the lap of honour they so richly deserved. There had been some good performances, but they hadn't earned promotion playing sizzling football – they had crushed their opponents with consistency. Only once all season in the league had there been consecutive defeats.

Did this City team play with the same style as the Championship winners of recent years, the likes of Queens Park Rangers and Newcastle? No, certainly not, but after 46 games the table doesn't lie – and City were streets ahead of their opponents. Unlike during the Dave Jones days, there were no prolonged periods of bad form. Yes, there were bad results – a 5-4 defeat at Charlton after being 2-0 up felt disastrous at the time – but the response was always good, and swift.

The mastermind behind City's first promotion in ten years was Malky Mackay. It was the Scot's second season with City after being poached from Watford, and he had brought an incredible focus and intensity to the club. You could see the steely determination in his eyes. Malky's philosophy was to win at all costs. If at times that meant playing direct, or keeping a clean sheet or even getting stuck in, he was fine with that.

He didn't get carried away after a win, or distraught after defeat, it was all about the next game – and then the one after that. In short, he was an inspired choice for the job at a time when the likes of Roberto Di Matteo, Chris Hughton and Alan Shearer were all available.

Mackay started the rebuilding process the season before by signing the likes of Aron Gunnarsson, Don Cowie, Andrew Taylor and Ben Turner, and he had been busy again during the summer. In came promising midfielder Jordon Mutch, experienced striker Heidar Helguson, promotion veteran Matthew Connolly and tricky Tommy Smith. Backed by chairman Vincent Tan, Malky was also able to sign Craig Noone from Brighton, South Korean Kim Bo-Kyung, £2.75m man Nicky Maynard and, of course, home hero Craig Bellamy, who returned to City from Liverpool on a free. In the January transfer window he was also able to add former Manchester United star Fraizer Campbell to his ranks on a £650,000 transfer from Sunderland.

It was a strong squad, but it would never have worked without Mackay's discipline. He managed to get a group of players working together as a team, desperate to support each other by grafting hard and grinding out results relentlessly.

City started the season a little edgily, even falling to a 4-2 away defeat against rivals Bristol City in August, and the Robins would go on to finish bottom of the table. But City were soon in among the leading pack and never relinquished top spot from November 24 onwards after a 2-1 win at Barnsley.

After so many false dawns in recent years, Bluebirds fans were reluctant to believe that promotion was on the cards until it became abundantly clear that the teams hanging on to City's coat-tails were simply incapable of the consistency needed to bridge the gap.

After a crucial stalemate at chasers Watford, followed by a useful point at home to Barnsley and a wonderful 3-0 success against Nottingham Forest, City needed just a solitary point against Charlton to book their place in the big time. Even a defeat would have done the job if Gianfranco Zola's Watford failed to win at Millwall. Fifty-three years to the day since City last earned promotion to the top division with a win over Aston Villa, the prize was within touching distance.

A sell-out crowd packed into the Cardiff City Stadium in the hope of witnessing history. City were not without their injury problems. Star striker Maynard had missed the whole season after injuring his knee on only his third appearance for the club. Campbell, who had bagged six crucial goals in his first 11 games, was also missing, as was tough battler Helguson. That left Malky with the choice of Joe Mason or Rudy Gestede up top, and he went for Benin international Gestede, who had scored twice in the Forest win.

In defence Leon Barnett, on loan from Norwich, continued to deputise for injured skipper Mark Hudson and McNaughton filled in for Connolly, who was also crocked. Kim and Mutch had both recently forced their way into the team after being used sporadically throughout the season and Noone was chosen ahead of Craig Conway, leaving Peter Whittingham warming the bench. Whitts had started the season in electric form but seemed to lose his confidence towards the end of the campaign and, subsequently, his place in the starting line-up.

It was immediately clear from the buzz around the ground that this was to be a special night in Cardiff City's history. And City started positively, though it was Charlton who had the first shot on goal through Ricardo Fuller, but Marshall was able to turn the experienced marksman's dipping long-range attempt out for a corner.

Seven minutes in Bellamy was not too far off target with a 30-yard free kick after McNaughton had been hacked down, while at the other end Turner had to stop a dangerous whipped cross by Callum Harriott from reaching Fuller.

City were playing some neat football along the ground with Bellamy and Kim lively, but the final ball was lacking. On 18 minutes Noone sprayed a good pass out to Bellers on the left wing. Bellamy found Noone again with a decent looking cross, but the former Brighton man had stepped offside.

But there was a heart-stopping moment just around the corner on 21 minutes as the Addicks came within a whisker of silencing the home fans. A free kick was awarded after Barnett had clattered into Yann Kermorgant. It was a good 25 yards from goal and quite far out on the right, yet Charlton skipper Johnnie Jackson was able to curl a beauty up and over the wall – and only the post prevented it from hitting the back of the net.

After 28 minutes it was City back on the attack after good battling by Mutch. The midfielder fought well to win the ball on the edge of the area, and back-heeled to Gunnarsson, who scrambled it on to Bellamy in a wide position inside the area. Bellamy looked to curl the ball into the far corner with the inside of his boot, but just got under it and was a foot or so over.

Just minutes later came a huge opening for the Bluebirds when Noone burst over the halfway line and sent Kimbo free darting down the right. Athletic were exposed and Chris Solly had to come charging over towards the South Korean, leaving Bellamy unmarked in the middle. Kim just had to find his team-mate and it was surely 1-0 – but Solly did just enough to block his pass.

On 33 minutes Mutch and Gestede got in each other's way and neither could direct Bellamy's deep cross towards goal, before three minutes later Kim hit a daisy cutter from 25 yards. City were getting forward regularly and passing the ball around nicely, but Charlton were showing enough quality to suggest they could be party poopers.

Five minutes from half-time City were awarded a free kick on the edge of the area, just right of goal. It was a position which would have had Whittingham salivating, but with the midfielder benched, responsibility fell to Kim. The 23-year-old, who cannot speak English, whipped his effort up and over well but it brushed the side netting.

City started the second half on the front foot and left-back Taylor, who had scored just one goal in 81 appearances for the Bluebirds since his move from Middlesbrough, struck the stanchion behind the goal after tricky Noone's cross fell nicely for him just outside the box.

But just three minutes later, as chants of "the blues are going up" swirled around the ground, Michael Morrison rolled Turner too easily on the penalty spot and City fans were relieved to see the centre-back's shot screw high and wide.

City should have made more of an opening close to the hour when Gunnarsson, who had been excellent all season, jinked his way into the box and found Bellers with another cheeky back-heel, but the Welshman's cross was easily plucked from the air by Ben Hamer. A couple of minutes later Hamer was in action again, diving to catch Barnett's deflected drive from long range.

The excitement was increasing around the CCS with every minute that passed – but the job was not yet done. Eighteen minutes into the second half Jamaican Fuller, a top goalscorer for 14 years, cut inside Kim and Turner with a neat Cruyff turn and curled a left-footed shot which Marshall saved spectacularly with one hand. The Scottish keeper had enjoyed an outstanding campaign, raising his game several notches from the previous season, and was a significant reason why City had kept more clean sheets than any other team in the division.

All the game needed to take the roof off was a City goal – and it looked like it had one with 70 on the clock when Mutch chipped the ball over the Addicks back-line and unmarked Noone kneed into the corner of the net. The 25-year-old was well into his celebration dash when he noticed the linesman's flag on the far side. It was a correct decision. That was Noone's last involvement as Smith came on in his place.

Then with seven minutes remaining excited chatter gradually built into a roar as the news spread like a wave – Shaun Batt had given Millwall the lead over Watford. That was it – the job was done. There was more chance of Leighton James getting a bluebird tattooed on his neck than City playing Bournemouth instead of Manchester United the next season.

The final minutes were a party in all four stands. Rarely had a 0-0 draw been so excitedly received. It is just as well there wasn't a Cardiff winner – St John's Ambulance would have been overwhelmed by hyperventilations. Gestede came closest with an overhead kick which, frankly, wasn't that close at all.

Three minutes of added time were announced, but there were no real nerves among the fans. It passed in a flash and soon supporters were hurdling advertising hoardings. An emotional McNaughton provided the iconic image from the night which will be shown time and time again over the next 100 years but everywhere all across the pitch there were incredible scenes.

Barnett, who had only played seven games for the club, was lifted high like the hero he undeniably was. The 27-year-old had huge shoes to fill when he was brought in to cover the injured Hudson – and he had been brilliant. Little Kimbo was mobbed by jubilant fans, as was Gunnarsson. They had earned this moment, the lot of them.

Champagne corks popped in an ecstatic dressing room. There were smiles galore and, in Bellamy's case, a few tears, too. Like many of us, he had gone down Ninian Park with his old man and wondered if the sleeping giant would ever stir. "It was an emotional night because I had people I truly love around me to share this with me," the City talisman said, clearly choked.

"To see my dad afterwards and all the heartache he has been through over the years. I have lost count how many games I used to go to with him to watch Cardiff on a Tuesday night. He'd pull me to the side to say we were leaving 10 minutes before the end, and say we would never go back. Then on the Saturday we would be there again. For him to see this and for his son to play a part in that makes it even more special. Dad said to me, 'I will die a happy man'. It really hit home to me."

The players re-emerged for a lap of honour, joined by Malky and Vincent Tan. Malaysian billionaire Tan, who was keeping the club afloat to the tune of £1m a month, was given a warm hand. It had been a turbulent season in some respects after Tan's decision to change the club colours from blue to red. Some old-timers had even given up on the club. But for one glorious night none of that mattered. Some wore red, some wore blue, but we were all Cardiff City – and we were heading for the greatest league in the world. The dream which Sam Hammam had reignited in 2000 had finally been realised.

Now there was just the small matter of the Championship title to deal with.

50 v Burnley 1-1

20 April 2013. Attendance: 13,264
Championship. Turf Moor

CARDIFF CITY:	BURNLEY:
David Marshall	Lee Grant
Kevin McNaughton	Kieran Trippier
Andrew Taylor	Danny Lafferty
Ben Turner	Jason Shackell
Leon Barnett	Kevin Long
Craig Conway	Chris McCann
Kim Bo-Kyung	Ross Wallace (Martin Paterson 46)
Craig Noone (Craig Bellamy 66)	Dean Marney (Keith Treacy 83)
Aron Gunnarsson	Junior Stanislas (David Edgar 46)
Jordon Mutch (Don Cowie 74)	Sam Vokes
Rudy Gestede	Danny Ings
Subs not used: Joe Lewis, Ben Nugent, Peter Whittingham, Simon Lappin, Joe Mason	Subs not used: Brian Jensen, Luke O'Neill, Marvin Bartley, Brian Stock

Referee: Stuart Attwell

FOUR DAYS after sealing promotion with a draw against Charlton, City travelled to Burnley to clinch their first ever second tier championship title. If only every week could be as good as this.

Hull City's dismal 0-0 draw against already relegated Bristol City on the Friday night meant the Bluebirds needed just one point at Turf Moor to make certain of top spot. A 1-1 draw for Malky Mackay's heroes did the job, and the club could celebrate only its third ever championship success – and the first in 20 years.

It had been a long, grind of a season. Mark Hudson's late, late winner against Huddersfield Town on the opening day felt like an age ago. But now, with two games to spare, City had won one of the most prestigious pieces of silverware in English football – the Football League Championship trophy.

Only the most short-sighted of football observers could dispute that City deserved their success. They had been top for five months and had taken teams apart one by one. Early challengers Crystal Palace, Leicester City, and Middlesbrough all fell by the wayside and in the end, even Hull and Watford succumbed to City's relentless consistency. As Mackay was given the bumps by his loyal players on the Burnley pitch, there was no doubt City were worthy champions.

With hindsight, the title was won during a stunning mid-November to late February period, during which City notched up 13 wins and three draws from 18 games. Things got just a little jittery through March and April, yet City continued to pick up crucial points and others around couldn't capitalise. Going into this clash at Burnley, a ground City had not won at since 1988, the Bluebirds had won just one of the last five – though they were also unbeaten in that run.

Mackay made one change to the starting line-up after that Charlton draw, Craig Conway coming in for Craig Bellamy on the left wing. The players were allowed to party after promotion was assured in the week and Kevin McNaughton admitted that getting up for this game was like climbing Everest, so it is to their credit that they started with such hunger.

Less than two minutes in the ball bobbled to Rudy Gestede 25 yards out and the Benin striker, making his 50th appearance for the club (41 from the bench), hit a sweet half-volley which skimmed the top of the net. By the ten-minute mark City had already taken control of the game with possession beyond 60 per cent. The players may well have been celebrating all week, but there were no hangovers on show in Lancashire.

After 14 minutes a long free kick from halfway by Andrew Taylor was nodded down by Gestede, laid off by Kim Bo-Kyung and Aron Gunnarsson's low right-footed drive wasn't too far off target.

Kim, making his sixth consecutive start, powered into the Burnley half before drilling a left-footed shot a yard wide on 19 minutes, before seconds later the South Korean went down in the box under a challenge by Junior Stanislas but the referee waved play on. You have seem them given.

Burnley looked nervous, no surprise when you consider they had won twice in 15, slipping from mid-table into a relegation scrap. Without their injured 28-goal front man Charlie Austin they were a poor side.

It was no shock on 26 minutes when the Bluebirds went ahead. Skilful Kim sliced a killer ball forward for Conway, who cut inside Kieran Trippier and Kevin Long and bent an outstanding shot into the corner from the edge of the area. One hand on the trophy and the 1,600 travelling fans burst into chants of "Championes" for the first time since the days of Eddie May.

Kim, the classiest player on the pitch, was coming in for some rough treatment from Ross Wallace and two blows to the face went unnoticed.

Conway then found himself in a similar position to the one from which he scored earlier, but this time he leant back slightly and shot over. Burnley, a Premier League club themselves just three seasons previously, were marginally better after the interval and David Marshall was finally called into some action on the hour when Trippier's deep free kick was won by Sam Vokes, but the Welshman's header had little power.

Mackay sent on Bellamy for Craig Noone with 24 minutes to play and he took the captain's armband from Taylor. A couple of minutes later the home side had half a chance when a long throw was flicked on by Dean Marney but substitute Martin Paterson could only send his close-range header over.

Grafter Don Cowie came on for Jordon Mutch in the 74th minute. Moments later Burnley thought they had a penalty when Marney went flying over Gunnarsson's outstretched leg, but instead the Burnley man was booked for diving.

City's best chance of the second half came on 83 minutes when Bellamy's dangerous free kick was met by Gestede, but he could only connect with the side of his head and it went well wide. Likeable Rudy was a real anomaly. At times he looked ungainly and lost at Championship level, yet he did have a goal in him and he did cause problems in the opposition's box.

With five minutes to go Marshall, who had been twiddling his thumbs for the entire game, pulled off a fantastic save to keep Cardiff ahead. Danny Ings got the better of Taylor and smashed a shot across goal from the edge of the six-yard box, but the Scottish keeper showed sublime reactions to stop with his left hand.

But there was to be a scarcely-deserved Burnley equaliser in the dying embers of the game. With 90 minutes played Trippier's cross was met by the head of Marney, who had squeezed in between Leon Barnett and McNaughton and found the bottom corner from deep inside a crowded area.

It wasn't the first time City had conceded in the dying minutes – a last-gasp leveller for Barnsley at the Cardiff City Stadium three games earlier could have been costly – but this time it didn't really matter. It was mission accomplished nonetheless.

Mackay gathered his players and coaches in a circle on the pitch. What did he say? Simply, "Remember days like this." Then they were left to celebrate with their adoring supporters. Malky was grabbed like a single girl at a gypsy wedding and was thrown in the air by Gestede, Mutch, Ben Turner and Gunnarsson. "I'm just glad the big men were involved," the City chief joked. "I wasn't holding out hope if it had been Noone and Bellamy catching me."

When Malky arrived at the club a mere 674 days earlier, he inherited just ten professionals and a bunch of kids. The rebuilding work required just to get to a point where City could compete in the Championship was massive, yet in his first season he defied the odds with a League Cup Final and a play-off berth. To follow that up by blitzing the league was a sensational achievement for a man who looks to have all the managerial skills to reach the very top of the game.

He was backed handsomely by Vincent Tan, as former boss Dave Jones was only too keen to point out, but plenty have tried and failed with money. Malky's success was built around togetherness and teamwork, and that was embodied in the post-match huddle.

When the long overdue celebrations had finally calmed, Malky, who won promotion from the Championship three times as a player, added, "There was a mix of everything. Relief, excitement, sheer joy. It's absolutely fantastic, I'm delighted for everyone at the football club. Very few people get to actually make history. For these players to do that for the city of Cardiff is something that I'm very proud of. They have been top since November and deserve to be champions."

A week later City received their trophy after drawing 1-1 with Bolton Wanderers in front of a full house at the Cardiff City Stadium. Eight days later, in scenes reminiscent of 1927, thousands thronged the streets of the capital as the players showed off their silverware on an open-top bus.

Mackay, though keen for his players to enjoy their moment of glory, warned of the challenges that lay ahead. But whatever the future may bring, whether immediate relegation or Champions League glory, this squad will always be remembered as legends, right from Mackay to Kim's translator. The dream which just 15 years ago had seemed such a long way away had been achieved and a new chapter in the club's history had begun.

Manchester United, Liverpool, Swansea – we're coming for you.

Bibliography

Cardiff City Chronology – John Crooks

Come on you Bluebirds – The South Wales Echo

Derby Days – Neil Palmer, Vertical Editions

From Shattered Dreams to Wembley Way – Annis Abraham Jnr, Headhunter
   Books

Make Some Noise for the Bluebirds – Gary Wharton, Lushington Publishing

Mr Cardiff City, The Autobiography of Phil 'Joe' Dwyer – Phil Dwyer, Fort
   Publishing Ltd

Ooh Ah Stantona – Phil Stant, John Blake Publishing Ltd

Passovotcha – David Downing, Bloomsbury Publishing

The Definitive Cardiff City FC – Richard Shepherd, Tony Brown

The Official History of The Bluebirds – John Crooks, Yore Publications

The Who's Who of Cardiff City – Dean Hayes, Breedon Books